本书为西安外国语大学2019春"一流专业"校级教材建设立项专项资助项目（项目编号：2019JC01）

新时代·新西部

高等院校英语专业创新系列教材

WAMEC

总主编 ◎ 姜亚军 董洪川

U0719630

基于研究的本科英语写作

Research-Based English Writing for Undergraduates

主编 黑玉琴

编者 林 琳 黑玉芬

西安交通大学出版社

XI'AN JIAOTONG UNIVERSITY PRESS

图书在版编目（CIP）数据

基于研究的本科英语写作 / 黑玉琴主编. --西安：
西安交通大学出版社，2024.10. --（"新时代·新西部"
高等院校英语专业创新系列教材）. --ISBN 978-7-5605
-8032-6

Ⅰ.H319.36

中国国家版本馆CIP数据核字第2024TQ6893号

基于研究的本科英语写作

Research-Based English Writing for Undergraduates

主　　编　黑玉琴
策划编辑　李　蕊
责任编辑　庞钧颖
责任校对　牛瑞鑫
封面设计　伍　胜

出版发行　西安交通大学出版社
　　　　　（西安市兴庆南路1号　邮政编码710048）
网　　址　http://www.xjtupress.com
电　　话　（029）82668357　82667874（市场营销中心）
　　　　　（029）82668315（总编办）
传　　真　（029）82668280
印　　刷　陕西思维印务有限公司

开　　本　889mm×1194mm　1/16　　印张　14.75　　字数　521千字
版次印次　2024年10月第1版　　　2024年10月第1次印刷
书　　号　ISBN 978-7-5605-8032-6
定　　价　59.80元

进入新时代以来，我国高等教育改革稳步推进，各级各类高等院校力求分类卓越，服务国家战略和区域经济社会的能力不断增强。就外语类专业而言，教育部于2018年发布的普通高等学校本科专业《外国语言文学类教学质量国家标准》（以下简称"《国标》"）和教育部高等学校外国语言文学类专业教学指导委员会（以下简称"外指委"）于2020年编制的《普通高等学校本科外国语言文学类专业教学指南》（以下简称"《教学指南》"），成为新时期我国外语教育教学承担新使命、形成新理念、探索新模式、开创新格局的重要指导性文件。

近年来，我国西部各高校在力促《国标》和《教学指南》生根落地的过程中，深刻认识到构建新发展格局所面临的诸多挑战，采取协同发展等手段，推动高等教育发展模式转变和服务能力提升。2019年9月，经西安外国语大学和四川外国语大学倡议，西部高等院校外语教育教学联盟在西安成立，成为西部高校通过区域内部协作、激发内生动力、深入推进"四新"建设和"三个一流"建设、构建西部高等外语教育集群式发展模式的重要平台。联盟成立短短两年多以来，中国高校外语慕课平台（UMOOCs）"西部外语"正式开通，目前上线西部各高校在线课程50余门；"西部外国语言文学博士研究生论坛"已成功举办两届；覆盖西部12省市的"西部高等外语教育发展研究"项目也正在有序推进，西部高等外语教育共同体雏形初见。

教材建设是推动《国标》和《教学指南》生根落地的重要手段之一，西部高等院校外语教育教学联盟成立之初就将此纳入议事日程。经过联盟专家团队广泛调研、充分论证，我们决定陆续出版"新时代·新西部"高等院校英语专业创新系列教材。本系列教材坚持马克思主义指导地位，贯彻《关于新时代振兴中西部高等教育的若干意见》精神，以《国标》和《教学指南》为依据，充分体现立德树人原则和课程思政理念，反映中西部外语教育特色和实际。具体而言，本系列教材具有如下特点：

1. 坚持价值导向，落实立德树人的根本任务

外语教育在真实、有效、立体、全面展示中国，服务我国国际传播能力建设，讲好中国故事，推动中国更好走向世界上，担负着重大的使命与责任。本系列教材在整体设计和素材选取等方面充分融入课程思政建设理念，引导学生了解世情、国情、党情、民情，增强学生对党的创新理论的政治认同、思想认同、情感认同，坚定中国特色社会主义道路自信、理论自信、制度自信、文化自信，教育引导学生积极践行社会主义核心价值观，深刻理解中华优秀传统文化，牢固树立法治观念，深刻理解并自觉实践各行业的职业精神和职业规范。同时，本系列教材在教学理念和教学方法上，引导任课教师树立课程思政意识，提升课程思政教学能力，提高立德树人成效。

2. 落实《国标》《教学指南》要求，明确素质、知识和能力的关系

《国标》和《教学指南》对素质、知识和能力三个方面的要求做了明确的界定。因此，如何通过知识的传授，培养学生正确的世界观、人生观和价值观，家国情怀与国际视野，跨文化能力和创新能力等，就成了推动《国标》和《教学指南》理念在教材中生根落地的首要任务。在整体设计上，本系列教材力促专业技能课程的专业化，一是在素材选择上贯穿以内容为依托的设计理念，让学生在习得外语技能的同时，获取某一学科的专业基本知识；二是在课程习题中有针对性地培养学生的跨文化能力、思辨能力、创新意识和社会责任感。在教学理念和教学方法上，本系列教材引导教师以知识传授为手段，注重学生素质和能力的培养。

3. 体现"分类卓越"思想，充分考虑不同类别学校的实际

本系列教材主要由熟悉外语教育改革方向，理解《国标》和《教学指南》理念和西部外语教育实际，且对外语教材有一定研究的高校骨干教师编写。在教材整体设计上，我们把握《国标》中所提出的"专业准入"要求，力求陆续做到专业核心课程和专业方向课程全覆盖。在内容安排和习题设计上，我们也力争体现出一定的区分度，从而给各级各类的学校留出一定的选择空间，也给教师在课堂教学中提供一定的灵活度。

4. 开发多元平台，提供全方位的学习体验

本系列教材依托现代信息技术手段，着力开展立体化教材建设。编写团队在展开内容编写之前，便同步设计了与教材内容适配的自主学习平台、多媒体课件、音频、视频等多元立体的课程资源，可满足教师开展微课、慕课、翻转课堂等基于网络多媒体教学的需求。此外，学生还可以随时随地在电脑、手机上学习，有利于教学效果的提升。

今年，教育部将发布振兴中西部高等教育的若干意见，实施新时代振兴中西部高等教育攻坚行动，全面提升中西部高等教育发展水平。这促使我们进一步思考如何激发中西部高等教育的内生动力和发展活力，进一步提升服务国家战略和区域经济发展的能力。希望本系列教材的顺利出版，能够为中西部高等教育振兴尽绵薄之力。

2022 年 1 月

当前，全球范围内新一轮科技革命和产业变革正以前所未有的广度和深度重塑着社会发展格局，加剧了科技领域的竞争与国际舞台的较量，科学研究范式、学科发展模式正经历着深刻变革，社会各领域对拔尖创新人才的需求愈发强烈，为高等教育人才培养模式改革与人才供给带来了新机遇和新挑战，推动了拔尖创新人才培养模式的探索向更深、更广的领域迈进。党的二十大报告指出，要"加快建设教育强国、科技强国、人才强国，坚持为党育人、为国育才，全面提高人才自主培养质量，着力造就拔尖创新人才"。这一重要论述为新时代我国教育发展、科技进步、人才培养指明了前进方向。《基于研究的本科英语写作》正是在这样的背景下设计编写的，教材旨在提高英语专业课程尤其是卓越拔尖人才实验班课程的挑战度，进一步推动研讨式教学，加强学生科研训练的系统性，助力拔尖创新人才培养。

目前，国外主要英语国家的大学都设立了本科生科研机构，如美国高校的 CUR（Council on Undergraduate Research）、英国的 BCUR（British Council of Undergraduate Research）和澳大利亚的 ACUR（Australian Council of Undergraduate Research），并创办了针对本科生学术发表的期刊，出版了一系列相关著作，内容涵盖本科研究型教学的课程设置、教学模式和培养方法，涉及人文社科及理工农医等各个学科。针对具体课程而编写的教材也陆续出版并应用于实际教学中，使一线教师能更好地将教学与科研深度融合，同时有助于学生在课程学习中参与实际科研活动，增强学生的创新精神和科研能力。《基于研究的本科英语写作》以国外本科生研究型教学的课程设置和培养目标为参考，针对国内外相关教材编写及使用现状，以英语写作课教学为依托，将本科生的研究能力培养纳入写作课堂教学，力求促成研究型教学（research-based/oriented teaching），将单纯写作内容教学拓展至相关的写作研究（writing studies/research）。与国外相关教材不同，本教材针对以英语为外语的学习者，编写内容和目标设置更符合国内教学状况。此外，不同于国内大部分仅针对写作方法、写作内容而编写的教材，本教材除了介绍、讲解具体研究方法，更注重引导学生开展自己的研究，在写作课堂教学中通过具体研究项目设计和研究过程，培养学生的研究意识、创新思维、科研能力，这一编写理念也符合新一轮高等教育改革和《外国语言文学类教学质量国家标准》（《国标》）对英语专业培养目标、教学内容及教学水平等不同层面的新要求，将专业课程学习内容与科研过程和人才培养过程紧密结合，强化科研对人才培养的支撑作用。

我们衷心希望本教材能为学生的英语写作与研究提供有益的方法，激发学生与教师的科研热情，提升学生知识探究的高度，并期待能推动高层次、高水平的英语教学建设，促成科研成果向优质教学资源转化。在本教材的编写过程中，我们参阅并借鉴了大量国内外相关文献资料和同类教材，在此向所有相关作者致以深深谢意。本书虽经反复打磨，但由于编者水平有限，难免有疏漏之处，恳请广大专家、读者批评指正！

编　者

2024 年 8 月 15 日

Part 1　Introduction to Writing Studies

Part 2　Key Areas of Writing Studies

Part 3   Approaches to Research on Writing

Part 1

Introduction to Writing Studies

▶ ▶ ▶ ▶ ▶

Writing Studies, an umbrella term, is an interdisciplinary field that includes scholars, researchers and teachers who are interested in the study of writing. Writing Studies can be traced to the ancient Greeks' studies in rhetoric, logic, and grammar; in modern times generations of scholars across disciplines (e.g., education, communication, linguistics, language learning, etc.) have investigated the role of writing in creativity, communication, learning, and human development. More recently, since about the 1970s, U.S. institutions of higher education have developed masters and doctoral degrees that specialize in the study of writing. Perhaps because it's such a new field, it tends to go by different names at different higher education institutions in the United States, including Rhetoric and Composition, and Composition Studies. While the names of these programs may differ, they do share commonalities: they typically have an interdisciplinary focus and are chiefly concerned with the study of writing pedagogy, theory and research. Nowadays, the field also includes teaching and research of English as a Second Language (ESL) writing.

Unit ①

Composition Studies

1.1 Introduction

Composition Studies, also referred to as rhetoric and composition, or simply composition, is an academic field of writing, research, and instruction, focusing especially on writing at the college level in the United States and the processes writers use to compose and share texts. As a discipline, Composition Studies is chiefly concerned with scholarly inquiry and teaching related to rhetoric, composition, professional and technical writing, writing center studies, writing across the curriculum, and writing assessment. Though a sub-discipline of Writing Studies, Composition Studies is a rapidly growing and constantly changing field. The world's largest professional organization for this field is the Conference on College Composition and Communication.

In most U.S. and some Canadian colleges and universities, undergraduate students take freshman— sometimes higher—composition courses. To support the effective administration of these courses, the development of basic and applied research on the acquisition of writing skills, and an understanding of the history of the uses and transformation of writing systems and writing technologies (among many other subareas of research), over seventy American universities offer doctoral study in rhetoric and composition. These programs usually include study of composition pedagogical theory, research methodologies in rhetoric and composition, and the history of rhetoric. Many composition scholars study not only the theory and practice of post-secondary writing instruction, but also the influence of different writing conventions and genres on writers' composing processes. Composition scholars also publish in the fields of Teaching English as a Second (ESL) or Foreign Language (EFL), writing centers, and new literacies.

1.2 Major Areas in Composition Studies

▶ Basic writing

First described by Mina Shaughnessy in the 1970s, Basic Writing (BW) is a division of Composition Studies that strives to bring disadvantaged students entering college to a more complete understanding of the rhetorical aspects of the writing process. Many of the courses focused on what used to be core concepts of formal English, like spelling, usage, and organization, though as the field has advanced these courses are increasingly aligned with the curricula found in mainstream first-year composition. Basic Writing coursework has diversified considerably since its beginnings in non-credit-bearing "pre" college courses, which remain typically understood as precursors to or supplements for mainstream first-year composition.

▶ First-year composition

First-Year Composition (FYC, sometimes known as first-year writing, freshman composition or freshman writing) is an introductory core curriculum writing course in American colleges. This course focuses on improving students' abilities to write in a university setting and introduces students to writing practices in the disciplines and professions. Traditionally, these courses are the basic requirement for incoming students, thus the previous name, "Freshman Composition." Scholars working within the field of composition-rhetoric often have teaching first-year composition courses as the practical focus of their scholarly work.

First-Year Composition is designed to meet the goals for successful completion set forth by the Council of Writing Program Administrators. To reach these goals, students must learn rhetorical conventions, critical thinking skills, information literacy, and the process of writing an academic paper. While there is no American standard curriculum for first-year composition, curriculum is developed at several levels, including the state, institution, department, and writing program.

Writing curricula vary considerably from institution to institution, but it may emphasize many stages of different writing processes (invention or brainstorming, drafting, revision, editing, proofreading), different forms of writing (narration, exposition, description, argumentation, comparison and contrast), different portions of the written product (introductions, conclusions, thesis statements, presentation and documentation of forms of evidence, inclusion of quotations, etc.), along with different modalities of composing to expand the concept of "writing." Students are encouraged to interact with classmates and receive feedback to be used for revision. These practices can take the form of essay peer review or workshops. Portfolios are a common way of assessing revised student work.

There are a number of identifiable pedagogies associated with FYC, including: current-traditional, expressivist, social-epistemic, process, post-process and Writing about Writing (WAW), all grounded in a range of different traditions and philosophies. Each of these pedagogies can generate a multitude of curricula. The second edition of *A Guide to Composition Pedagogies* identifies 17 different composition pedagogies, a few of which that relate to first-year composition are summarized below (Tate, 2014).

Genre

Genre pedagogy is meant to focus the student's attention on the purpose of a given piece of text through the lens of genre. Some perspectives favor instruction on the specific traits of a given established genre, particularly for those who are learning English as a second language. Others espouse the view that students should learn to identify elements of writing—style and conventions, for example—which denote its usefulness in a given setting as genre elements and know when to use them appropriately. Another form of genre pedagogy involves evaluating the characteristics of given genres, including the sensibilities they instantiate and which individuals or perspectives are excluded by them.

Literature and composition

Literature and composition, as an approach to teaching, is premised upon the integration of literature as the content for a composition course. Literature is strategically threaded through the writing course providing learners with in-depth comprehensive information, empowering their contribution to a variety of literary conversations. In this approach, literature provides learners with a plethora of opportunities for the development of writing skills including topics for debates, arguments, discussions, and general exploration of humanity. Discourses for discovery with this methodology are inclusive of gender, race, ethnicity, culture, feminism, social issues, politics, and religion.

Process

As the name suggests, process pedagogy utilizes classroom time by discussing the entire writing process. A class that implements process pedagogy aims to improve students' skills as writers by working in one or more groups on brainstorming, revising, proofreading, and "workshopping" students' work before they submit a final draft. After first-year composition students will have learned strategies for the skills. Before submitting a final successful draft, students would complete multiple drafts. Through the use of process pedagogy, the students' own writing acts as a text for the class which they use and learn from in order to become better writers. Each college has its own curriculum that doesn't easily transfer from one course to another; students will have trouble applying the skills they learned to other contexts.

Researched writing

The original purpose of assigning research papers in first-year composition was to assist students in developing research skills. Along with these skills came the emphasis of learning to incorporate sources to strengthen a paper's thesis. In recent years, a shift towards teaching information literacy skills and including multimedia has become more common in academia, and traditional research papers assigned to students have been on a decline since the 2000's (Tate, 2014).

▶ Advanced composition

Some universities require further instruction in writing and offer courses that expand upon the skills developed in First-Year Composition. Second level or advanced composition may emphasize forms of argumentation and persuasion, digital media, research and source documentation formats, and/or genres of writing across a range of disciplines and genres. For example, the skills required to write business letters or annual reports will differ significantly from those required to write historical or scientific research or personal memoirs.

▶ Graduate studies

Doctoral and Masters' programs in Composition Studies are available in some universities. Such programs are commonly housed within English Studies or Education programs. However, recently there are an increasing number of departments specifically dedicated to this field of study (e.g. Composition Studies, Writing & Rhetoric, Composition & Linguistics, etc.).

▶ Second language writing

Second language writing is the practice of teaching English composition to non-native speakers and writers of English. Teaching writing to ESL students does not receive much attention because even in ESL classes teachers focus on speaking, listening and reading, not just writing.

▶ Writing across the curriculum

Because there are curricula that address academic discourse and can be applied to specific parts of a writing curriculum, many compositionists have created a Writing Across the Curriculum (WAC) movement that situates writing-intensive instruction in specific academic discourse communities.

▶ Writing in the disciplines

Many university writing programs include Writing in the Disciplines (WID) courses, which focus on the genres and writing procedures that occur within specific fields of research.

▶ Writing center

Many colleges and universities have a writing center, which offers supplementary tutorial support for writing specifically in English classes and/or across the curriculum. Many universities in Europe only offer writing instruction via writing centers. The European Association for the Teaching of Academic Writing (EATAW), for example, specifically concerns itself with the study and advancement of writing centers in Europe. Since multimodality has resonated with Composition Studies, many writing centers have developed associated centers to support students' multimodal, multimedia composing. Some models for this work include the digital studio and the multiliteracy center.

1.3 Key Theories in Composition Studies

In the United States, the academic discipline of composition or composition-rhetoric has evolved rapidly over the past 50 years. Composition Studies emerged as a scholarly research discipline during the 1970s as (1) empirical methods became available to investigate the problem of meaning in discourse and, concomitantly, (2) the work of an international writing research community became institutionalized in the form of new journals and graduate programs.

From 1870 to 1900, as the American college system moved from small schools to a larger, diverse set of universities with distinct academic disciplines, the field of composition studies grew from traditional rhetorical studies. As pioneers in the field of composition studies, Harvard University enacted a new program in their English department that, for the first time, made a total commitment to writing, though the initial focus was on personal writing and did not include rhetoric or literary analysis. However, the field of composition studies soon became paired with the field of rhetoric as the modern university developed, because scholars began to realize that elements of rhetoric and not systematic grammatical study were necessary to improve writing and composition abilities. While rhetoric traditionally concerned matters related to verbal orations or speeches, both rhetoric and composition are related to the expression of ideas, often in an attempt to influence one's audience. In addition, composition is also concerned with the principles of invention, arrangement, style, and delivery traditionally associated with rhetoric; even memory can become an element of composition when one is writing a speech or a scholarly paper to be delivered orally. Thus, rhetoric and composition—colloquially termed "rhet/comp" or "comp/rhet"—became a field of its own and remains a burgeoning discipline in universities today. Scholars in composition studies identify their research with a variety of broader knowledge enterprises besides or instead of rhetoric. These include, for instance, literacy, linguistics, or discourse studies; cultural studies; English; English education; and communication. College composition itself (originally "freshman English"), once used to refer to the whole field, is now only one focus within rhetoric and composition, which has become progressively more intertwined with multiple, parallel, or transdisciplinary studies of discourse.

Below is an overview of the development of key theories underpinning the field of composition studies from the 1940s to today.

▶ Current-traditionalism

This is also known as formalism, which is the predominant form of composition pedagogy from the 1940s until the 1970s. Educators adhering to formalism focus on teaching students to model "correct" writing and to avoid grammatical errors. With instruction emphasizing formal features of writing, the formulaic five-paragraph essay becomes the standard for academic writing. Formalists view texts as having fixed meanings that can be discovered through close reading and explication. Having composition students do "close readings" of other writers' use of rhetoric and/or providing students with models of successful texts is one way formalist pedagogy may still be useful in the classroom. John Warriner's *English Grammar and Composition* (1950) serves as a primary example of the kind of instruction that was dominant at this time, and James Kinneavy and Gary A. Olson are representative scholars in this movement.

▶ Expressivism

It is also known as expressionism, which can be radical or moderate. Expressivism rose in popularity in the 1960s and 1970s as a reaction to formalism. Expressivists believe that writing should be taught as art, and they consider all writers artists. The individual "genius" is prized, and, under expressivism, writing is highly individualized. Teachers should merely act as facilitators of writers' personal growth. Freewriting and clustering as brainstorming techniques stem from expressivism and are still helpful for some students. Peer review and non-traditional grading also emerged from expressivism and are still considered valuable pedagogical tools. Peter Elbow and Donald Murray are key figures in the expressivist movement.

▶ Cognitivism

Also called socio-cognitivism, constructivism, or social constructivism, cognitivism gained attention in the 1970s and 1980s. Cognitivists work with psycholinguistics and cognition studies to focus on the individual writing process. Under the scientifically focused pedagogy of cognitivism, there are "correct" and "incorrect" writing processes. Reader response and structuralist theories under cognitivism place importance on the individual as a writer and a reader, and meaning is thought to be determined by the individual. Discussion of students' writing processes and modeling of "ideal" writing processes can be helpful in the classroom as long as students understand that writing processes can be very different from individual to individual. Linda Flowers and John Hayes are notable figures in the cognitivist movement.

▶ Cultural studies

Also known as multiculturalism, cultural studies rose to popularity in the 1970s and 1980s, around the same time as cognitivism. Cultural studies theorists recognize marginalized and/or oppressed groups and the importance of their voices to the field of composition studies. Writing instruction becomes less about "correct" grammar and standard English and more about student identity and voice. Writing instructors using cultural studies as a lens may focus more on personal narratives and writing about students' life experiences. Henry Giroux, Joe Hardin, Cary Nelson, Paula A. Treichler and Lawrence Grossberg have made much contribution to the development of this trend.

▶ Critical pedagogy

Critical pedagogy followed social constructionism and became popular in the 1980s and 1990s. Composition theorists who advocate critical pedagogy are interested in the power structures of writing instruction. Paulo Freire's "banking model" of education posits that institutions or teachers "deposit" knowledge into students, effectively removing students' agency within the education system. Critical pedagogy examines the power structures behind the education system and seeks to disrupt those structures by taking power away from instructors and giving more agency to students. Writing is viewed as a tool for activism. In the classroom, critical pedagogy encourages discussions about power dynamics, social issues, and activism. Students are urged to question their thinking and write to affect social and political change. Paulo Freire's *Pedagogy of the Oppressed* is a seminal text in the critical pedagogy movement.

▶ Social constructionism

Also known as social epistemicism, social constructionism emerged in the 1980s as a reaction to the internal focus of cognitivism. Under social constructionism, community becomes the focus of attention, as writers are perceived to be members of specific discourse communities, and those communities are believed to shape the individual. Writing instruction is geared towards helping writers gain access to and move between discourse communities. Texts and knowledge are thought to be products of society, and meaning is contingent on community standards. Applications of social constructionism in the classroom include engaging students in class discussion, encouraging collaborative writing, and providing students with rationales behind assignments. James Berlin is one of the most well-known proponents of social constructionism.

▶ Post-process

Also called post-structuralism, it became popular in the 1990s and remains a contemporary theory of composition. Post-process theory is difficult to pin down due to its lack of structure and the tendency of post-process theorists to disagree. However, post-process theory is generally considered a reaction against cognitivism/process theory, which upholds the idea that there is a right and wrong writing process that students should follow. Another characteristic of post-process theory is its rejection of universalism and expressivism. Some scholars also consider it anti-pedagogical. Sidney Dobrin and Thomas Kent are two of the early figures in the post-process movement. John Whicker is a well-known critic of the term post-process, which he claims is a sort of "catch all" term for theorists to apply to any new or trendy theoretical concept.

Unit ②

Second/Foreign Language Writing Studies

2.1 Introduction

Second language writing is the practice of teaching English composition to non-native speakers and writers of English. Teaching writing to English as a Second Language (ESL) students does not receive much attention because even in ESL classes teachers focus on speaking, listening and reading, not just writing. But it is important that teaching writing should understand the needs of ESL students so as to help them improve their writing.

The field of second language (L2) writing has come of age. The formal study of L2 writers, writing, and writing instruction has a relatively short but fruitful history going at least as far back as the 1960s. Research in L2 writing has grown exponentially over the last 40 years and, during the late 1980s and the early 1990s, L2 writing began to evolve into an interdisciplinary field of inquiry with its own disciplinary infrastructure— replete with a journal, monographs, edited collections, a book series, annotated bibliographies, graduate courses, and conferences as well as symposia (Matsuda, et al., 2003).

2.2 Major Teaching Approaches to Second Language Writing (SLW)

Teaching writing has progressed through several approaches during the history of education in the United States. ESL teachers might need to explore common methods which are the cognitive, social and expressive theories to create an approach that meets the needs of ESL writers and help them to overcome their difficulties.

▶ Cognitive approach

The cognitive view believes that writing is progressing from one stage to another in a series of single steps. That means "good" writing is a planned process, which includes planning, translating and reviewing. But the composition of writing occurs as a recursive process, where writers return to "backwards" parts of the process in order to move "forward" with the overall composition. ESL teachers may find this approach helpful at first in teaching beginning ESL students because at this level students do not have large amounts of vocabulary and grammar or knowledge of the style of essays which is the basis of writing English. However, many kinds of grammar make ESL students confused, especially because there are many exceptions. Because writing styles are different in different languages, ESL students need time to master them. Therefore, ESL teachers should find an effective way to teach ESL students vocabulary, grammar and style as required in English writing. With the emphasis on the steps, organization and process of writing, the cognitive approach can meet these needs.

▶ Social approach

Another approach is the social view which shows the importance of teaching writing by making students learn the different languages of discourse communities. Discourse community can be thought of as members of an academic discipline or a select audience. When the ESL students have become good at grammar and style, they face a large problem when they enter their chosen academic field since each academic community has a particular language or vocabulary of its own, which differs from one to another. This problem is faced not only by ESL students, but almost all students who are native English speakers will struggle with this when they begin the first year of their academic life. The social approach can be used by ESL teachers as a second step but they should make sure that their students master the basics of English writing such as grammar and style.

▶ Expressive approach

The expressive view is focused on wittier creating and freer movement. There are three elements for "good" writing which are integrity, originality, and spontaneity. However, it is difficult to evaluate them in a paper. Therefore, these standards cannot be relied upon to judge writing. In addition, these elements are not the important elements that help to assess "good" writing. ESL teachers might use this approach but it can only be used for highly advanced ESL students. It is difficult to ask ESL students to write freely if they possess limited vocabulary or grammar. They need examples to help them which they can find in the cognitive approach.

ESL teachers may use these common ways of teaching writing, but they need first to understand their students' difficulties. Learning writing is one of the essential difficulties that ESL students find in studying English, especially since writing is important in an academic community. Some ESL students may need to jump from being a student who does not speak English ever to a student who uses academic language in a short time which may put a large burden on their shoulders. Hence, teaching writing to ESL students is different than teaching native speakers. ESL teachers need to choose an effective way to meet the needs of ESL students. It would be helpful if ESL teachers look at these different ways of teaching writing to see which one addresses ESL students' difficulties in the best way or if a combination of these theories may be better.

②.③ An Overview of L2 Writing Research

A considerable variety of methods have been used to understand the complex, multifaceted nature of L2 writing. Often driven by pedagogical imperatives and informed by particular views of writing, texts and writers, these methods themselves raise questions regarding what we believe writing is and about our interpretive practices. With increasing numbers of teachers and scholars turning to investigate writing in their classrooms or courses of further study, it may be helpful to be aware of what options are available for studying writing and how these relate to key methodological designs. More than this, however, it is important to be aware of what our choices imply about our understanding of what writing is and how it can be known. Ken Hyland in the paper "Methods and Methodologies in Second Language Writing Research" (*System* 59, 2016, pp. 116–125), slightly adapted and presented below, sets out the main approaches to studying writing for novice researchers, providing examples of key studies, and then situates these methods within the main theories about writing arguing that methods are not neutral options but allow us to see certain things but not others. They do not just tell us different things about writing but reveal what we believe writing to be.

▶ Methods and methodologies in writing research

Research generally begins by isolating something that interests or worries us and then asking questions about it. The kinds of questions we ask, however, and how we collect, analyze and interpret the data to answer them, depend on our preferences and preconceptions, the topic and the purpose we have for studying it, the context, our access to data, the time and resources we have, and the energy we are prepared to invest. There is no "one-size-fits-all" formula to carrying out research on writing (or on anything else) but nor is there a perfect approach to every question. While research can answer questions that interest us, there is rarely only one answer or one "truth" waiting to be revealed. In fact, almost any research design can answer any research question. But while the research approach we adopt will tell us something about the thing we are studying, it is important to be aware of the assumptions we are making when we design our research and select our tools for collecting data.

Here, we need to distinguish between *methods*, or ways of collecting data (such as observations, surveys and interviews), and *methodologies*, the principles and understandings that guide and influence our choice and use of methods (like experimentation and ethnography). Methods are the front-line techniques and methodologies the systematic application of them.

Methodology, therefore, concerns how research is done, how we find out about things, and how knowledge is gained. While it clarifies, explains and justifies the choice of certain methods in our research, researchers (and journals) often tend to favour some methodologies over others and regard those as uniquely legitimate or effective. In fact, the choice of methodology we adopt to study L2 writing will largely depend on what we believe writing is, the model of language we subscribe to, and how we understand learning. Methodology, then, is a general strategy or operating model for conducting research: a plan which contains a logical organization and the directions to answer a research question. It shapes how methods are used but does not determine the data required, how these data are to be collected or how they should be analyzed. Thus collecting naturally-produced student texts, a method, might be done as part of a wider ethnographical study, as part of a controlled experiment to compare groups of writers, or as data for studying learner improvement over time (methodologies).

▶ Research methods

Because method is often used to refer to all research processes, it is helpful to clarify the differences so that we can see the research options available to us. First, there are four broad ways of collecting data related to writing and these are set out in Table 2.1 and elaborated briefly below.

Table 2.1   Major methods used in researching writing

Methods	Elaboration
Elicitation	Ways of prompting self-report and performance data
Introspection	Ways of collecting verbal or written reports by text users
Observation	Direct or recorded data of "live" interactions or writing behavior
Text data	Collections of naturally produced samples of writing

Elicitation

Elicitation refers to methods for prompting self-report and performance data.

- **Questionnaires** are useful for collecting large amounts of structured, easily analysable information about text users' characteristics, beliefs or attitudes, information that is not usually available from observation of their behavior or from their texts. Like interviews, they allow researchers to tap people's views and experiences of writing, but are more quantitative and restrictive. They have been widely used in writing research to discover the kinds of writing target communities require. One study, for example, employed a questionnaire design to survey 5,000 Chinese Hong Kong students about the difficulties they experienced when studying through the medium of English, identifying problems of style, grammar and cohesion.

- **Interviews** offer more interactive and less predetermined ways of eliciting information than surveys and so allow greater flexibility and potential for elaboration. Although sometimes simply oral questionnaires, highly structured and limiting responses, interviews generally represent a very different way of understanding human experience. Semi-structured formats, which loosely follow a set of guidelines and allow extensive follow-up, or unstructured types, which observe an outline of issues but follow the direction of interviewee responses, regard knowledge as generated between people rather than as objectified and external to them. Participants are able to discuss their interpretations and perspectives, sharing what writing means to them rather than responding to preconceived categories. This flexibility and responsiveness means that interviews are used widely in writing research to learn more about attitudes to writing, about teaching and learning and about reasons for rhetorical choices. They are therefore helpful in learning about how writers understand what it is they do when they write and are particularly valuable in revealing issues that might be difficult to predict, such as how students interpret teacher written feedback.

- **Focus groups** are more interactive and less threatening than interviews as participants are free to talk with other group members. They therefore take some control away from the interviewer, but can produce richer data as a result, although what participants tell the researcher is shared with other group participants as well, raising privacy concerns and limiting the kinds of topics that the researcher can pursue. Usually conducted face-to-face, they may also be held in synchronous computer-mediated venues or on chatrooms where transcripts can be saved and considered later. Groups have been used to discover students' academic writing needs and difficulties.

- **Tests**, or **one-shot writing tasks**, elicit performance information from students, discovering what it is they know, can do or are able to remember in writing. They therefore offer insights into students' writing ability and knowledge of genre, language forms and rhetorical understandings and, indirectly, can also provide information about rater behavior and judgements of good writing. Previous research, for example, investigated how experienced and inexperienced raters scored essays written by ESL writers on two different prompts, finding that inexperienced raters were more severe on one prompt but that differences between the two groups were eliminated following rater training.

Introspection

The use of verbal reports as data reflects the idea that the process of writing requires conscious attention and that at least some of the thought processes involved can be recovered, either by talking aloud while writing or as retrospective recalls.

- **Think aloud protocols** (TAPs) involve participants writing in their normal way but instructed to verbalize what they are doing at the same time, so that information can be recorded on their decisions, strategies and perceptions as they work. This kind of data has been criticized as offering an artificial and incomplete picture of the complex cognitive activities involved in writing as many such processes are routine and not available to verbal description while the act of reporting may create reactive effects, distorting the process being reported on. However, it was found that verbalization had little impact on students' writing in controlled conditions. In the absence of alternatives, the method has been widely used to reveal the strategies writers use when composing, particularly what students do when planning and revising. Stimulated recalls, on the other hand, involve videotaping the writer while writing and then discussing the writer's thought processes while watching the video together immediately afterwards. This is the approach taken in previous research to study student writing strategies.

- **Diaries** are first-person entries in a journal or blog and then analyzed for recurring patterns or significant events. Diarists can be asked to produce "narrative" entries which freely introspect on their learning or writing experiences, or follow guidelines to restrict the issues addressed. These can be detailed points to note (Who is your reader for this essay?) or a loose framework for response (note all the work you did to complete this task). Alternatively, researchers may ask diarists to concentrate only on "critical incidents" of personal significance or to simply record dates and times of writing and what it was they wrote. While some diarists may resent the time and intrusion this involves, diaries provide a rich source of reflective data which can reveal processes difficult to access in other ways. Thus previous research, for example, used a Chinese scholar's blog entries to discover how he went about writing a paper in English for publication.

Observation

While elicitation and introspective methods report what people say they think and do, observations give evidence of it. They are based on conscious noticing and precise recording of actions as a way of seeing these actions in a new light.

- **Recording behavior** can be done live or from taped recordings. Again, the researcher can impose different degrees of structure on the mass of data that this method can often produce, from simply checking pre-defined boxes at fixed intervals or every time a type of behavior occurs, to writing a full narrative of events. The most structured observations involve a prior coding scheme to highlight significant events but one problem here is that all observations privilege some behaviours and neglect others, as we only record what we think is important. Ticking pre-selected actions gives more manageable data, but it may ignore unexpected behavior. This explains why the method is often combined with others, as in one study of a Business Manager's activities through one day. In addition to observation, she recorded oral encounters, analyzed copies of written materials and conducted interviews to gain as full a picture as possible.

- **Keystroke logging** is a more reliable, and less intrusive, way of tracking writing behavior than a researcher looking over a writer's shoulder as software such as Inputlog or Scriptlog can record and playback what writers do as they write. This logs and time stamps keystrokes, pauses, cutting, pasting, and deleting and mouse activity, allowing the researcher to reconstruct text production processes and sites visited. Closely associated with psycholinguistic aspects of writing, the method can show how a writer juggles the complexities of cognitive activities in real time, planning content, choosing forms, considering audience and style, and so on. One study, for example, reveals how a group of Master's students and experts used sources when writing short texts, describing the organization of writing processes that involve searching, reading, and copying from multiple digital sources.

Text data

A major source of data is writing itself: the use of texts as objects of study. Approaches which analyze texts see writing as an outcome of activity, as words on a page or screen and can be descriptive (revealing what occurs), analytical (interpreting why it occurs) or critical (questioning the social relations which underlie and are reproduced by what occurs). Because they can be approached in different ways for different purposes, text analyses can be seen as both methodology and method as researchers seek to understand what language choices writers make, why they make them and what they mean. Before the discussion of data analyses, first data collection is presented below.

- **Single text.** Some studies focus on a single text as an instance in action, either because the text seems interesting or represents a particular genre or author, such as Martin's (2004, qtd. in Hyland, 2016) analysis of the ways a writer negotiates solidarity with his readers in a lifestyle magazine.

- **Chain of texts.** Another source of text data is the collection of a series of texts gathered. This may be to observe the changes made by a single writer over several drafts, such as previous research's account of the transformations over six drafts of a research paper by a Chinese scholar. Alternatively, chains can be observed to see how different purposes, audiences and genres influence rhetorical choices. Previous analysis of revisions made in parallel passages from introductions in six humanities and social science dissertation-monograph pairs, for example, highlights the revisions transforming a PhD dissertation into a book. Studies have also explored historical changes in a single genre over time.

- **Corpora.** Perhaps most commonly now, analysts study collections of texts, to get a more representative picture of a genre or a group of writers. A corpus represents a writer's experience of language in some restricted domain, providing an alternative to intuition, initially looking at the frequency with which words or patterns occur and how features commonly associate in collocational patterns, pointing to common usage in the genre.

▶ Methodologies

Together with these sources of data and the methods used in data collection are some major methodological designs, summarized in Table 2.2.

Table 2.2　Major design methodologies in L2 writing research

Methodologies	Elaboration
Experimentation	Controlled context to discover the effect of an intervention
Ethnography	Prolonged engagement with a community to capture participant perspectives
Auto-ethnography	Author reflects on personal experience and social meaning of writing
Critical analysis	Study connections between situated writing and wider socio-political contexts
Text analysis	Study of authentic examples of writing used for communication in natural settings
Meta-analysis	An empirical synthesis to provide and overview of results of studies in an area
Case studies	Detailed study of a specific subject to gain a better understanding

Experimentation

Experimental methods are set up to discover the effect of something on something else. Experimentation is a deductive method in that the researcher intervenes to test a theory by isolating and studying a single feature under controlled conditions. Most simply, this involves applying some treatment to one of two groups while holding other factors constant. The two groups are then given a post-test to see the effect of the treatment and statistical tests are carried out to find out if differences between the control and the experimental groups are significant. More complex treatments such as factorial designs can be used to explore several treatment variables at several levels of interactions. Experimental researchers are particularly concerned with internal validity, or whether changes are only due to the issue under study, and external validity, whether the results are generalizable to other populations. The use of test measurements also has to be carefully monitored to minimize threats to the reliability and validity of the research.

Writing research, however, largely follows a "relativist" orientation and favours more qualitative, natural, and "thicker" data collection techniques. Although experimental research is not possible to capture the rich complexity of writing, the method has been used to look at the overall impact of instruction or feedback on writing. In an experimental study on peer review, for instance, Lundstrom and Baker (2009) divided students into those who reviewed anonymous papers but received no peer feedback and those who received feedback but did not review other students' writing. An analysis of students' writing over a semester showed that the givers made more significant gains in their own writing than the receivers did, especially at lower proficiency levels. Experimental studies should be treated cautiously, however, as it is difficult to hold all non-experimental variables constant in natural settings so differences in teaching styles, learner preferences, teacher attitudes, peer relationships, and so on can all influence results.

Ethnography

Ethnography seeks to provide a rich (or "thick") description and interpretive account of what people do in a classroom, workplace or other social setting, the outcome of their interactions in that setting and how they understand what they are doing. Researchers use a range of diverse methods, particularly observation and elicitation, to understand behavior from participants' perspectives. As far as possible, they attempt to collect and analyze data over a period without pre-set categories or explicit hypotheses. Because it uses multiple methods and involves sustained engagement with a context, it is labor-intensive and time-consuming, demanding considerable know-how and resources. While sometimes criticized for a lack of generalizability, ethnography allows for a detailed explanation of what is specific to a particular group. Researchers generally study language practices within familiar communities and institutions rather than in far flung exotic locations, as in anthropological ethnographies. Language is always considered within the context of its production and reception, rather than in isolation, simply as text. An approach to studying writing which highlights text analysis within more traditional ethnographic techniques, such as informal interviews and observations, is textography. This aims to provide a more contextualized basis for understanding writing in the social, cultural and institutional settings in which it takes place than might be obtained by looking only at texts themselves. An example is Paltridge's (2008, qtd. in Hyland, 2016) study of the exegeses that art and design students write in their masters degrees, interviewing students, supervisors and examiners and studying their texts.

Auto-ethnography

Auto-ethnography focuses on the researcher-writer's subjective experience rather than the beliefs and practices of others, connecting this to wider cultural and social meanings. Potentially this might provoke insight into often overlooked problems, such as the nature of identity, race, sexuality, life in academia, etc. Involving recall or diary methods, auto-ethnography seeks to assist the researcher make sense of his or her individual experience. They are, however, also critical or even political as they often challenge us to consider things, or do them differently. Previous research found auto-ethnography to be a valuable tool for L2 learners in a writing class, allowing them to explore and reflect on their cultural background and identities in a U.S. university.

Critical analysis

Critical analysis is a methodology employing a range of methods to "identify linkages, broadly construed, between local occasions of language learning and use to broader social processes, formations and discourses" (Talmy, 2015, p.153). Essentially the prefix critical can be added to other methodologies such as discourse analysis or ethnography to empirically explore these linkages. In writing research, methods such as text analysis, observations and interviews have been used widely. All three methods, for example, were used in one study of two Chinese students exhibiting agency and identity investment through resistance to the practices of an American writing classroom, with the authors relating their actions to ideological implications about ethnicity, race, and class.

Text analysis

Texts can be approached in different ways and for different purposes: looking at systems of choices, institutional ideologies, L1 and L2 practices, what they say about communities of users and how they link to other texts. Broadly, texts can be understood in two ways. First, they can be looked at as systems of forms, focusing on grammatical items or patterns to better understand the regularities we find in texts or student errors. Second, and more usually, texts are treated as discourse, or how they work to communicate in particular settings. Here texts are resources to accomplish writer goals and understood as language in action, generally focusing on particular genres, such as a newspaper editorial, business report or an argumentative essay.

Central to discourse analysis is the idea that forms express functions and this also underpins the highly productive notion of genre. Genres are abstract, socially recognized ways of using language and represent how writers typically respond to recurring situations. The ways people write are often not a matter of conscious awareness, but of routine and habit, acquired and changed through repeated interactions. Evidence for this routine behavior is often sought in specialized corpora using concordance programmes which bring together all instances of a search word or phrase in the corpus as a list of unconnected lines of text, showing instances of actual language use when read horizontally but regularities of system when read vertically. Corpora can be analyzed using corpus-based or corpus-driven procedures. The former is where the researcher begins with a pre-selected list of potentially productive items and examines the corpus for their frequencies and behavior, such as the uses of passive voice. Less common in writing studies are corpus-driven methods where the corpus is treated as the basis for any discovery, as in the previous research to identify the most common multi-word patterns in textbooks.

Meta-analysis

This is an empirical synthesis or systematic review which aims to provide an exhaustive summary of current literature relevant to a research question. While it is customary to distinguish between research which is primary (gathers new data) and secondary (reviews existing studies), meta-analysis differs from traditional literature reviews by adopting an empirical perspective, being as thorough as possible, and not taking the claims of report authors at face value. It uses an explicit approach and aims to identify what can reliably be said on the basis of these studies and the criteria used to evaluate them. They therefore go beyond the individual results contained in the original studies to produce synthetic findings. Norris and Ortega (2006, qtd. in Hyland, 2016) have published a collection which exemplifies the methodology for conducting synthesis research in applied linguistics and a good example of a study in writing is Truscott's (2007, qtd. in Hyland, 2016) review of error correction studies which shows teacher feedback on errors has a negative effect on learners' accuracy.

Case studies

A case-study is "an instance in action"; a means of portraying what a particular situation is like by capturing the close-up reality of participants' lived experiences and thoughts about a situation. They typically combine methods to explore a particular bounded phenomenon. The purpose of most case studies is to gain a better understanding of a person, process, group or context rather than to statistically generalize to other populations, although they do allow theoretical generalizations which can be valuable in other research contexts. Essentially, case studies blend a rich description of events with interpretive analysis that draws on participants' own perspectives. Such a thorough portrayal of local writing behaviors characterizes a great deal of L2 writing research. One example is a study of how two first year Chinese Hong Kong undergraduates understood plagiarism and their strategies based on these understandings in writing the same source-based assignment. The study drew on textual comparisons between student texts and source texts, interview data, and observation notes. These data suggested that while both students seemed to understand the university's plagiarism policy, their texts displayed patchwriting and inappropriate citation which the authors discuss in relation to the complexity of sources in introductory courses and the difficulties of attribution for novice writers.

▶ Research choices and research methodologies

One of the main considerations of research methodology is to ensure that the study will answer the questions it has set itself, providing a credible explanation or characterization of the issue. To achieve this, many writing researchers combine several methods, both quantitative and qualitative, to gain a holistic picture of what is always a complex reality. In fact, the concept of triangulation, the use of multiple sources of data or analytical methods, can bring greater plausibility to the interpretation of results. It obviously makes sense to view research pragmatically, adopting whatever tools seem most effective, mixing methods to increase the validity of the eventual findings. Thus, text analysts, for example, often supplement studies of writing by interviewing writers and readers to better understand how these texts are typically produced and received. It is the combination of methods which help make explicit the tacit knowledge or strategies that writers and readers bring to acts of composing or assessing writing.

However, while methods have been discussed as a list of discrete instruments, they are not an open set of options in free combination. Research of any kind begins with some major decisions, concerning the degree of intervention, quantification, replication, objectivity and generalization which is thought desirable or even possible. An important feature of writing research, for example, is that it tends to favour data gathered in naturalistic rather than controlled conditions. This is not to say that methods that elicit data through questionnaires, structured interviews or experiments are not employed or that they have nothing to tell us about writing. It is simply that there has been a strong preference for collecting data in authentic circumstances not specifically set up for the research, such as via classroom observations or analyses of naturally occurring texts.

Most importantly, our choice of methods is influenced by our preconceptions: our personal view of what writing is and how it might best be understood. Methods are inseparable from methodologies and methodologies are underpinned by philosophical assumptions about the nature of the world and how we can know it. The selection of methods must therefore be made with regard to a range of personal and contextual factors, as shown in Table 2.3.

Table 2.3   Factors influencing choice of methods in writing research

Factors	Examples
What are you going to study	writer, reader, community, text, genre, context, modality
What stance will you take	disinterested, interested, participatory, interventionist
What theoretical framework will you use	linguistic, cognitive, sociocultural, critical, literary
What data will you collect	corpora, interviews, diary entries, think aloud protocols
How will you collect the data	observation, elicitation, experimental, text compilation
How will you analyze it	statistical, interpretive, stylistic
How will you present it	report, conference presentation, research article, blog

If we try and isolate methods from this complex, to see data collection instruments as something separate from how we see our role as researchers and our view of writing, then we remove them from the assumptions which influence our research and inform our interpretations. In other words, focusing on methods alone disguises their epistemological aspects and sees them only as tools for collecting and analyzing data rather than ways of testing our preconceptions. In sum, our views about writing influence the methods we select while our methods reinforce our views about writing.

▶ Major perspectives in writing research

Language research methodologies can be compared across a number of dimensions. Most obviously, we often see quantitative research, which involves statistics and manipulating numerical data, being contrasted with qualitative research, which is more holistic and process-oriented. The questions raised in Table 2.3, moreover, imply other divergences, such as *theoretical* vs *applied*, *objective* vs *subjective*, *experimental* vs *ethnographic*, *psychometric* vs *naturalistic* and *system* vs *instance*. Each of these contrasts can help us interrogate different methods and evaluate their value in particular contexts. When considering writing research, we can fold these polar distinctions into a number of predominant paradigms. These are six broad ways of viewing writing to which research is often oriented and which lead to choice of some methods over others. Though some of these already mentioned earlier in this unit, all the six are summarized in Table 2.4 and discussed below for emphasis and convenience.

Table 2.4 Perspectives on writing and research methods

Perspectives	Views of writing	Main methodologies	Research methods
expressive activity	writing is a creative act	ethnograph, case study	elicitation, observation
cognitive activity	writing is a thinking process	experiment, ethnography	observation, introspection, elicitation
completed activity	texts are rule-structured objects	text analysis	text analysis
situated activity	writing is contextual performance	ethnography, autoethnography	observation, introspection elicitation, text analysis
social activity	texts express community purposes	discourse analysis, case study	text analysis, elicitation
ideology	texts reinforce power relations	critical analysis, case study	text analysis, observation

Writing as expressive activity

The expressivist view rejects a definition of writing based on correct grammar and usage and considers it as a creative act of discovery in which the process is as important as the product to the writer. Writing is learnt and not taught; it is an act of imagination and self-discovery. This idea, however, is challenging to L2 writers from cultures which place less emphasis on individualism.

Writing as cognitive activity

For many researchers, writing is a cognitive performance which can be modelled by analogy with computer processing. Essentially writing is seen as a problem-solving activity: how writers approach a writing task as a problem and bring intellectual resources to solving it. It is through writing that individuals discover and formulate their ideas. A great deal of research has revealed the complexity of planning and editing activities, the influence of different writing tasks and the value of examining what writers do through a series of writing drafts. Observation and self-report are widely used methods in this paradigm. In particular, these studies have made considerable use of writers' verbal reports while composing, keystroke logging of writers, task observation, and retrospective interviews.

Writing as completed activity

Once the main approach to the study of writing, this is still an active research agenda which sees texts as a product or an artefact of activity independent of particular contexts and outside the personal experiences of writers and readers. Researchers follow de Saussure's (1986) famous binary and see texts as langue, or language as an abstract system which preexists users, rather than parole or instances of communication. They therefore tend to count features and infer rules of usage. Once this involved enumerating the T-unit length of a text to determine the overall syntactic complexity of language samples or measure the maturity of learners' writing. More recently, large corpora have been used to identify how features such as evaluative adjectives like *nice*, *good* and *great* are typically used or to assess improvement in student essays by measuring increases in morphemes, words and clauses. Alternatively, learner corpora can be studied to see the effect of L1 transfer. Such research describes language rather than writing, neglecting the fact that all texts include what writers suppose their readers will know, and how they will use the text. Thus no text can be fully explicit or universally "appropriate" so such analyses are limited to a static product not the result of a writer's dynamic effort to make meaning.

Writing as situated activity

For others, writing is a situated activity, placing emphasis on the physical and experiential contexts in which writing occurs—what Nystrand (1987) calls the "situation of expression." This view regards writing as influenced both by the personal attitudes and prior experiences that the writer brings to writing and the impact of the specific political and institutional contexts in which it takes place. Prior (1998, p. xi) puts it like this:

> When seen as situated activity, writing does not stand alone as the discrete act of a writer, but emerges as a confluence of many streams of activity: reading, talking, observing, acting, making, thinking and feeling as well as transcribing words on paper.

Ethnographic approaches are often used in an attempt to give a holistic explanation of behavior using a variety of methods and drawing on the understandings of insiders themselves to minimize the assumptions brought to the event by the researcher.

By using detailed observations of acts of writing, participant interviews, analyses of surrounding practices and other techniques, researchers have developed accounts of local writing contexts. These descriptions give significant attention to the experiences of writers and their understandings of the immediate context as they write. An example is the investigation of six ESL writers' reactions to, and uses of, teacher written feedback at a New Zealand university. This study used a longitudinal approach which drew on a variety of data sources including observation notes, interview transcripts, think aloud protocols and written texts. However, concentrating on the local setting fails to capture the culture and event within which the action is embedded and which their writing must invoke. Texts do not function communicatively at the time they are composed but when they are read, as they anticipate particular readers and the responses of those readers to what is written. Texts evoke a social milieu which intrudes upon the writer and activates specific responses to recurring tasks.

Writing as social activity

Once again, this perspective understands writing as a noun rather than as a verb, but the focus shifts from the formal features of isolated texts toward the whole text as an instance of language functioning in a context of human activity. The emphasis is on discourse rather than texts as objects, so here the linguistic patterns of texts point to contexts beyond the page or screen, implying a range of social constraints and choices which operate on writers in any context. Here the writer is neither a creator working through a set of cognitive processes nor an interactant engaging with a reader, but a member of a socially and rhetorically constituted community. The writer has certain goals and intentions, certain relationships to his or her readers, and certain information to convey, and the forms of a text are resources used to accomplish these. A variety of approaches have considered texts as discourse, but all have tried to discover how writers organize language to produce coherent, purposeful prose for particular groups of readers.

Writing as ideology

A final perspective on writing also emphasizes the importance of social context but stresses that the key dimension of a context are the relations of power that exist in it and the ideologies that maintain these relations. The importance of power as mediating discourse and social groups has been explored most extensively by researchers working in Critical Discourse Analysis (CDA) which attempts "to unpack the ideological underpinnings of discourse that have become so naturalized over time that we begin to treat them as common, acceptable and natural features of discourse" (Teo, 2006, qtd. in Hyland, 2016, p. 123). So while this approach typically involves analyses of texts, it also considers their relationship to the wider social environment and the part they play for individuals within specific situations.

Essentially, ideology is concerned with how individuals experience the world and how these experiences are reproduced through their writing. Fairclough (1992) uses the term "orders of discourse" to refer to the relatively stable configurations of discourse practices found in particular domains or institutions. These are frames for interaction such as lab reports, newspaper editorials, student records, academic articles, and so on, which have prestige value in different institutions and which are ideologically shaped by its dominant groups. They provide writers with templates for appropriate ways of writing, which means that any act of writing, or of teaching writing, is embedded in ideological assumptions. While CDA does not subscribe to any single method, some researchers draw on discourse analysis informed by Systemic Functional Linguistics (SFL). This is because the model sees language as a system of linguistic features which offer choices to users, but which are circumscribed in situations of unequal power. SFL thus offers CDA a way of analyzing the relations between language and social contexts, making it possible to ground concerns of power and ideology in the details of discourse.

▶ Conclusions

In closing, (1) there is no perfect research design or research method as the tools a researcher selects will depend on the purpose and context of the study; and (2) methods are inseparable from theories and how we understand writing. We may select methods in order to understand writing but at the same time we select them because of the way we understand writing. Our assumptions drive our interests and our research choices so that we cannot say that any method is better than any other in unpacking the intricacies of writing and telling us what it "really is." Different methods and methodologies have been developed to do certain things and they differ in their capacity to do the same things. They not only answer different questions, but also give us different answers to the same questions. It makes no sense, in other words, to say what writing is independently of a theory.

The connections suggested here between writing paradigms and inquiry methods encourage us to spell out our views about writing and about our role in the research process. This not only helps us think about our project more clearly, but is also a valuable professional development exercise in itself, sharpening our perceptions and clarifying our thinking. What questions are worth asking? What counts as appropriate data? Should it be collected naturalistically or in controlled conditions? What role will statistics play in interpreting it? How generalizable and replicable should the study be? These questions are asked by all those undertaking research and depend on what they understand writing to be and how it can be known. Clearly the complexity of writing requires multiple methods, viewing a writer, a context or set of texts through multiple lenses. But we need to be aware of the different ways of knowing that underpin our choices and make these explicit in our interpretations. The bottom line is that perspectives don't determine methods, but they do influence how we approach research, particularly the things we think it might be interesting to study, the kinds of questions we ask about them, and the data we need to answer those questions.

Part 2

Key Areas of Writing Studies
▶ ▶ ▶ ▶ ▶

This part introduces the key areas of writing studies selected and adapted from Hyland's "An overview of writing" in *Teaching and Researching Writing* (2009, pp. 7–42). Hyland discusses the major frameworks used to explore writing as well as different perspectives on writing research and teaching. More importantly, Hyland questions the widely held views that writing is either simply words on a page or an activity of solitary individuals. Rather, modern conceptions see writing as a social practice, embedded in the cultural and institutional contexts in which it is produced and the particular uses that are made of it. When we pick up a pen or sit at a computer, we adopt and reproduce certain roles, identities and relationships to engage in particular socially approved ways of communicating: to write an essay, make an insurance claim, or complain about a supermarket delivery. So while every act of writing is in a sense both personal and individual, it is also interactional and social, expressing a culturally recognized purpose, reflecting a particular kind of relationship and acknowledging an engagement in a given community.

Unit ③

Text-Oriented Research and Teaching

The first area of writing studies discussed in Hyland's work is text-oriented studies, which focus on the tangible, analysable aspects of writing by viewing it as a textual product. By looking at surface forms, these theories have in common an interest in the linguistic or rhetorical resources available to writers for producing texts, and so reduce the intricacies of human communication to the manageable and concrete. Text-focused theories have taken a variety of forms, but two broad approaches will be described here, together with the beliefs about the teaching and learning of writing that they imply.

3.1 Texts as Objects

The dominant model for many years saw writing as a textual product, a coherent arrangement of elements structured according to a system of rules. Based on ideas inherited from structuralism and implicit in the transformational grammar of Noam Chomsky, a basic premise of this approach is that texts are autonomous objects which can be analyzed and described independently of particular contexts, writers, or readers. Texts have a structure, they are orderly arrangements of words, clauses and sentences, and by following grammatical rules writers can encode a full semantic representation of their intended meanings.

▶ Focus on form/Structuralism view

The ideas that texts can function independently of a context clearly reflects the mechanistic view that human communication works by transferring ideas from one mind to another via language. Writing is disembodied. It is removed from context and the personal experiences of writers and readers because meanings can be encoded in texts and recovered by anyone who speaks the same language as the writer. Writers and readers conform to homogeneous practices so writing is treated like an object, and its rules imposed on passive users. This view of writing is still alive in a great deal of teaching of business writing and, indeed, is implicit in some notions of learning in western education systems. In many schools students are asked to write simply to demonstrate their knowledge of decontextualized facts with little awareness of a reader beyond the teacher-examiner. In these situations grammatical accuracy and clear exposition are often the main criteria of good writing.

Such a focus on form has led to considerable research into the regularities we find in texts. In recent years, for example, computer analyses of large corpora have been used to identify how functions such as stance and negation are commonly expressed in writing. An orientation to formal features of texts has also underpinned a great deal of research into students' writing development. From this perspective, writing improvement can be measured by counting increases in features such as relative clauses, modality and passives through successive pieces of writing. Some studies sought to assess language improvement in student writing by measuring increases in the number of morphemes, words and clauses in student essays, and some looked at features of academic writing such as impersonality, hedging and formality, and discovered "a general move from a spoken to a written style" in essays in a three-month EAP (English for Academic Purposes) professional course.

► Habit formation/Behaviorism view

From a perspective that regards texts as autonomous objects, then, learners' compositions are seen as *langue*, that is, a demonstration of the writer's knowledge of forms and his or her awareness of the system of rules to create texts. The goal of writing instruction therefore becomes training in accuracy, and for many years writing was essentially an extension of grammar teaching. Informed by a behavioral habit formation theory of learning, guided composition and substitution exercises became the main teaching methods, and these needed no context but the classroom and only the skill of avoiding errors. The teacher was an expert passing on knowledge to novices and there was a prescribed view of texts. This approach can still be found in classes around the world and survives in style guides, "how to write effectively" books, and some textbooks.

► Decontextualized approach to teaching

While this has been a major classroom approach for many years, the claim that good writing is context-free, that it is fully explicit and takes nothing for granted, draws on the rather old-fashioned and discredited belief that meaning is contained in the message. This lies behind the familiar conduit metaphor of language: that we have thoughts which we form into words to send to others which they receive and find the same thoughts—so meanings correspond with words and writing is transparent in reflecting meanings rather than constructing them. So we transfer ideas from one mind to another through language and meanings can be written down and understood by anyone with the right encoding and decoding skills. A text says everything that needs to be said—so there are no conflicts of interpretations, no reader positions, no different understandings, because we all see things in the same way. Clearly this fails to take account of the beliefs and knowledge writers assume readers will draw on in reading their texts.

Even academic articles, the most seemingly explicit of genres, draw on readers' assumed understandings. Through features such as references to prior research, technical lexis and familiarity with particular argument forms, writers work to establish a coherent context and enrich propositional meanings. Equally, this is how lawyers justify their fees, by disputing the exact meaning of even the most precisely written contracts and other legal documents.

In sum, inferences are always involved in recovering meanings: no text can be both coherent and context-free.

▶ Autonomous view of writing

Teachers' responses to writing in this perspective tend to focus on error correction and identifying problems in students' control of language rather than how meanings are being conveyed. Moreover, we can see an autonomous view of writing reflected in the design of many large international exams. Indirect assessments, typically multiple choice, cloze or error recognition tasks, are widely used in evaluating writing. But while they are sometimes said to be reliable measures of writing skill and facilitate reliability, they have little to do with the fact that communication, and not accuracy, is the purpose of writing. Moreover, even direct writing tasks, which require students to write one or two timed essays of a few hundred words, may lack "authenticity" and provide little information about students' abilities to produce a sustained piece of writing for different audiences or purposes.

▶ Focusing on accuracy

In fact, focusing on accuracy is exactly the wrong place to look for writing improvement as there is little evidence to show that either syntactic complexity or grammatical accuracy are the best measures of good writing. Many students can construct syntactically accurate sentences and yet are unable to produce appropriate written texts. Moreover, while fewer errors might be seen as an index of progress, this may equally indicate the writer's reluctance to take risks and reach beyond a current level of competence. To put this more directly, focusing exclusively on formal features of texts as a measure of writing competence ignores how texts are the writer's response to a particular communicative setting. Written texts cannot be autonomous precisely because they participate in a particular situation and reflect that situation in their pages.

What this means for teaching is that no particular feature can be said to be a marker of good writing because what is "good" varies across contexts. We can't just list the features needed to produce a successful text without considering appropriate purpose, audience, tone, formality, and so on. Simply, students don't just need to know how to write a grammatically correct text, but how to apply this knowledge for particular purposes and genres.

3.2 Texts as Discourse

While an autonomous model views texts as forms which can be analyzed independently of any real-life uses, another way of seeing writing as a material artefact looks beyond surface structures to see texts as discourse—the way we use language to communicate, to achieve purposes in particular situations. Here the writer is seen as having certain goals and intentions and the ways we write are resources to accomplish these. So instead of forms being disembodied and independent of contexts, a discourse approach sees them as located in social actions. Teachers following this line aim to identify the ways that texts actually work as communication by linking language forms to purposes and contexts.

► Discourse

Discourse refers to language in action, and to the purposes and functions linguistic forms serve in communication. Here the linguistic patterns of texts point to contexts beyond the page, implying a range of social constraints and choices which operate on writers in any situation. The writer has certain goals and intentions, certain relationships to his or her readers, and certain information to convey, and the forms of a text are resources used to accomplish these. These factors draw the analyst into a wider perspective which locates texts in a world of communicative purposes and social action, identifying the ways that texts actually work as communication.

► Functional perspective

A variety of approaches has considered texts as discourse, but all have tried to discover how writers organize language to produce coherent, purposeful prose. An early contribution was the "functional sentence perspective" of the Prague School which sought to describe how we structure text to represent our assumptions about what is known (given) or new to the reader. This was taken up and elaborated in the work of Halliday (Halliday & Matthiessen, 2004) in the concept of theme-rheme structure. Roughly, theme is what the writer is talking about and rheme what he or she is saying about it: the part of the message that the writer considers important. Theme and rheme help writers organize clauses into information units that push the communication forward through a text and make it easy for readers to follow. This is because we expect old information to come first as a context for new, but breaking this pattern can be confusing. In the following example, the writer establishes a pattern in which the rheme of the first sentence becomes the themes of the next three, clearly signposting the progression. The theme of the final sentence, however, breaks the sequence, surprising the reader and disturbing processability.

> Non-verbal communication is traditionally divided into paralanguage, proxemics, body language and haptics. Paralanguage refers to the non-verbal vocal signs that accompany speech. Proxemics concerns physical distance and orientation. Body language describes expression, posture and gesture. The study of touch is called haptics.

► Large textual patterns

A different strand of research has tried to identify the rhetorical functions of particular discourse units, examining what pieces of text are trying to do and how they fit into a larger structure. Some studies, for example, distinguish several patterns which they label problem–solution, hypothetical–real and general–particular. They show that even with no explicit signalling, readers are able to draw on their knowledge of recognizable text patterns to infer the connections between clauses, sentences or groups of sentences. For example, we all have a strong expectation of how a problem–solution pattern will progress, so that we look for a positive evaluation of at least one possible solution to complete the pattern. This pattern is illustrated below.

> **Problem–solution pattern**
>
> 1. *Situation*: We now accept that grammar is not restricted to writing but is present in speech.
>
> 2. *Problem*: This can lead to assumptions that there is one kind of grammar for writing and one for speech.
>
> 3. *Response*: A large-scale corpus survey of English has been undertaken.
>
> 4. *Evaluation of response*: Results show the same system is valid for both writing and speech. (Example based on a conference abstract.)

▶ Cognitive model

Descriptions of textual patterns lead us to the idea that we must draw on some notion of shared assumptions to account for what we recognize as connected text. That is to say, part of what makes writing coherent lies in the reader's background knowledge and interpretive abilities rather than in the text. One model of how this is done suggests that readers call on their conventionalized knowledge to impose a coherent frame on a message. They interpret discourse by analogy with their earlier experiences which are organized in their heads as scripts or schemata. Thus we carry around stereotypical understandings which we use as "scaffolding" to interpret the texts we encounter every day, allowing us to read texts as diverse as detective thrillers and postcards.

▶ Relevance model

A second approach, more pragmatic than this cognitive model, proposes that writers try to create texts which are as relevant to readers as possible, and that readers anticipate this when recovering meaning. This approach originates with Grice's (1975) principles of conversational inference, which try to explain successful communication in terms of interactants' mutual assumptions of rationality and cooperation. Building on this idea, Sperber and Wilson (1986) argue that readers construct meanings by comparing the information they find in a text with what they already know about the context to establish meanings that are relevant. In other words, when we interpret a text, we assume that the writer is being cooperative by thinking of what it is we need to know to fully understand what is going on, and so we look for ways of interpreting what we read as relevant to the ongoing discourse in some way. In these theories, interpretation depends on the ability of readers to supply needed assumptions from memory, but the text itself also plays an important part in this process. Kramsch (1997) argues that the construction of meaning from texts is a rhetorical and not just a cognitive process, and proposes seven principles of text interpretation which draw on current theories of discourse analysis.

The idea that forms express functions and that they vary according to context is a central notion of discourse analysis and underpins the key notion of genre.

Unit ④

Writer-Oriented Research and Teaching

The second broad approach discussed by Hyland takes the writer, rather than the text, as the point of departure. The theories in this section address the general issue of what it is that good writers do when confronted with a composing task, and seek to formulate the methods that will best help learners acquire these skills. Hyland here sketches the main contours of three positions which together have contributed to the hugely influential process writing movement: the first focuses on the personal creativity of the individual writer, the second on the cognitive processes of writing, and the third on the writer's immediate context.

4.1 Writing as Personal Expression

▶ Expressivist view of writing

Originating with the work of Elbow (1998), Murray (1985) and others, this view encourages writers to find their own voices to produce writing that is fresh and spontaneous. There is an underlying assumption that thinking precedes writing and that the free expression of ideas can encourage self-discovery and cognitive maturation. Writing development and personal development are seen as symbiotically interwoven to the extent that "good therapy and composition aim at clear thinking, effective relating, and satisfying self-expression" (Moffett, 1982, p. 235).

The expressivist view strongly resists a narrow definition of writing based on notions of correct grammar and usage. Instead it sees writing as a creative act of discovery in which the process is as important as the product to the writer. Writing is learnt, not taught, and the teacher's role is to be non-directive and facilitating, providing writers with the space to make their own meanings through an encouraging, positive, and cooperative environment with minimal interference. Because writing is a developmental process, teachers are encouraged not to impose their views, give models, or suggest responses to topics beforehand. On the contrary, they are urged to stimulate the writer's thinking through pre-writing tasks, such as journal-writing and analogies, and to respond to the ideas that the writer produces. This, then, is writing as self-discovery.

Unfortunately, this approach offers no clear theoretical principles from which to evaluate "good writing," nor does it furnish advice that can help accomplish it. This is because good writing, for expressivists, does not reflect the application of rules but that of the writer's free imagination.

▶ Extreme learner-centered perspective

The expressivist manifesto is essentially a romantic one. It promotes vague goals of "self-actualization" and even vaguer definitions of good writing which depend on subjective, hazy and culturally variable concepts such as originality, integrity and spontaneity. This, then, is the extreme learner-centred stance. The writer is the centre of attention, and his or her creative expression the principal goal. Unfortunately, the basic assumption that all writers have similar innate intellectual and creative potential and simply require the right conditions to express this, now seems rather naive. Essentially the approach is seriously under-theorized and leans heavily on an asocial view of the writer, operating in a context where there are no cultural differences in the value of "self-expression," no variations in personal inhibition, few distinctions in the writing processes of mature and novice writers, and no social consequences of writing.

While expressivism has helped to move writing teaching and research away from a restricted attention to form, it ignores communication in the real-world contexts where writing matters. But despite its limitations, the expressivist approach is still influential in many U.S. first language classrooms, underpins courses in creative writing, and has helped inspire research to support a cognitive view of writing.

4.2 Writing as a Cognitive Process

Interest in writers' composing processes has been extended beyond notions of creativity and self-expression to focus on the cognitive aspects of writing. This is a very different view of process as it draws on the techniques and theories of cognitive psychology and not literary creativity. Essentially it sees writing as a problem-solving activity: how writers approach a writing task as a problem and bring intellectual resources to solving it. This view of writing has developed a range of sophisticated investigative methods, generated an enormous body of research, and was, until recently, the dominant approach to teaching writing.

▶ Writing process

At the heart of this model is the view that writing is a "non-linear, exploratory and generative process whereby writers discover and reformulate their ideas as they attempt to approximate meaning" (Zamel, 1983, p. 165). Following the description of composing as "recursive," rather than as an uninterrupted, Pre-writing–Writing–Postwriting activity, a great deal of research has revealed the complexity of planning and editing activities, the influence of different writing tasks and the value of examining what writers do through a series of writing drafts. Case-studies and think-aloud protocols, rather than just texts themselves, have been widely used as research methods to get at these processes.

Flower and Hayes' (1981) model was decisive here. It suggested that the process of writing is influenced by the task and the writer's long-term memory. Its main features are that

- writers have goals;
- they plan extensively;
- planning involves defining a rhetorical problem, placing it in a context, then exploring its parts, arriving at solutions and finally translating ideas on to the page;
- all work can be reviewed, evaluated and revised, even before any text has been produced;
- planning, drafting, revising and editing are recursive, interactive and potentially simultaneous;
- plans and text are constantly evaluated in a feedback loop; and
- the whole process is overseen by an executive control called a monitor.

This, then, is a computer model typical of theorizing in cognitive psychology and artificial intelligence, giving priority to mechanisms such as memory, central processing unit, problem-solving programs and flow-charts.

Clearly, the Flower and Hayes's model helped to promote a "science-consciousness" among writing teachers which promised a "deep-structure" theory of how writing could be taught. The beauty of the model is its simplicity as the wide range of mental activities which can occur during composing can be explained by a fairly small number of sub-processes. The model also purports to account for individual differences in writing strategies, so immature writers can be represented as using a composing model that is a reduced version of that used by experts and so guided towards greater competence by instruction in expert strategies.

▶ Computer-based composing

The process approach to teaching writing was also assisted by the increasing availability and affordability of personal computers in the early 1980s. Word processing was not just a new form of typing, but a different way of manipulating texts, making it easier to re-draft, revise and edit. Teachers were quick to see the pedagogical possibilities of this and specialist programs emerged such as Daedalus which contained modules to support the stages of the writing process: questions for generating material, multi-screens for editing, and connectivity for peer review and discussion. As Bloch (2008: 52) observes: "The ease with which one could make changes or incorporate new ideas made it clear how all of these aspects of the writing process were now integrated."

The impact on research and teaching has been enormous and we now know much more about composing processes. Process approaches also extended research techniques beyond experimental methods and text analyses to the qualitative methods of the social sciences, often seeking to describe writing from an emic perspective by taking account of the views of writers and readers themselves. In particular, these studies have made considerable use of writers' verbal reports while composing, task observation, and retrospective interviews. Often research is longitudinal, following a few students over an extended period of their writing development and uses multiple techniques which may include recall protocols and product analyses of several drafts.

▶ Process approach to L2 writing

The extension of this research into studies of L2 writers, however, has been disappointing. Many teachers will find little that is surprising in the findings of process writing studies. Silva (1993) summarizes the main results of research into composing practices as

- general composing process patterns seem to be similar in L1 and L2;
- skilled writers compose differently from novices;
- skilled writers use more effective planning and revising strategies;
- L1 strategies may or may not be transferred to L2 contexts;
- L2 writers tend to plan less than L1 writers;
- L2 writers have more difficulty setting goals and generating material;
- L2 writers revise more but reflect less on their writing; and
- L2 writers are less fluent, and produce less accurate and effective texts.

The research generally supports our intuitions about the practices of skilled and unskilled writers. Even less encouraging for teachers is the fact that different studies often produce contradictory findings, often because they are limited to small samples of writers in a particular context and so lack generalizability to wider populations of writers. Moreover, despite the massive output of this research serious doubts have been raised about the methods used to explore cognitive models of writing.

One serious problem is that these results often rely heavily on think-aloud protocols, a method where researchers ask writers to report their thoughts and actions while involved in a writing task. These have been criticized as offering an incomplete picture of the complex cognitive activities involved, not least because many cognitive processes are routine and internalized operations performed without any conscious recognition and therefore not available to verbal description. In addition, asking subjects to simultaneously verbalize and carry out complex operations is likely to overload short-term memory due to "a crowding of the cognitive workbench" (Afflerbach & Johnson, 1984, p. 311). As a result, such reports may only provide a partial record of processes. Worse, the act of reporting itself may merely be a narrative that participants construct to explain, rather than reflect, what they do, potentially distorting the thought processes being reported on.

▶ Novice vs expert writing models

Reservations have also been expressed about the status of the models themselves. It is argued that such models do not represent fully worked-out theories and fail to either explain or generate writing behavior. The models do not tell us why writers make certain choices and therefore cannot help us to advise students on their writing practices. In fact, Flower and Hayes's original model was too imprecise to predict the behavior of real writers or to carry the weight of the research claims based on it and they have subsequently emphasized the importance of appropriate goal-setting and rhetorical strategies far more. But such refinements cannot obscure the weaknesses of a model which seeks to describe cognitive processes common to all writers, both novice and expert and all learners in between these poles.

Bereiter and Scardamalia (1987) suggest that because skilled and novice practices differ so radically, two models, knowledge-telling and knowledge-transforming, account for the research findings better than one, as shown below:

- A **knowledge-telling model** addresses the fact that novice writers plan less often than experts, revise less often and less extensively, and are primarily concerned with generating content from their internal resources. Their main goal is simply to tell what they can remember based on the assignment, the topic, or the genre.

- A **knowledge-transforming model** suggests how skilled writers use the writing task to analyze problems and set goals. These writers are able to reflect on the complexities of the task and resolve problems of content, form, audience, style, organization, and so on within a content space and a rhetorical space, so that there is continuous interaction between developing knowledge and text. Knowledge transforming thus involves actively reworking thoughts so that in the process not only text, but also ideas, may be changed.

Bereiter and Scardamalia's model certainly adds psychological insight to writing activity and helps explain the difficulties often experienced by unskilled writers because of the complexity of the writing task and their lack of topic knowledge. It also helps account for reflective thought in writing, and therefore suggests that students should participate in a variety of challenging writing tasks and genres to develop their skills. It also draws attention to the importance of feedback and revision in the process of developing both content and expression. It remains unclear, however, how writers actually make the cognitive transition to a knowledge-transforming model, nor is it spelt out what occurs in the intervening stages and whether the process is the same for all learners. Many students, for example, continue to have considerable difficulty with their writing despite intensive teaching in expert strategies.

▶ Individualism in process writing

It is, however, difficult to exaggerate the impact of process ideas on both L1 and L2 writing classrooms. There are few teachers who do not set pre-writing activities to generate ideas about content and structure, encourage brainstorming and outlining, require multiple drafts, give extensive feedback, facilitate peer responses, delay surface corrections until the final editing, and display finished work. Process research has meant that cooperative writing, teacher conferences, problem-based tasks, journal-writing, group discussions, and mixed portfolio assessments are now all commonplace practices in our methodological repertoire.

However, while there is a great deal of case-study and anecdotal support for this model, there is actually little hard evidence that process-writing techniques lead to significantly better writing. This is not really surprising as "the approach" is actually many different approaches applied unevenly and in different ways. In addition, there are serious reservations about whether the underlying individualistic emphasis of the methods, which say little about social aspects of either language use or language learning, may handicap ESL students from more collectivist cultures. But we should not expect any method automatically to produce good writers. The process of writing is a rich mix of elements which, together with cognition, include the writer's experiences and background, as well as a sense of self, of others, of situation and of purpose. Writers, situations and tasks differ, and no single description can capture all writing contexts or be applied universally with the same results.

▶ Pros and cons of process teaching approaches

Pros:

- Major impact on the theory and methodology of teaching writing to L1 and L2 students
- A useful corrective to preoccupations with "product" and student accuracy
- Important in raising teachers' awareness of what writing involves—contributing to a professionalization of writing teaching
- Gives greater respect for individual differences among student writers
- Raises many new research questions which remain to be answered

Cons:

- Overemphasizes psychological factors in writing
- Focuses on the writer as a solitary individual and fails to recognize social aspects of writing
- Based on individualistic ideologies which may hamper the development of ESL students
- Ignores important influences of context, especially differences of class, gender and ethnicity
- Downplays the varied conventions of professional and academic communities
- Uncertain whether this approach greatly improves student writing

In sum, the process-writing perspective allows us to understand writing in a way that was not possible when it was seen only as finished products. It does, however, overemphasize psychological factors and fails to consider the forces outside the individual which help guide problem-definition, frame solutions and ultimately shape writing.

4.3 Writing as a Situated Act

A third writer-oriented perspective goes some way to addressing the criticisms levelled at cognitive modelling by giving greater emphasis to the actual performance of writing. Less a single theory than several lines of enquiry, this research incorporates the writer's prior experiences and the impact of the immediate, local context on writing and has had an important influence on both the ways we see writing and how it might be studied.

▶ Introduction

Writing is a social act that can occur within particular situations. It is therefore influenced both by the personal attitudes and prior experiences that the writer brings to writing and the impact of the specific political and institutional contexts in which it takes place. By using detailed observations of acts of writing, participant interviews, analyses of surrounding practices and other techniques, researchers have developed interesting accounts of local writing contexts. These descriptions give significant attention to the experiences of writers and to their understandings of the demands of the immediate context as they write.

This perspective takes us beyond the possible workings of writers' minds and into the physical and experiential contexts in which writing occurs to describe how "context cues cognition" (Flower, 1989). Of crucial importance is the emphasis placed on a notion of context as the "situation of expression" (Nystrand, 1987). Flower (1989) elaborates this as the effects of prior knowledge, assumptions and expectations together with features of the writing environment which selectively tap knowledge and trigger specific processes. The goal is to describe the influence of this context on the ways writers represent their purposes in the kind of writing that is produced. As Prior (1998, p. xi) observes:

> Actually writing happens in moments that are richly equipped with tools (material and semiotic) and populated with others (past, present and future). When seen as situated activity, writing does not stand alone as the discrete act of a writer, but emerges as a confluence of many streams of activity: reading, talking, observing, acting, making, thinking and feeling as well as transcribing words on paper.

Studies therefore seek to analyse, often in considerable detail, how writing is constituted as a feature of local situations.

To accomplish such exhaustive or "thick" descriptions (Geertz, 1973) of writing contexts, researchers have relied heavily on ethnographic studies. The term "ethnographic" remains somewhat fuzzy and contested, but essentially it refers to research which is highly situated and minutely detailed, attempting to give an holistic explanation of behavior using a variety of methods and drawing on the understandings of insiders themselves to avoid any prior assumptions of the researcher.

▶ Ethnographic research

Ethnography is a type of research which undertakes to give, insider-oriented description of individuals' cultural practices. It relies on the view that collecting and analyzing a variety of different kinds of data makes possible a more valid description of complex social realities than any single kind of data alone. Applying this method to an understanding of how and why people write means gathering naturally occurring data under normal conditions from numerous sources, typically over a period of time, without interfering with either writers or the writing context.

Ethnographic methods typically include detailed, longitudinal, observations of a setting and the writing that occurs within it, interviews with participants on their writing and relevant autobiographical issues, recursive analyses of students' process logs and diaries, questionnaires and close examination of classroom interactions. Texts such as coursebooks, manuals and course outlines are also often studied, as is student writing itself and teacher responses to this. Sometimes the researcher participates in the class and follows students around to observe their daily activities and gain insights into the contexts and practices which might illuminate the writing process.

Ethnography, however, is not a term that everyone feels comfortable with. Its origins in anthropology mean it carries connotations of the researcher's total immersion in another culture rather than simply an attitude to research and use of varied methods. Because of this, Swales' (1998) coining of the term textography in his case studies of particular departments and academics and their discipline specific texts in a university building, has offered a more manageable way of exploring the richness of the working contexts while avoiding a full cultural description.

▶ Swales' Textography

> As textographer of the second floor I have tried to do justice to a number of themes that have emerged over a three-year involvement with its practices, rhythms, texts and personalities. One is a sense of locale, a sense of autonomous place ... Juxtaposed to that, I have tried to capture a feeling of the academic personalities, and especially the scriptural personalities, of those I have chosen for inclusion ... And juxtaposed to the partial accounts of careers that a textography engenders, the use of close, but nontechnical, analysis of particular stretches of text, illuminated on occasion by text-based interview data, shows how the language of normal science can ... reveal the individual humanities of the authors. (Swales, 1998, pp. 141–142)

The features of local setting that have particularly interested "situated" researchers have been the roles individual writers perform and how writers' interactions with local participants feed into the writing task, especially in collaborative contexts. Contexts are sites for interactions where relationships, and the rules which order them, can both facilitate and constrain composing. The social routines surrounding acts of writing have therefore been studied in detail and attention given to certain tangible features of the local environment which have meaning for writers. Thus research has shown how students on a journalism course saw the use of physical space in their department as barriers which excluded them and restricted access to the material resources they needed for writing. Similarly, research has revealed how the absence of resources like libraries and computers can serve to exclude Third World scholars from publishing their writing.

▶ Wider factors in writing

There is little doubt that this research has produced rich, detailed descriptions of particular contexts of writing, expanding greatly our understanding of the personal, social and institutional factors which can impinge on writing. One problem, of course, is that while these methods might illuminate what goes on in a particular act of writing, they cannot describe everything in either the writer's consciousness or the context which might influence composition, so we can never be certain that all critical factors have been accounted for. More importantly, this approach runs the risk of emphasizing writers' perceptions and the possible impact of the local situation to the detriment of the rhetorical problems to which writing responds. In other words, by focusing on the context of production, we might be neglecting the effects of the wider social and institutional orders of discourse which influence writers' intentions and plans for writing.

One potential impact of such wider social worlds is the experiences writers might bring to the classroom as a consequence of prior negative evaluation of their writing. Social inequalities of power, educational and home backgrounds, and so on can result in what has been called writing apprehension where individuals experience high degrees of anxiety when asked to write. These anxious feelings, about oneself as a writer, one's writing situation, or one's writing task can seriously disrupt the writing process and educational success. The term is used to describe writers who are intellectually capable of the task at hand, but who nevertheless have difficulty with it, feeling their writing isn't sufficiently creative, interesting, sophisticated, or well expressed. This can result in students avoiding courses or careers which involve writing, low self-esteem and confidence, or the production of poor texts.

Overall, then, a focus on writers lacks a developed theory of the ways experience is constituted and interpreted in social communities and underplays the workings of wider factors. As a result, it fails to move beyond the local context to take full account of how an evolving text might be a writer's response to a reader's expectations. This neglect of the social dimension of writing has eventually led research away from internally directed process models to more socially situated approaches.

Unit 5

Reader-Oriented Research and Teaching

A final broad approach expands the notion of context beyond features of the composing situation to the purposes, goals and uses that the completed text may eventually fulfill. The perspectives discussed in this section share the view that writers select their words to engage with others and to present their ideas in ways that make most sense to their readers. This involves what Halliday refers to as the interpersonal function of language, and it is encoded in every sentence we write. Readers must be drawn in, influenced and often persuaded by a text that sees the world in similar ways to them. In other words, writing is an interactive, as well as cognitive, activity which employs accepted resources for the purpose of sharing meanings in that context. Hyland (2009) discusses three approaches for this social view:

- Writing as social interaction
- Writing as social construction
- Writing as power and ideology

5.1 Writing as Social Interaction

The idea that writing is an interaction between writers and readers adds a communicative dimension to writing. It moves away from our stereotype of an isolated writer hunched over a keyboard to explain composing decisions in terms of the writer's projection of the interests, understandings, and needs of a potential audience. This view has been developed by Martin Nystrand, who argues that the success of any text is the writer's ability to satisfy the rhetorical demands of readers: we have to embed our writing in a non-local discourse world.

▶ Nystrand on writing as social interaction

> The process of writing is a matter of elaborating text in accord with what the writer can reasonably assume that the reader knows and expects, and the process of reading is a matter of predicting text in accord with what the reader assumes about the writer's purpose. More fundamentally, each presupposes the sense-making capabilities of the other. As a result, written communication is predicated on what the writer/reader each assumes the other will do/has done. (Nystrand, 1989, p. 75)

In a social interactive model, meaning is created via "a unique configuration and interaction of what both reader and writer bring to the text" (Nystrand et al., 1993: 299). A discourse is shaped by writers attempting to balance their purposes with the expectations of readers through a process of negotiation. For Nystrand, a text has "semantic potential," or a variety of possible meanings, all but a few of which are closed down by a combination of the writer's intention, the reader's cognition and the objective properties of the text itself. Meaning, in other words, is not transmitted from mind to mind as in the model of autonomous texts, nor does it reside in the writer's cognition as in process models. Instead it is created between the participants themselves.

▶ Recursive writing process

Essentially the process of writing involves creating a text that we assume the reader will recognize and expect and the process of reading involves drawing on assumptions about what the writer is trying to do. Skilled writers are able to create a mutual frame of reference and anticipate when their purposes will be retrieved by their audiences, providing greater elaboration where they expect that there may be misunderstanding. The recursiveness of the drafting process thus becomes a way of responding to an inner dialogue with readers, part of how the writer monitors the evolving text for potential troublespots. Writing, then, is not an act of an isolated individual but a joint endeavour between writers and readers, co-constructed through the active understanding of rhetorical situations and the likely responses of readers.

Audience can be a difficult concept for teachers. Clearly, a writer who understands something of the needs and interests of his/her audience possesses important rhetorical knowledge about appropriate genre, content, stance and style. The ability to analyze an audience, however, obviously becomes more problematic the larger and less immediately familiar it gets. Texts are often addressed to a plurality of audiences. As mentioned by Hyland (2009), when he writes the book *Teaching and Researching Writing*, he is picturing you, the reader, as someone with more than a passing interest in writing, but he cannot predict your cultural background, your knowledge of the subject, or what you want from this book. Perhaps you are a teacher, a student, a trainer; maybe a casual bookshop-browser, or someone supervising a thesis on writing. In other words, he is aware that his book could be read by specialists, novices, practitioners and lay people, and while he tries to make the subject as explicit as he can, he knows that not all readers will recover every intended meaning.

The notion of audience is a contentious area of debate in literary studies, has been much discussed in rhetoric, and has become more complex in the era of electronic writing. Audience is, in fact, rarely a concrete reality, particularly in academic and professional contexts, and must be seen as essentially representing a construction of the writer which may shift during the composing process.

▶ Two types of audience

Two models of audience have dominated much of the writing literature. Ede and Lunsford (1984) refer to these as *audience addressed*, the actual or intended readers who exist independently of the text, and *audience invoked*, a created fiction of the writer rhetorically implied in the text which can be persuaded to respond to it in certain ways. Park's more sophisticated conception focuses less on people and more on the writer's awareness of the external circumstances which define a rhetorical context and requires the text to have certain characteristics in response. Audience therefore exists in the writer's mind and shapes a text as "a complex set of conventions, estimations, implied responses and attitudes" (Park, 1982, p. 251).

Issues of audience have encouraged a growing interest in the use of peer and teacher feedback among teachers so that students get an idea of how others understand their texts. Equally, however, teachers recognize that they can promote a sense of audience among students by exposing them to examples of texts in target genres. This is because an understanding of audience largely involves exploiting readers' abilities to recognize intertextuality between texts. This idea originates in Bakhtin's (1986) view that language is dialogic: a conversation between writer and reader in an ongoing activity. Writing reflects traces of its social uses because it is linked and aligned with other texts upon which it builds and which it anticipates. "Each utterance refutes, affirms, supplements, and relies on the others, presupposes them to be known and somehow takes them into account" (ibid.: 91). Here written genres are regarded as parts of repeated and typified social situations, rather than particular forms, with writers exercising judgement and creativity in responding to similar circumstances.

▶ Intertextuality

Bakhtin's notion of intertextuality suggests that discourses are always related to other discourses, both as they change over time and in their similarities at any point in time. This connects text-users into a network of prior texts and so provides a system of options for making meanings which can be recognized by other texts-users. Because they help create the meanings available in a culture, the conventions developed in this way close out certain interpretations and make others more likely, and this helps explain how writers make particular rhetorical choices when composing. Fairclough (1992, p. 117) distinguishes two kinds of intertextuality:

- **Manifest intertextuality** refers to various ways of incorporating or responding to other texts through quotation, paraphrase, irony, and so on.

- **Interdiscursivity** concerns the writer's use of sets of conventions drawn from a recognizable text type or genre. Texts here then are associated with some institutional and social meanings.

A major pedagogical implication of an interactionist approach is obviously that a cultivated sense of audience is crucial to the development of effective writing strategies, and that this can only be accomplished through a sense of social context. This means teachers have tried to employ contexts for writing which reflect real life uses as far as possible, with a clear purpose and a specified external audience. Some scholars advocate that students should engage in writing tasks that involve researching potential readers for their written arguments and show how collaborative tasks can improve essays by helping writers predict readers' problems with a text. The central importance of the social-interactionist orientation to teachers is therefore to encourage a focus on context as a set of recognizable conventions through which a piece of writing achieves its force. The text, in sum, is the place where readers and writers meet.

5.2 Writing as Social Construction

Another way of thinking about readers is to step back and see interaction as a collection of rhetorical choices rather than as specific encounters. Here the writer is neither a creator working through a set of cognitive processes nor an interactant engaging with a reader, but a member of a community. The communicating dyad is replaced by the discourses of socially and rhetorically constituted groups of readers and writers.

▶ Social construction

Social construction is based on the idea that the ways we think, and the categories and concepts we use to understand the world, are "all language constructs generated by knowledge communities and used by them to maintain coherence" (Bruffee, 1986, p. 777). The everyday interactions that occur between people produce the world that we take for granted. Language is not just a means of self-expression then, it is how we construct and sustain reality, and we do this as members of communities, using the language of those communities. The features of a text are therefore influenced by the community for which it was written and so best understood, and taught, through the specific genres of communities.

Originating in sociology and postmodern philosophy, this approach takes the view that what we know and do is relative to a collectively organized conceptual schema. Writing is a social act, and to understand it fully we must go beyond the decisions of individual writers to explore the regular features of texts as the preferences of particular communities. A text carries certain meanings and gains its communicative force only by displaying the patterns and conventions of the community for which it is written. Essays produced by biology students, for example, draw on very different forms of argument, interpersonal conventions and ways of presenting facts and theories than those written by business students. So, whereas interactionists work from individuals to groups, constructionists proceed from social group to individuals: writing is a form of cultural practice tied to forms of social organization.

▶ Community

Another way of putting this is that writers always have to demonstrate their credibility, that their text has something worthwhile to say, by positioning themselves and their ideas in relation to other ideas and texts in their communities. The notion of discourse community draws attention to the idea that we do not use language to communicate with the world at large, but with other members of our social groups, each with its own norms, categorizations, sets of conventions, and ways of doing things. The value of the term lies in the fact that it offers a way of bringing writers, readers and texts together into a common rhetorical space, foregrounding the conceptual frames that individuals use to organize their experience and get things done using language.

More than this, however, through notions of community we can see writing as a means by which organizations actually constitute themselves and individuals signal their memberships of them. By engaging with others through writing we enter into a culture of shared belief or value concerning what is worth discussing and how things should be discussed. Through our language choices we align ourselves with, challenge, or extend what has been said before. In institutional contexts then, community is a means of accounting for how communication succeeds through the individual's projection of a shared professional context. Such language choices help us see that institutional practices are not just conventional regularities of a particular style. Instead they evoke a social environment where the writer activates specific recognizable and routine responses to recurring tasks. In a real sense, therefore, through these repeated practices, we "construct" the institutions we participate in. Texts are created in terms of how their authors understand reality and, in turn, these understandings are influenced by their membership of social groups. Discourse is therefore a reservoir of meanings that give identity to a culture.

▶ Discourse community

The term "discourse community" is perhaps one of the most indeterminate in the writing literature. It is possible to see communities as real, relatively stable groups whose members subscribe, at least to some extent, to a consensus on certain ways of doing things and using language. On the other hand, community can be regarded as a more metaphorical term for collecting together certain practices and attitudes. Swales (1990), for instance, sets out criteria for using language to achieve collective goals or purposes, while other writers have suggested a weaker connection. Barton, for example, defines it as a loose association of individuals engaged in either the reception or production of texts, or both:

> A discourse community is a group of people who have texts and practices in common, whether it is a group of academics, or the readers of teenage magazines. In fact, discourse community can refer to the people the text is aimed at; it can be the people who read a text; or it can refer to the people who participate in a set of discourse practices both by reading and writing. (2007, pp. 75–76)

To see discourse communities as determinate and codifiable runs the risk of framing them as closed, self-sufficient and predictable arenas of shared and agreed-upon values and conventions. On the other hand, reducing them to mere collections of competing voices reduces the idea's explanatory authority. Clearly, we have to avoid the strong structuralist position of a single deterministic consensus which separates a community from its moments of creation in writing, but at the same time we need to acknowledge the obvious effects of groups on the ways individual communicative practices are realized.

The fuzziness of the term means that it is often unclear where to locate a discourse community. Can it, for example, refer to all academics, a university, a discipline, or just a specialism? We also have to account for the ways these groupings come into being, how they admit variable degrees of membership, exercise power over participants, accommodate differences, resolve conflict, and how they develop and change. Clearly the term is only useful if it is seen as connected to real individuals and the cultural frames that carry meaning for them. As a result, some writers have sought to "localise" the concept into "place discourse communities" (Swales, 1998) or "communities of practice" defining a community in terms of the literacy practices and relations which emerge in some mutual endeavour over time.

Despite the term's imprecision, there is a core meaning of likemindedness or membership, and this concept has proved central to research on writing. It has contributed to how we understand writing in business settings, the law, health care, technology, and other professional contexts. Constructionism has been most influential, however, in describing academic writing.

▶ English for academic purposes (EAP)

Academic disciplines use language in different ways and might therefore be seen as academic tribes with their own particular norms and practices. Through the use of these disciplinary conventions and practices, members construct academic knowledge, as they galvanize support, express collegiality, resolve difficulties, and negotiate disagreement through patterns of rhetorical choices which connect their texts with their disciplinary cultures. Persuasion, then, is accomplished with language. But it is language that demonstrates legitimacy. Writers must recognize and make choices from the rhetorical options available in their fields to appeal to readers from within the boundaries of their disciplines. This approach tells us that essays, reports, memos, dissertations, and so on, are not the same in all fields and disciplines and that the ability to produce them does not involve generic writing skills. Only when we use a language to create genres in specific contexts does our competence in writing cease to be a display of control of a linguistic code and take on significance as discourse. Expert writers are obviously better able than novices to imagine how readers will respond to a text because they are familiar with the ways experience is typically constructed in their communities. The role of the writing teacher is therefore to help students discover how valued text forms and practices are socially constructed in response to the common purposes of target communities. Johns (1997) calls this a "socioliterate" approach to teaching.

▶ "Socioliterate" approaches to teaching

In socioliterate views, literacies are acquired principally through exposure to discourses from a variety of social contexts. Through this exposure, individuals gradually develop theories of genre.

> Those who can successfully produce and process texts within certain genres are members of communities, for academic learning does not take place independent of these communities ... What I am advocating, then, is an approach in which literacy classes become laboratories for the study of texts, roles, and contexts, for research into evolving student literacies and developing awareness and critique of communities and their textual contracts. (Johns, 1997, pp. 14–19)

Rather than modelling the practices of experts, this approach offers students a guiding framework for producing texts by raising their awareness of the connections between forms, purposes and roles in specific social contexts. Teaching methods vary, but generally seek to give students experience of authentic, purposeful writing related to the kinds of writing they will need to do in their target communities. Johns (1997), for example, stresses the value of students researching both texts and community informants and of compiling mixed-skills portfolios. Some point out the advantages of examining changes in pre-publication drafts, and underline the benefits of student text analyses.

The danger of a constructionist perspective, of course, is that practitioners may represent, in their teaching or research, particular conventions as normative, static and natural. There is a risk that particular forms and practices will not only be seen as somehow fixed and "correct," but uncritically regarded as naturally superior forms of communication, blessed with the prestige of the social groups which routinely employ them. This can only make the learning task harder for novice writers since they may view the indigenous literacies that they bring with them to the classroom as a deficit which has to be rectified and replaced. This brings us to the final perspective in this unit.

5.3 Writing as Power and Ideology

A third reader-oriented view of writing also emphasizes the importance of social context to writing but stresses that the key dimension of context is the relations of power that exist in it and the ideologies that maintain these relations.

▶ Critical discourse analysis (CDA)

The importance of power as a force which mediates discourse and social groups has most extensively been explored by researchers working in critical discourse analysis (CDA). CDA links language to the activities which surround it, focusing on how social relations, identity, knowledge and power are constructed through written and spoken texts in communities, schools and classrooms. Discourse is thus a mediator of social life: simultaneously both constructing social and political reality and conditioned by it.

> By "critical" discourse analysis I mean analysis which aims to systematically explore often opaque relationships of causality and determination between (a) discursive practices, events and texts, and (b) wider social and cultural structures, relations and processes; to investigate how such practices, events and texts arise out of and are ideologically shaped by relations of power and struggles over power; and to explore how the opacity of these relationships between discourse and society is itself a factor securing power and hegemony. (Fairclough, 1992, p. 135)

A central aspect of this view is that the interests, values, and power relations in any institutional and sociohistorical context are found in the ways that people use language.

▶ Principles of critical discourse analysis

- CDA addresses social problems and not simply language use by itself.
- Power relations are discursive.
- Discourse constitutes society and culture, and every instance of language use contributes to reproducing or changing them.
- Discourse does ideological work, representing and constructing society in particular ways.

- Discourse is historical, and must be related to other discourses.
- The link between texts and society is mediated by "orders of discourse."
- Discourse analysis is interpretive and explanatory, requiring systematic methods.
- Discourse is a form of social action, and CDA is a socially committed paradigm.

(Wodak, 1996, p. 17–20)

The notion of ideology is important because it is concerned with how individuals experience the world and how these experiences are, in turn, reproduced through their writing. Fairclough (borrowing from Foucault) uses the term "orders of discourse" to refer to the relatively stable configurations of discourse practices found in particular domains or institutions. These are frames for interaction such as patient case-notes, lab reports, newspaper editorials, student records, academic articles, and so on, which have prestige value in different institutions and which are ideologically shaped by its dominant groups. They provide writers with templates for appropriate ways of writing and this means that any act of writing, or of teaching writing, is embedded in ideological assumptions.

But while these frameworks help enforce the authority of particular forms of discourse in any community, they do not exclude possibilities for change. This is because when we write we not only take up socially ratified social roles and relationships, but also draw on our personal and social experiences which cross-cut what we write.

Of importance in this perspective is the view that writing is both texts and contexts, the work of both individuals and institutions. This requires us to consider not only texts but also their relationship to the wider social environment and the part they play for individuals within specific situations. CDA is, therefore, analysis with attitude. It proclaims an interest and sets an agenda, as Fairclough and Wodak (1997, p. 259) make clear: "What is distinctive about CDA is both that it intervenes on the side of the dominated and oppressed groups and against dominating groups, and that it openly declares the emancipatory interests that motivate it."

▶ Model of analysis: systemic functional linguistics (SFL)

While CDA does not subscribe to any single method, Fairclough and Wodak draw on systemic functional linguistics (SFL). This is useful as the model sees language as systems of linguistic features offering choices to users, but these choices are considerably circumscribed in situations of unequal power. Young and Harrison (2004, p. 1) claim that SFL and CDA share three main features:

- a view of language as a social construct, or how society fashions language;
- a dialectical view in which "particular discursive events influence the contexts in which they occur and the contexts are, in turn, influenced by these discursive events"; and
- a view which emphasizes cultural and historical aspects of meaning.

SFL thus offers CDA a sophisticated way of analyzing the relations between language and social contexts, making it possible to ground concerns of power and ideology in the details of discourse. In practice CDA typically examines features of writing such as

- vocabulary—particularly how metaphor and connotative meanings encode ideologies;
- transitivity—which can show, for instance, who is presented as having agency and who is acted upon;
- nominalization and passivization—how processes and actors can be repackaged as nouns or agency otherwise obscured;
- mood and modality—which indicate relationships such as roles, attitudes, commitments and obligations;
- theme—how the first element of a clause can be used to foreground particular aspects of information or presuppose reader beliefs;
- text structure—how text episodes are marked; and
- intertextuality and interdiscursivity—the effects of other texts and styles on texts, which lead to hybridization, such as where commercial discourses colonize those in other spheres.

Unfortunately much CDA analysis has relied exclusively on the researcher's interpretations of texts, cherry-picking both the texts it studies and the features it chooses to discuss. This has the effect of simply confirming the analyst's prejudices while reducing pragmatics to semantics in assuming just one possible reading of the text. Moreover, this privileging of the analyst's viewpoint is often reinforced by appeal to an explanatory level of social theory which lies above any analysis of the text itself. In other words, there is little dialogue with real readers; interpretation becomes a black box rather than a product of analysis. The plausibility of any interpretation of a text ultimately depends on our willingness to accept it, and this is best enhanced by obtaining the intentions and interpretations of participants. So, although it might be acknowledged that no analysis can be neutral, and that a clear political agenda helps to redress the invisible ideological presuppositions in much writing research, we need to go beyond good intentions. It is essential that any theory of writing is thoroughly grounded in the contextual understandings of the users that give it significance.

▶ Application of CDA to writing practices

From a pedagogical perspective, a major task of CDA is to help students to gain an awareness of how writing practices are grounded in social (and especially institutional) structures. This means that teachers must build on the perceptions and practices of writing that students bring with them to the classroom to expose the authority of the prestige discourses that they seek to acquire. By the close study of texts and their contexts, students might become more aware of the ideological assumptions which underlie texts and the forms of persuasion found in an array of current discourses they encounter in their everyday lives. More directly, CDA helps to reveal writing as relative to particular groups and contexts, and so encourages teachers to assist students in unpacking the requirements of their target communities. What appear as dominant and superior forms of writing can then be seen as simply another practice, one among many, and thus open like others to scrutiny and contestation.

Part 3

Approaches to Research on Writing

▶▶▶▶▶

Research approaches or methods are the tools and techniques for doing research. Research is a term used liberally for any kind of investigation that is intended to uncover interesting or new facts. As with all activities, the rigour with which this activity is carried out will be reflected in the quality of the results. Part III presents a basic review of the nature of research and the methods which are used to undertake a variety of investigations relevant to education and the humanities, especially second language writing or academic writing. Obviously, almost every university course includes an element of research that students must carry out independently, in the form of projects, term papers, and theses. The more advanced the degree, the greater the research content.

Research methods are a range of tools that are used for different types of enquiries, just as a variety of tools are used for doing different practical jobs. So, it is necessary to know what the correct tools are for doing the job, and how to use them to best effect. This part provides the basic information about the tools used in research, the situations in which they are applied and indicates briefly how they are used by giving practical examples.

Unit 6

Discourse Analysis

Discourse analysis is a research method for studying written or spoken language in relation to its social context. It aims to understand how language is used in real life situations. When we do discourse analysis, we might focus on

- the purposes and effects of different types of language;
- cultural rules and conventions in communication;
- how values, beliefs and assumptions are communicated; and
- how language use relates to its social, political and historical context.

Discourse analysis is a common qualitative research method in many humanities and social science disciplines, including linguistics, sociology, anthropology, psychology and cultural studies.

6.1 Introduction

Discourse analysis (DA), the study of situated language use, involves exploring texts for what they tell us about the purposes and functions of language use and the constraints operating on writers in particular contexts (Matsuda et al., 2003). The analysis describes texts and evaluates their quality, both from the viewpoint of texts that learners produce as well as the kinds of texts they need to learn to produce. Text analysis can help ESL researchers, teachers, and language learners identify rules and principles of written or spoken texts at a variety of levels: sentences, sentence relations, and complete texts. This research orientation differs from traditional linguistic analysis in two major ways: (1) It extends analysis beyond the level of sentence grammars, and (2) it considers the multidimensional, communicative constraints of the situation (Connor, 1994)

Discourse analysis has been a significant method both in understanding language use and in literacy education since the early 1970s. In second language contexts, it has contributed to the emergence and development of English for Specific Purposes, where research conducted helps reveal some of the common features of texts of different genres and has established an empirical basis for teaching both first and second language writing.

6.2 Application of Discourse Analysis

Conducting discourse analysis means examining how language functions and how meaning is created in different social contexts. It can be applied to any instance of written or oral language, as well as non-verbal aspects of communication such as tone and gestures.

Materials that are suitable for discourse analysis include

- books, newspapers and periodicals;
- marketing material, such as brochures and advertisements;
- business and government documents;
- websites, forums, social media posts and comments; and
- interviews and conversations.

By analyzing these types of discourse, researchers aim to gain an understanding of social groups and how they communicate.

▶ Possible areas of DA studies

Hyland discussed discourse analysis in L2 writing research in "Changing currents in second language writing research: A colloquium" (Matsuda et al., 2003, pp. 151–179). Here is a list of major areas of DA adapted and summarized from his discussion.

Student writing

Discourse analysis has examined the writing of secondary school learners and university students. Research has been focused on expository genres of various kinds with an emphasis on the development of topic and argument, features of cohesion and coherence, and pragmatic and interpersonal aspects of language.

DA does not just look at how sentences fit together; it tries to show how they are related to their contexts. This means linking discourse features to issues of writer purpose, identity, audience expectations, cultural schemata, disciplinary perceptions, and so on. DA gives us a theoretical and research platform to study the meanings learners are trying to express through their choice and arrangement of forms. By providing information about differences between learners and native speakers, analysis of student texts provides insights for more effective teaching, helping teachers to target students' more frequent and intractable errors. It also encourages us to explore student writing as a valid form of discourse in its own right, rather than as a hybrid interlanguage of L1 interference.

Learner corpora

Nowadays compiled and stored corpora of students' writing open up new possibilities for discourse analysis by revealing how particular groups of students typically express certain meanings and approach rhetorical problems. Frequency counts can expose the features that students often over- or under-use, while collocations reveal typical patterns of co-textual association, indicating how particular groups of learners understand and use various features. Some generalizations from the work on learner corpora show that second language writers make greater use of a smaller range of vocabulary, that they overuse items of high generality, and that they favour features which are more typical of spoken English. Overall, the value of corpora of learner language is that it gives us the power to go beyond the instance of the individual case to explore systematic variation in authentic learner language with greater confidence.

Cultural differences in writing

Research in this area is closely related to contrastive rhetoric (CR), which aims to identify the differences in rhetorical preferences between cultural and linguistic groups. Discourse-based research has explored the persuasive practices of different language groups, and shown how credibility is differently negotiated, how patterns of argument make use of different appeals to objectivity or personality, and how control over reader awareness features, such as questions, directives, and inclusive and second person pronouns, differ.

In addition to CR, studies are also conducted from functional and systemic perspectives to explore some of the ways that L2 students establish relationships with their readers through patterns of stance, engagement, and the construction of academic identity. This discourse research undermines some established cultural stereotypes about L2 writing. For example, in a study of 700 school leavers in China and U.K., it was found that Chinese writers didn't conform to the stereotype of Asian indirectness but made far stronger commitments and used about half the number of hedges than the L1 writers.

Multiple literacies

DA shows culture to be an important contextual constraint on the expression and interpretations of meanings, and it is not monolithic or deterministic. No contexts are static or homogeneous and the fact that we all belong to multiple groups means that communities cannot be distilled down to sets of discourse features. However, DA emphasizes that both texts and the activity of writing are embedded in culture and are inseparable from linguistically encoded cultural meanings.

By showing that writing always takes place in and for particular social groups, DA provides an empirical basis for the idea of multiple literacies. There is no single, self-evident, and non-contestable literacy, as dominant ideologies suggest, but a wide variety of practices relevant for particular times and purposes. Recognizing these pluralities not only reveals that potentially contested cultural assumptions underlie texts, but replaces the native versus non-native writer distinction with one emphasizing the variable expertise of novices and experts in particular contexts.

With comparable samples, the study of parallel corpora can provide information about what different groups of language users actually do, revealing their linguistic and interactive schemata. In turn, this throws light on an increasing amount of work which has supported analyses of texts with interview data to go beyond description and link surface patterns to particular cultural or social schemata—how students understand English and how they use it to express particular meanings and concepts.

Some future directions

Many areas of L2 discourse remain to be explored. First, we need to consider areas of learner preference and difficulty. We know little about the lexical, syntactic, or rhetorical features of writing by particular learners in a range of different genres and professional and institutional contexts. There is the need for research on the extent to which these features differ from those of other learners or native speakers, and investigations into whether patterns can be explained by proficiency, by L1 conventions, or by cultural assumptions. Second, we should study areas of overlap and difference. DA research has the potential to expand our understanding of the hybridity and heterogeneity of communities and cultures, revealing the ways that communities influence writing and how these vary. Third, we can focus on areas of change and manipulation. This concerns questions of generic integrity and flexibility, the extent to which individuals can successfully challenge the conventions or ethos of the L2 by manipulating its discourse conventions. DA can tell us more about the ways L2 writers draw on their vernacular rhetoric and what is required for these features to become recognized as new conventions.

Conclusion

While discourse analysis is mainly concerned with language, it has much to tell us about interaction. DA can tell us about how students construct texts, how their rhetorical choices reflect their purposes and relationships with readers, and how these texts compare with those of other groups. Discourse analysis reminds us that writing involves writers making language choices in social contexts peopled by readers, prior experiences, and other texts. Bringing together action, activity, and language in a single concept, discourse analysis is an indispensable tool for understanding second language writing.

6.3 Features of Discourse Analysis

Unlike linguistic approaches that focus only on the rules of language use, discourse analysis emphasizes the contextual meaning of language. It focuses on the social aspects of communication and the ways people use language to achieve specific effects (e.g. to build trust, to create doubt, to evoke emotions, or to manage conflict). Instead of focusing on smaller units of language, such as sounds, words or phrases, discourse analysis is used to study larger chunks of language, such as entire conversations, texts, or collections of texts. The selected sources can be analyzed on multiple levels (see Table 6.1).

Table 6.1　Discourse analysis

Level of communication	What is analyzed?
Vocabulary	Words and phrases can be analyzed for ideological associations, formality, and euphemistic and metaphorical content
Grammar	The way that sentences are constructed (e.g. verb tenses, active or passive construction, and the use of imperatives and questions) can reveal aspects of intended meaning
Structure	The structure of a text can be analyzed for how it creates emphasis or builds a narrative

Level of communication	What is analyzed?
Genre	Texts can be analyzed in relation to the conventions and communicative aims of their genre (e.g. political speeches or tabloid newspaper articles)
Non-verbal communication	Non-verbal aspects of speech, such as tone of voice, pauses, gestures, and sounds like "um," can reveal aspects of a speaker's intentions, attitudes, and emotions
Conversational codes	The interaction between people in a conversation, such as turn-taking, interruptions and listener response, can reveal aspects of cultural conventions and social roles

6.4 Conducting Discourse Analysis

Discourse analysis is a qualitative and interpretive method of analyzing texts (in contrast to more systematic methods like content analysis). You make interpretations based on both the details of the material itself and on contextual knowledge.

There are many different approaches and techniques you can use to conduct discourse analysis, but the steps below outline the basic steps you need to follow.

▶ Step 1. Defining your research question and select the content of analysis

To do discourse analysis, you begin with a clearly defined research question. Once you have developed your question, select a range of material that is appropriate to answer it.

Discourse analysis is a method that can be applied both to large volumes of material and to smaller samples, depending on the aims and timescale of your research.

This type of analysis sees writing as an outcome of activity, as words on a page or screen and can be descriptive (revealing what occurs), analytical (interpreting why it occurs) or critical (questioning the social relations which underlie and are reproduced by what occurs).

Choosing your research topic

First you have to come up with some ideas. Your topic can start out very broad. Think about the general area or field you're interested in—it's often a good idea to choose a topic that you already know a bit about.

Start with a broader topic, and then do some reading to begin narrowing down your topic. Look for the top journals in your field and skim through some recent issues. If an article interests you, check the reference list to find other relevant sources.

As you read, take notes and try to identify problems, questions, debates, contradictions and gaps. Your aim is to narrow down from a broad area of interest to a specific niche.

Make sure to consider the practicalities: the requirements of your project, the amount of time you have to complete the research, and how difficult it will be to access sources and data on the topic. Before moving onto the next stage, it's a good idea to discuss the topic with your instructor or the members of your group.

▌• Task

♦ Research topic

1. Individual work: Go over the possible areas of study in this unit, choose a topic that interests you, for example, student writing, and think about the aspects that you want to explore as well as the material that you can collect for your investigation.

2. Group work: Work in small groups, share with each other the topic selected and discuss any problems or difficulties that may appear in actual research.

Identifying a problem

Now you've settled on a topic and found a starting point—but what exactly will your research investigate, and why does it matter? To give your project focus and purpose, you have to define a research problem.

The problem might be a practical issue, for example, a process or practice that isn't working well, an area of concern in students' writing practice, or a difficulty faced by a specific group of learners in school.

Alternatively, you might choose to investigate a theoretical problem—for example, an underexplored phenomenon or relationship, a contradiction between different models or theories, or an unresolved debate among scholars.

Writing research questions

When you have a clearly-defined problem, you need to formulate one or more questions. Think about exactly what you want to know and how it will contribute to resolving the problem. To put the problem in context and set your objectives, you can write a problem statement. This describes who the problem affects, why research is needed, and how your research project will contribute to solving it.

Based on the problem statement, you need to write one or more research questions. These target exactly what you want to find out. They might focus on describing, comparing, evaluating, or explaining the research problem.

A strong research question should be specific enough that you can answer it thoroughly using appropriate textual or discourse analysis. It should also be complex enough to require in-depth investigation and argument. Questions that can be answered with "yes/no" or with easily available facts are not complex enough for a research paper.

At this state, write out the single research question to guide your reading and thinking. The answer that you develop is your thesis statement—the central assertion or position that your paper will argue for.

A good research question is essential to guide your research project. It pinpoints exactly what you want to find out and gives your work a clear focus and purpose. A good research question should be

- focused on a single problem or issue;
- researchable using primary and/or secondary sources;
- feasible to answer within the timeframe and practical constraints;
- specific enough to answer thoroughly;
- complex enough to develop the answer over the space of a paper; and
- relevant to your field of study and/or society more broadly.

> **Research problem:** People increasingly engage in the Wechat for communication instead of text messaging, but there is little research into their use of language in these different forms of interaction.
>
> **Research question:** What are the features of their language use in the Wechat? What are the main factors that influence peoples' language use? Do age and educational level have an effect on the type of interaction?

Types of questions in relation to your research

- Descriptive research: What are the characteristics of X?
- Comparative research: What are the differences and similarities between X and Y?
- Correlational research: What is the relationship between variable X and variable Y?
- Exploratory research: What are the main factors in X? What is the role of Y in Z?
- Explanatory research: Does X have an effect on Y? What is the impact of Y on Z? What are the causes of X?
- Evaluation research: What are the advantages and disadvantages of X? How well does Y work? How effective or desirable is Z?

▸ Task

♦Problem statement and research questions

1. Individual work: Read the following sample, and then write your own problem statement and specific research questions by referring to the guidelines given in this section as well as your selected topic.

Sample 1: Topic, problem statement, and research questions*

Topic: Nominal stance in academic writing

Previous research (Baratta, 2010; Barton, 1993; Charles, 2003, 2007) has shown that stance expression through nouns is a feature of competent academic writing. These studies have analyzed a variety of academic text types, including coursework (Aull & Lancaster, 2014; Mei, 2007), theses (Baratta, 2010; Charles, 2003, 2007), argumentative essays (Jiang, 2015) and research articles (Jiang & Hyland, 2015; Mu et al., 2015).

Problem Statement

However, there are no known studies that have investigated the use of stance nouns in scripts produced by writers in a high-stakes test, such as the IELTS test. Writing produced in such settings may constitute a different register from other types of academic writing and thus be associated with different linguistic and functional characteristics (Staples, Egbert, Biber, & McClair, 2013).

One of the few studies on stance construction in IELTS scripts was conducted by Kennedy and Thorp (2007). This study investigated "hedging" as one aspect of stance in the IELTS Writing Task 2 and focused on how writers at levels 4, 6 and 8 used modal auxiliary verbs, adjectival/adverbial/ nominal modal expressions, modal lexical verbs and it-clauses in hedging. However, nominal stance construction was not the focus of this study.

Research Question

The present study addresses the need for further research on how stance is constructed through nouns as a "neglected feature of metadiscourse" (Jiang & Hyland, 2016, p. 1) in test scripts written by L2 writers of different English proficiency levels. I specifically aim to investigate if and to what extent nominal stance construction differentiates highly proficient writing from less proficient writing. To this end, I aim to explore the following question:

What differences, if any, are there in the distribution, form, functions and premodification of stance nouns in scripts at three proficiency levels (4, 6 and 8) in the IELTS test?

2. Classwork: Present in class your research project, including the research topic, problem statement and research questions, trying to get some suggestions and feedback from your peers or instructors.

▶ Step 2. Gathering information and theory on the context

Here in this step, you must establish the social and historical context in which the material was produced

---

*The sample here is taken from a research paper "Nominal stance construction in IELTS tests" by Elvan Eda Isık-Tas, published in *Journal of English for Academic Purposes*, 34 (2018), pp. 1–11. For the purpose of illustration, parts of the paper in this sample are marked with specific headings to demonstrate how to write the problem statement and ask research questions.

and intended to be received. Gather factual details of when and where the content was created, who the author is, who published it, and whom it was disseminated to.

While understanding the real-life context of the discourse, you can also conduct a literature review on the topic and construct a theoretical framework to guide your analysis. For example, you study L1 (Chinese) and L2 (English) organizational patterns in the argumentative writing of Chinese EFL student-writers. You also research theory on the transfer of organizational patterns from L1 to L2 and the relationship between student writing background and textual organization.

Conducting a brief literature review

A literature review is a survey of scholarly sources on a specific topic. It provides an overview of current knowledge, allowing you to identify relevant theories, methods, and gaps in the existing research. A good literature review doesn't just summarize sources—it analyzes, synthesizes, and critically evaluates to give a clear picture of the state of knowledge on the subject.

Conducting a literature review involves collecting, evaluating and analyzing publications (such as books and journal articles) that relate to your research question. There are five main steps in the process of writing a literature review.

Step 1. Searching for relevant literature

When searching for the relevant literature, use keywords and citations. Start by creating a list of keywords related to your research topic and question. There are some useful databases to search for journals and articles:

- Web of Science
- JSTOR
- CNKI
- Scopus

Read the abstract to find out whether an article is relevant to your question. When you find a useful book or article, you can check the bibliography to find other relevant sources.

To identify the most important publications on your topic, take note of recurring citations. If the same authors, books or articles keep appearing in your reading, make sure to seek them out.

For example, you can find out how many times an article has been cited on Baidu Xueshu—a high citation count means the article has been influential in the field, and should certainly be included in your literature review.

Step 2. Evaluating sources

You probably won't be able to read absolutely everything that has been written on the topic—you'll have to evaluate which sources are most relevant to your questions.

For each publication, ask yourself:

- What question or problem is the author addressing?
- What are the key concepts and how are they defined?
- What are the key theories, models and methods? Does the research use established frameworks or take an innovative approach?
- What are the results and conclusions of the study?
- How does the publication relate to other literature in the field? Does it confirm, add to, or challenge established knowledge?
- How does the publication contribute to your understanding of the topic? What are its key insights and arguments?
- What are the strengths and weaknesses of the research?

Make sure the sources you use are credible, and make sure you read any landmark studies and major theories in your field of research.

The scope of your review will depend on your topic and discipline: in the humanities you might take a long historical perspective (for example, to trace how a concept has changed in meaning over time).

Step 3. Taking notes and citing your sources

As you read, you should also begin the writing process. Take notes that you can later incorporate into the text of your literature review.

It is important to keep track of your sources with citations to avoid plagiarism. It can be helpful to make an annotated bibliography, where you compile full citation information and write a paragraph of summary and analysis for each source. This helps you remember what you read and saves time later in the process.

Use correct and consistent APA citations or MLA format citations.

Step 4. Organizing the literature review

Identifying themes, debates and gaps

To begin organizing your literature review's argument and structure, you need to understand the connections and relationships between the sources you've read. Based on your reading and notes, you can look for:

- **Trends and patterns (in theory, method or results).** Do certain approaches become more or less popular over time?
- **Themes.** What questions or concepts recur across the literature?
- **Debates, conflicts and contradictions.** Where do sources disagree?
- **Pivotal publications.** Are there any influential theories or studies that changed the direction of the field?
- **Gaps.** What is missing from the literature? Are there weaknesses that need to be addressed?

This will help you work out the structure of your literature review and (if applicable) show how your own research will contribute to existing knowledge.

Outlining the structure

There are various approaches to organizing the body of a literature review. You should have a rough idea of your strategy before you start writing.

Depending on the length of your literature review, you can combine several of these strategies (for example, your overall structure might be thematic, but each theme is discussed chronologically).

Chronological

The simplest approach is to trace the development of the topic over time. However, if you choose this strategy, be careful to avoid simply listing and summarizing sources in order.

Try to analyze patterns, turning points and key debates that have shaped the direction of the field. Give your interpretation of how and why certain developments occurred.

Thematic

If you have found some recurring central themes, you can organize your literature review into subsections that address different aspects of the topic.

For example, if you are reviewing literature about the multimodal discourse analysis of Chinese youth image construction in the official news media, the key terms or concepts might include image, image construction, modality and multimodality, multimodal discourse analysis, and approaches to multimodal discourse analysis.

The example below is taken from the literature review of the same research paper cited on p. 60, which is about nominal stance construction in L2 academic writing. The selected part here discusses how scholars in the field have approached the the concept of stance.

> ## 2. Stance in academic writing
>
> The two most frequent terms in studies on stance in academic writing are evaluation and stance. Thompson and Hunston (2000) use evaluation as a "broad cover term for the expression of the speaker or writer's attitude or stance towards, viewpoint on, or feelings about entities or propositions that he or she is talking about" (p. 5). Conrad and Biber (2000), on the other hand, prefer to use the term stance as a general term corresponding to the expression of personal feelings and assessments. Other terms used in studies of stance include modality (Halliday, 1985), evidentiality (Chafe & Nichols, 1986), voice (Hirvela & Belcher, 2001), hedging (Hyland, 1998), authorial identity (Ivanic, 1998) and appraisal (Martin & White, 2005).
>
> In using stance, writers do not only express their opinions and reflect their value systems but they also construct relationships with their readers and organize their texts (Thompson & Hunston, 2000). For L2 writers, one aspect of difficulty in the acquisition of pragmatic competence

is establishing an appropriate stance in academic writing. As evidenced in previous studies (e.g., Hyland & Milton, 1997), L2 writers have difficulty manipulating the linguistic resources to construct a stance in their writing. Studies that investigated epistemic stance in L2 learner production (e.g., Bartley & Hidalgo-Tenorio, 2016; Gabrielatos & McEnery, 2005; Hyland & Milton, 1997; Kecskes & Kirner-Ludwig, 2017) found that L2 learners had difficulty making epistemic comments, conveying statements with appropriate degrees of doubt and certainty and presenting assertions in acceptable and persuasive ways.

The effective construction of stance increases the quality of argumentation in academic essays (Mei, 2007; Wingate, 2012). Mei (2007) found significant differences in the way engagement resources were employed in high- and low-scoring essays of L2 learners and concluded that these differences "may underline the importance of the appropriate use of such resources to the evaluative quality of arguments" (p. 266). In this respect, to raise L2 writers' awareness of stance options in academic writing, we need a better understanding of the linguistic resources utilized in stance construction. To this end, nominal stance construction, as an understudied aspect of stance-taking in L2 academic writing, will be the focus of this study.

The example uses the thematic approach. As part of the literature review, it focuses on the theme of stance, as can be seen from the subheading.

Methodological

If you draw your sources from different disciplines or fields that use a variety of research methods, you might want to compare the results and conclusions that emerge from different approaches. For example:

- Look at what results have emerged in qualitative versus quantitative research.
- Discuss how the topic has been approached by empirical versus theoretical scholarship.
- Divide the literature into sociological, historical, and cultural sources.

Theoretical

A literature review is often the foundation for a theoretical framework. You can use it to discuss various theories, models, and definitions of key concepts.

You might argue for the relevance of a specific theoretical approach, or combine various theoretical concepts to create a framework for your research.

Step 5. Writing your literature review

Like any other academic text, your literature review should have an introduction, a main body, and a conclusion. What you include in each depends on the objective of your literature review.

Introduction

The introduction should clearly establish the focus and purpose of the literature review.

Body

The body, depending on the length of your literature review, can be divided into several paragraphs or subsections. You can use a subheading for each theme, time period, or methodological approach.

As you write, you can follow these tips:

- **Summarize and synthesize.** Give an overview of the main points of each source and combine them into a coherent whole.
- **Analyze and interpret.** Don't just paraphrase other researchers—add your own interpretations where possible, discussing the significance of findings in relation to the literature as a whole.
- **Critically evaluate.** Mention the strengths and weaknesses of your sources.
- **Write in well-structured paragraphs.** Use transitions and topic sentences to draw connections, comparisons and contrasts.

Conclusion

In the conclusion, you should summarize the key findings you have taken from the literature and emphasize their significance.

❗ Task

♦Literature review

1. Individual work: Based on your reading of relevant source materials, write your literature review, following the steps and guidelines given in this section.

2. Group work: After you have finished writing the literature review, work with a peer to read each other's writing, giving feedback on how to revise or improve, if necessary.

Constructing a theoretical framework

The goal of a theoretical framework

After refining your problem statement and research question(s), you have to explore what theories, ideas and models other researchers have already developed.

By presenting this information, you frame your research and justify your overall approach. The main goals of a theoretical framework are to

- define key concepts;
- evaluate, select, and/or combine relevant theories; and
- explain your assumptions and expectations.

The theoretical framework shows that your research has a clear rationale based on existing knowledge. The definitions and models you select give your project direction, and you will build on these choices at later stages. This part lays the foundations that will support your analysis, helping you interpret your results and make broader generalizations.

How to create a theoretical framework

To build your theoretical framework, follow these three steps.

Step 1. Identifying your key concepts

The first step is to pick out the key terms from your problem statement and research questions. Concepts often have multiple definitions, so the theoretical framework involves clearly defining what you mean by each term. The example below is taken from a student's BA thesis about language transfer in the Spanish passive voice learning of English majors in China. Note that the underlined places show the key concepts related to the study: transfer and passive voice, which are discussed further in the theoretical framework section.

> **Problem statement:** In recent years, an increasing number of college students in China study Spanish as a second foreign language after learning English for several years, so more and more Chinese scholars and teachers are concentrated on English (L2) transfer effects on Spanish (L3) acquisition these years. Many studies have covered both positive and negative transfer of English on Spanish, particularly in phonetics, morphology, syntax, and pragmatics. However, previous studies are mostly conducted by teacher researchers from their teaching experience. For one thing, they mainly discuss how to deal with transfer effects as Spanish teachers but neglect students' thinking patterns and attitudes in the learning process. For another, those studies are too theoretical and general to fit in authentic language acquisition of individual students.
>
> **Objective:** Therefore, this empirical study aims to interpret English transfer effects on Spanish, particularly in the acquisition of passive voice. With the combination of grammar tests and questionnaires, the study can delve further into students' learning outcomes and reflection in Spanish study, which offers a new perspective to current studies on language transfer in the third language acquisition.
>
> **Research Questions:** This empirical study intends to answer the following research questions:
> (1) Are English majors influenced by their English grammatical knowledge in learning Spanish passive voice? If yes, what are the manifestations of transfer effects?
> (2) When learning Spanish, are students aware of transfer effects? If yes, what are their attitudes towards the transfer effects?

Step 2. Defining and evaluating relevant concepts, theories, and models

By conducting a thorough literature review, you can determine how other researchers have defined and drawn connections between these key concepts. As you write the theoretical framework, aim to compare and critically evaluate the approaches that different authors have proposed.

After discussing different models and theories, you establish the definitions that best fit your research and justify why it suits your own study. In more complex research projects, you might combine theories from different fields to build your own unique framework.

Make sure to mention the most important theories related to your key concepts. If there is a well-established theory or model that you don't want to apply to your own research, explain why it isn't suitable for your purposes.

Step 3. Showing what your research will contribute

Apart from discussing other people's theories and ideas, the theoretical framework should aim to show how your own project fits in.

- Will you test a theory or contribute new evidence by collecting original (qualitative or quantitative) data?
- Will you use theory as a basis for interpreting and understanding your data?
- Will you analyze, critique or challenge established theory?
- Will you combine theoretical approaches in a new or unique way?

If relevant, you can also use the theoretical framework to develop hypotheses for your research. A hypothesis makes a testable prediction about the outcome of a specific study, while a theory is the overarching explanation for why and how certain outcomes happen in general. That means you can use the theory to determine what you expect to happen.

The structure of the theoretical framework

There are no fixed rules for structuring a theoretical framework. The important thing is to create a clear, logical structure. One way to do this is to draw on your research questions/hypotheses and some of your key terms.

For example, you could create a section or paragraph that looks at each question, hypothesis, or key concept. Within each section, you would then explore the theories and models that are relevant to that particular item.

As in all other parts of your paper, make sure to properly cite your sources to avoid plagiarism.

Based on the above example, as the concepts of "language transfer" and "passive voice" play a major role in the investigation and will later be measured or examined, they are essential concepts to define within the theoretical framework.

Below is a (simplified) example of how the student describes and compares definitions as well as theories from the literature. The example focuses on the concepts , "transfer" and "passive voice."

Theoretical Framework

2.1 Language Transfer in Third Language Acquisition

Dating back to the 1950s, language transfer emerged, mainly on the basis of contrastive analysis and behaviorism. Linguists such as Charles Fries and Robert Lado (85–87) claimed that differences among languages made learning a second language totally different from acquiring the first language. Difficulties and errors in the second language acquisition could be predicted by analyzing the relationship of the first and the second language. In the past decades, some researchers regarded "language transfer" as simply "native language influence" (Odlin 25). With the further study of cross-linguistic influence on multilingual speakers, linguists gradually realized that transfer impacts not necessarily came from learners' mother tongue.

Language transfer, according to Terence Odlin, is "the influence resulting from similarities and differences between the target language and any other language that has been previously (and perhaps imperfectly) acquired" (27). To learners of a new language, transfer impacts can be both helpful and adverse. On the one hand, similarities in different languages facilitate language acquisition, which is referred as positive transfer. On the other, differences among languages bring about negative transfer, which hinders language learning and may cause errors (Odlin 26).

Language transfer in third language acquisition is not exactly the same as that in the process of second language acquisition. Third language acquisition, according to Jasone Cenoz, is "acquisition of a non-native language by learners who have previously acquired or are acquiring two other languages" (71). With interactions of more languages, cross-linguistic influence in over two languages is more complicated, compared with studies in which only two languages are involved, as more variables are taken into consideration (Aronin 33–47). In addition, language transfer in L3 acquisition differs from that in L2 acquisition in learners' metalinguistic awareness. Studies show that learners with previous language learning experience, compared with monolingual learners, present higher sensitivity and awareness of linguistic features, which benefits overall language learning (Park 5).

2.2 Passive Voice in Spanish and English

Passive voices, used frequently in both English and Spanish, occur when people "have little interest in, or knowledge of, the doer of the action but are more interested in what happens to, or is done to, the person or thing thus affected" (Espinoza 230). Despite great similarities in usages and structures, the passive voice in English is not exactly the equivalent of that in Spanish. In this section, basic forms and usages of passive voices in English and Spanish are introduced respectively.

In English, there is simply one construction of the passive voice, where the subject can be nouns and pronouns of both human beings and objects. Unlike English, there are two types of passive voice in Spanish: passive voice with *se* and with *ser*. Generally speaking, the former form is far more commonly used, in which subjects receive the action of the verbs without mentioning the performer of the move (Serigos "Passive Voice"). In this structure, nouns or pronouns of human beings normally cannot work as subjects. As people tend to use active constructions, passive voice with *ser* are not widely used. In this passive construction, agents can be mentioned with the preposition *por*, which serves as "by" in English. The syntactic structure of this type of sentences is the closest one to that of English passive voice (Espinoza 231). Table 2.1 below demonstrates structures and examples of passive voice in English and Spanish.

Table 2.1   Passive voice in English and Spanish

English	Spanish
Passive voice: be+past participle of verb+(by somebody/something) Example: These works were made by a Mexican artist. Example: This novel is widely read.	(1) Passive voice with *ser*: *ser*+past participle of verb+(*por* somebody/something) Example: Estas obras fueron realizadas por un artista mexicano. (2) Passive voice with *se*: *se* + third person of active verb forms Example: Esta novela se lee mucho.

(Serigos "Passive Voice")

Besides the two forms of passive voice in Spanish, impersonal sentences sometimes can also be used to express passive meaning, as shown in Table 2.2. The most typical instance is "*Se dice...*" or "*Dicen...*", which means "It is said..." or "It is reported..." in English.

Table 2.2   Impersonal structures expressing passive meaning in Spanish

English	Spanish
Example: It is said that his/her son is very intelligent.	(1) *se* + third person singular form of verb Example: Se dice que su hijo es muy inteligente.
Example: It is said that his/her son is very intelligent.	(2) third person plural form of verb Example: Dicen que su hijo es muy inteligente.

Of course, you could analyze the concepts more thoroughly and compare additional definitions to each other. You could also discuss the theories and ideas of key authors in greater detail and provide several models to illustrate different concepts.

It is just critical that you correctly cite all of your sources throughout the theoretical framework; the APA or MLA Style can guide you on how to do this.

If you do not cite your sources you risk committing plagiarism. Read more about the consequences of plagiarism and how to avoid plagiarism.

Checklist: Theoretical framework

- Key concepts have been defined.
- The most relevant theories and models have been analyzed.
- The theories and models chosen to answer the research questions or develop hypotheses have been justified.
- Notable relationships between concepts have been explained.
- The theoretical framework has a logical structure.
- Relevant and recent sources have been cited.
- The theoretical relevance of the research has been made clear.

▌ Task

♦ Building the theoretical framework

Individual work: Read this section carefully, and then start building the theoretical framework for your own research based on your research question and the literature review. Finally, write this part following the structure guidelines as well as the sample provided.

▶ Step 3. Analyzing the data for themes and patterns

This step involves closely examining various elements of the material—such as words, sentences, paragraphs, and overall structure—and relating them to attributes, themes, and patterns relevant to your research question.

You analyze the selected material for wording and statements that reflect or relate to certain textual patterns, ways of thinking, writing conventions or traditions, and even ideologies, including attitudes toward authority, traditional or widely held values, and popular opinion.

> **Sample 2: Data collection and procedure***
>
> The corpus for this study comprises 40 introductions of research articles—20 Chinese and 20 English—in the field of educational psychology. The English research articles, written by first language speakers, were selected from *The Journal of Educational Psychology*, published by the American Psychological Association, Washington, DC. The Chinese research articles written by first-language Chinese speakers were selected from *Psychological Development and Education*, a leading academic journal published in Beijing, China by Children's Psychology Research Institute of Beijing Normal University, and Children's

*The sample here is taken from an article "Cultural differences in the organization of research article introductions from the field of educational psychology: English and Chinese" by Chek Kim Loi and Moyra Sweetnam Evans, published in *Journal of Pragmatics*, 42 (2010), pp. 2814–2825.

Educational Psychology Research Institute of China Education Society. The journal has published research articles in educational psychology since 1985 with four issues yearly. The two journals were selected as being representative of prestigious refereed journals in the field of educational psychology in the respective countries.

Initially, 60 articles were selected from each journal based on judgment sampling. Later, 20 articles were extracted from the 60 articles for each language to form the actual corpus of the present study. To obtain a random-stratified sample, the total population of 60 articles was first stratified into five subgroups based on publication in the five years preceding the year in which the sampling was made (2003–2007), followed by a simple random sampling to select articles from each of the five subgroups in proportion to their representation in the total population. A simple random sampling was employed within each stratum to ensure an unbiased representative sample. The modest size of 40 research article introductions was considered to be justified considering the present study is a combination of qualitative and quantitative research which includes both a description of generic structures and quantitative data. Observations are restricted to the corpus. It is thus not the aim of the present study to generalize about the generic patterns of research article introductions in the field of educational psychology.

The instrument

Swales' (1990, 2004) CARS (Create a Research Space) model was selected as the basis for the analysis and coding of the moves and steps in both sets of articles (see Appendix A for the coding scheme). Past studies (e.g. Najjar, 1990; Taylor and Chen, 1991; Ahmad, 1997; Jogthong, 2001; Ahmed, 2004) have confirmed Swales' move-analysis framework as a valid tool for analyzing research article introductions in particular and other research article sections (including complete research articles) in general. The CARS model consists of three stages termed "moves" by Swales. Swales and Feak (2000: 35) specify a move as "the defined and bounded communicative act that is designed to achieve one main communicative objective." The three moves in Swales's (1990, 2004) CARS model are:

i. Move 1—establishing a research territory

ii. Move 2—establishing a niche

iii. Move 3—occupying the niche (Swales, 1990)/Move 3—presenting the present work

As observed, Move 3 (occupying the niche) in Swales's (1990) version of the CARS model was re-labelled Move 3 (presenting the present work) in Swales's (2004) model, the latter term providing a more explicitly functional label. In Swales's (1990, 2004) CARS model, these three moves are further sub-divided into their constituent steps. A step is defined by Swales (1990) as a smaller unit of discourse that builds moves. In other words, each step supports and guarantees the validity of the move.

Appendix A

Table A.1

Coding scheme for English and Chinese research article introductions in educational psychology

Move 1	Specifying the topic	Step 1	*Claiming centrality
		Step 2	Defining terms/concepts
		Step 3	Presenting the theoretical basis
		Step 4	*Reviewing literature/findings of previous research
Move 2	Making links between past research and present research	Step 1	*Indicating a gap
		Step 2	*Raising a question
		Step 3	*Counter-claiming
Move 3	Introducing the present research	Step 1	*Announcing the purpose
		Step 2	Announcing the focus of the research
		Step 3	Presenting the background of the study
		Step 4	*Introducing the research hypothesis
		Step 5	*Introducing the research questions
		Step 6	*Presenting positive justification
		Step 7	Introducing the implications of the findings
		Step 8	*Claiming the significance of the study

Note: *refers to steps adapted from Swales's (1990, 2004) CARS model.

▌• Task

♦ Data analysis

1. Group work: Work in small groups, share with each other the kind of data and the analysis you are planning to use in your paper, focusing on the advantages and disadvantages of the analytical elements, and then decided on the appropriate analysis framework for your project.

2. Individual work: Based on the group discussion and the feedback from your peers and your instructor, if possible, write up this section by referring to the sample given above.

► Step 4. Reviewing your results and drawing conclusions

Once you have assigned particular attributes to elements of the material, reflect on your results to examine the function and meaning of the language used. Here, you will consider your analysis in relation to the broader context that you established earlier to draw conclusions that answer your research questions.

Sample 3: Findings and discussion*

Overall, the rhetorical structures employed in both English and Chinese research article introductions appear to be characterized by the three major features, namely explicitness, specifying the value of research and taking a critical stance. Both English and Chinese research article introductions establish the context explicitly by defining the terms/concepts (Move 1 Step 2), presenting the background of the study (Move 3 Step 3), reviewing literature/findings of previous research (Move 1 Step 4), announcing the purpose (Move 3 Step 1) and the focus of the study (Move 3 Step 2). The data show that these constituent steps help establish clear contexts. In defining the terms/concepts (Move 1 Step 2), writers provide explicit meanings to the terms and concepts related to the research topic. In presenting the background of the study (Move 3 Step 3), writers provide background information on issues closely related to the reported studies before they are dealt with in detail in the subsequent sections of the articles. In reviewing previous research or findings (Move 1 Step 4), writers refer to other studies in the specific domain which is addressed in the article. In announcing the purpose (Move 3 Step 1) and the focus of the research (Move 3 Step 2), writers present clear indications on the direction and the scope of their studies, while in introducing the research questions (Move 3 Step 5), writers offer the readers a yardstick by which to measure the success of the studies. In addition, the linguistic realizations of the aforementioned constituent steps explicitly signal the communicative intentions of the writers in both the English and Chinese introductions. For example, in order to indicate the importance of the research topic, writers employ expressions such as "significant," "the most critical," and "increasing evidence." The above steps are manifested in the data, as shown below:

Move 1 Step 2 Defining terms/concepts

[E-16]   Wineburg (1991a) defined heuristics as "sense-making activities [that help] their user resolve contradictions, see patterns and make distinctions among different types of evidence"(p.77).

[C-20]   自尊是个体人格的核心因素之一，也是人的基本需要之一。

(Individual self-esteem is one of the core personalities and it is also one of the basic human needs.)

Move 1 Step 4 Reviewing literature/findings of previous research

[E-15]   Mead (1934) elaborated on this account by arguing that it is not perceptions of specific significant others that influence the self-concept but rather the generalized other-the individual's assessment of how he or she is generally perceived by others.

[C-16]   本研究查阅了近十年来国内有关大学教师职业压力的研究报告……[2] 例如；有研究发现 [3]，……

(The study reviewed the recent ten years' research report concerning the work stress of university lecturers... For example，some research found out that[3], ...

(**Note:** For limited space, illustration of other steps is omitted.)

---

*The following excerpt is selected from the same research cited on pp. 69–70.

While English and Chinese research article introductions broadly share the communicative intentions characterized by the three major features, the sets of data differ in the degree of application of these features. This study found that rhetorical variations exist between the research article introductions written by Chinese L1 users and English L1 users. Chinese research article introductions generally use these three major features to a lesser degree than English introductions do. The degree of use of these features is reflected in the percentage of the introductions employing the steps. Generally (except for Move 1 Step 4 and Move 2 Step 2), the above steps were employed in fewer Chinese than in English introductions as shown in Figs. 1–3.

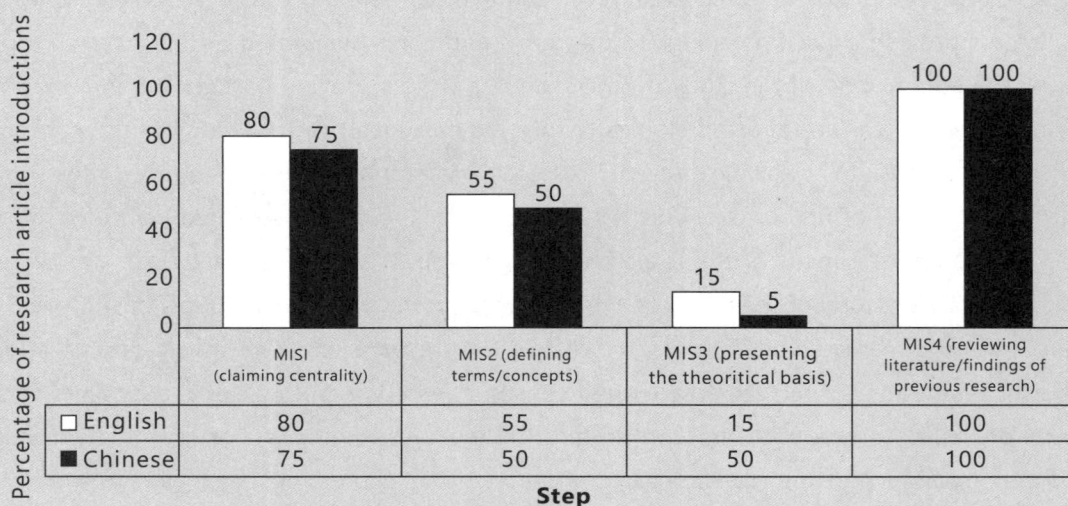

	MIS1 (claiming centrality)	MIS2 (defining terms/concepts)	MIS3 (presenting the theoritical basis)	MIS4 (reviewing literature/findings of previous research)
□ English	80	55	15	100
■ Chinese	75	50	50	100

Step

Fig. 1. The employment of steps in Move 1 of English and Chinese research article introductions

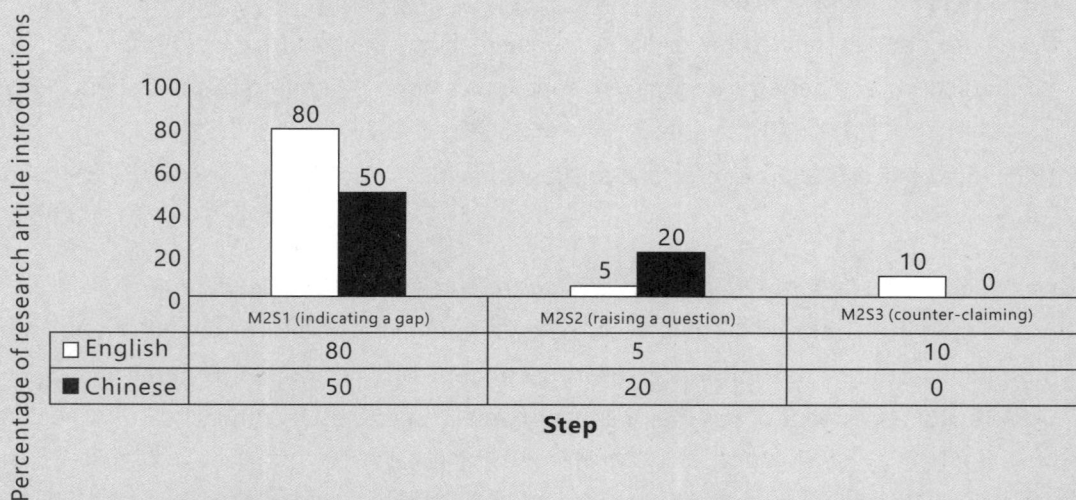

	M2S1 (indicating a gap)	M2S2 (raising a question)	M2S3 (counter-claiming)
□ English	80	5	10
■ Chinese	50	20	0

Step

Fig. 2. The employment of steps in Move 2 of English and Chinese research article introductions

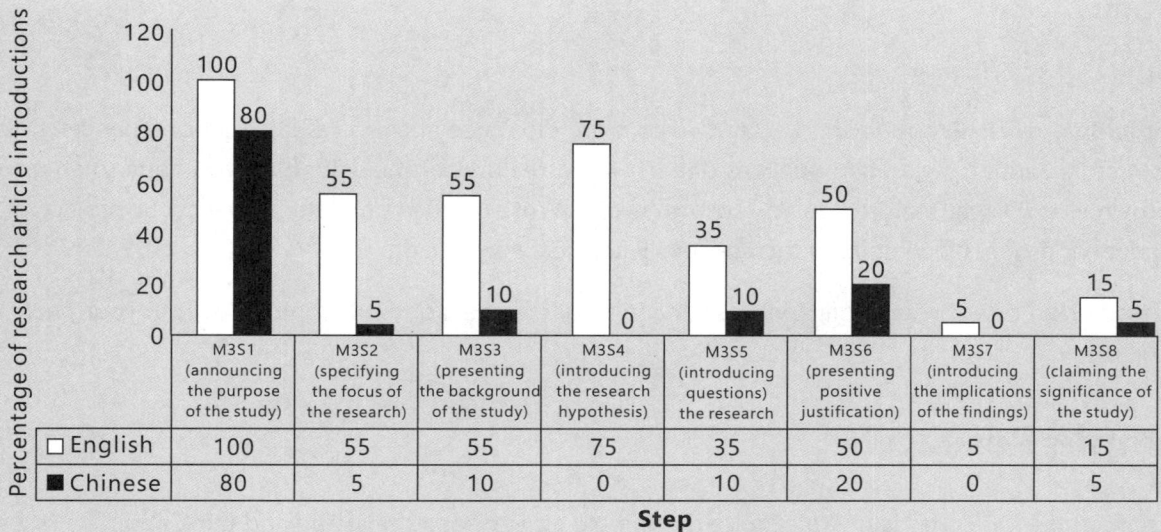

	M3S1 (announcing the purpose of the study)	M3S2 (specifying the focus of the research)	M3S3 (presenting the background of the study)	M3S4 (introducing the research hypothesis)	M3S5 (introducing questions) the research	M3S6 (presenting positive justification)	M3S7 (introducing the implications of the findings)	M3S8 (claiming the significance of the study)
☐ English	100	55	55	75	35	50	5	15
■ Chinese	80	5	10	0	10	20	0	5

Step

Fig. 3. The employment of steps in Move 3 of English and Chinese research article introductions

(*Note:* The results are followed by the discussion of socio-cultural factors underlying the differences in terms of the three dominant features identified: (1) Taking a critical stance, (2) Explicitness, and (3) Specifying the value of the research. For the limited space, it is omitted here.)

Conclusion

Despite the links postulated above between socio-cultural factors and rhetorical features in Chinese research article introductions, this study does not claim that the rhetorical organization of the corpus can or should be attributed solely to cultural conventions. Further research might shed more light on how written discourse can be viewed as at least partially influenced by the cultural background of the writer and the intended audience, in the same way that it is accepted that spoken discourse is so shaped (see, for e.g. Halliday, 1978; Halliday and Hasan, 1989).

With knowledge of the distinctive rhetorical features in each of these languages (English and Chinese), Chinese students will be aware that the expectations of native English-speaking readers are different from those of Chinese-speaking readers. This could perhaps make the rhetorical aspects of English academic writing more visible and attainable. EAP writing instructors should be aware that Chinese students might base their EAP writing on a set of rhetorical forms that differ from those of English. This should allow them to make informed pedagogical decisions that are grounded in the understanding of the preferred rhetorical strategies in both languages, to guide Chinese students in writing English academic writings which are acceptable and comprehensible to English audiences.

Task

♦ Writing up the final project

1. Individual work/Group work: Locate two or more discourse analysis research articles/papers. Discuss the structure, writing styles, and qualities of each. What features of the writing do you hope to emulate in your own work? What features do you wish to avoid? Write up the complete draft of your project, either individual or group, by combining the previously finished assignment.

2. Classwork: Present your project in class, trying to get suggestions and comments from your peers and instructor.

Sample Research

Please scan the QR code below to acquire the sample article. Read the article and think about its research methods.

Sample Article

Unit ⑦

Critical Discourse Analysis

As mentioned briefly in the previous section 5.3, the umbrella term "critical discourse analysis" (CDA) refers to a variety of overlapping methodologies associated with a somewhat different approach to discourse and world. The controlling theoretical idea behind CDA is that text, embedded in recurring "discursive practices" for their production, circulation, and reception which are themselves embedded in "social practice," are among the principal ways in which ideology is circulated and reproduced. The goal of CDA is thus to uncover the ways in which discourse and ideology are intertwined. Ways of talking produce and reproduce ways of thinking, and ways of thinking can be manipulated via choices about grammar, style, wording, and every other aspect of discourse. The goal of CDA is often explicitly political as well. Acknowledging that science is never value-free, CDA advocates social justice and social change (Johnstone, 2018).

⑦.1 Introduction

Discourse refers to expressing oneself using words. Discourses are ubiquitous ways of knowing, valuing, and experiencing the world. Discourses can be used for an assertion of power and knowledge, and they can be used for resistance and critique. Discourses are used in everyday contexts for building power and knowledge, for regulation and normalization, for the development of new knowledge and power relations, and for hegemony (excess influence or authority of one nation over another). Given the power of the written and spoken word, CDA is necessary for describing, interpreting, analyzing, and critiquing social life reflected in text. CDA is concerned with studying and analyzing written texts and spoken words to reveal the discursive sources of power, dominance, inequality, and bias and how these sources are initiated, maintained, reproduced, and transformed within specific social, economic, political, and historical contexts (Van Dijk, 1988). It tries to illuminate ways in which the dominant forces in a society construct versions of reality that favor their interests. By unmasking such practices, CDA scholars aim to support the victims of such oppression and encourage them to resist and transform their lives, the central tenet of critical theory and the critical science approach.

Stemming from Habermas's (1973) critical theory, CDA aims to help us understand social problems that are mediated by mainstream ideology and power relationships, all perpetuated by the use of written texts in our daily and professional lives. The objective of CDA is to uncover the ideological assumptions that are hidden in the words of our written text or oral speech in order to resist and overcome various forms of power over or to gain an appreciation that we are exercising "power over," unbeknownst to us. CDA aims to systematically explore often opaque relationships between discursive practices, texts, and events and wider social and cultural structures, relations, and processes. It strives to explore how these non-transparent relationships are a factor in securing power and hegemony, and it draws attention to power imbalances, social inequities, non-democratic practices, and other injustices in hopes of spurring people to corrective actions.

Task

1. Group work:

1) Discussion on the uses of the words "critical" and "criticism."

The words "critical" and "criticism" are used in several ways. "Criticism" can be evaluative. It can mean negative commentary (as in "She is too critical of her students"), or it can mean evaluative commentary whether negative or positive (like much literature, film, music, or theater criticism). "Criticism" can also be non-evaluative (at least in theory): "critical thinking" is careful, systematic, self-conscious thinking, without any necessary evaluative goals, and the goal of academic literacy criticism is not always overtly evaluative, either. Would you say it is just a historical accident that the same set of words should be used to refer to description and evaluation, or is there a necessary connection between description and evaluation? Is it possible to describe without evaluating?

2) Discussion on the uses of the term "Discourse."

The word discourse has come to be used with a number of different senses. Below are two uses of the term.

- The term has been used to indicate simply spoken interaction. This meaning of the term has a long history; *Shorter Oxford English Dictionary* refers to its use in 1559 to mean "communication of thought by speech, talk, conversation." Nowadays, we normally use the term in the more general sense to include written communication. Of course, where necessary, we can specify *spoken discourse* as distinct from *written discourse*.

- "Discourse" is frequently used to refer to the general communication that takes place in specific institutional contexts. For example, we can talk about the discourse of science, legal discourse, and so on. This is useful shorthand, but, of course, it is an abstract concept that does not bear much relationship to individual communicative events since each of these discourses is realized in different ways depending on the situations involved. Thus the discourse of science includes many types of interaction, including lectures, research reports, theoretical discussions, to name but a few. Similarly, legal discourse embraces actual written laws, statutes, contracts, wills, conventional courtroom exchanges, cross-examination, and so on.

Compare the two definitions carefully. Think about the kinds of discourse, either spoken or written, Chinese or English, that show its different uses. Then, work in small groups, sharing with each other your understanding of the term, giving examples to support your idea.

2. Individual work: Based on the group discussion, try to answer the following questions, thinking about how you will conduct your own analysis.

1) What are your goals as a discourse analyst?
2) How do you imagine being able to use discourse analysis to help answer the questions you are asking?
3) Are your goals descriptive, critical, or both?

7.2 Principles and Framework of CDA

▶ Principles: three central tenets

There are three central tenets of CDA (Fairclough, 2013). Discourse is shaped and constrained by social structure (class, status, age, ethnic identity, and gender); and by culture, both "big" and "small" cultures, for example, the language or national culture, professional culture. Discourse (the words and language we use) helps shape and constrain our identities, relationships, and systems of knowledge and beliefs. As foreign language learners, our identities, the nature of our social relationships, and our knowledge and belief systems are shaped and constrained by the language and words espoused by us and by others.

▶ Analytical framework

CDA tries to unite, and determine the relationship among three levels of analysis: (1) the actual text; (2) the discursive practices (that is the process involved in creating, writing, speaking, reading, and hearing); and (3) the larger social context that bears upon the text and the discursive practices (Fairclough, 2013).

Textual level analysis

In more detail, the text is a record of an event where something was communicated and involves the presentation of facts and beliefs (often ideological), the construction of identities of participants discussed in the communication, and strategies to frame the content of the message (to be discussed later).

Discursive practice

This refers to rules, norms, and mental models of socially acceptable behavior in specific roles or relationships used to produce, receive, and interpret the message. They are the spoken and unspoken rules and conventions that govern how individuals learn to think, act, and speak in all the social positions they occupy in life.

Gee (1990) clarifies that discursive practices involve ways of being in the world that signify specific and recognizable social identities. We have learned to "be" students, daughters, mothers, members of an ethnic group or gender, entrepreneurs, and volunteers.

Social practice

Finally, the social context comprises distinct settings where discourse occurs (marketplace, classroom, playground, church, conferences), each with a set of conventions that determine rights and obligations—what each is allowed and expected to do. Simply put, the text becomes more than just words on a page—it discloses how those words are used in a particular social context (Huckin, 1997).

▌• Task

Individual work: Here is a detailed illustration of social practice. Read the text carefully, and then do the activity that follows.

> People within specific domains engage in social practices. Technically, these people are often referred to as actors. Social practices are human behaviours which involve following certain socially established conventions (some might say "rules") within which the actors have some degree of individual freedom and opportunities for unique behavior.
>
> Examples of social practices include business meetings, religious services, birthday parties, and so on. Most social practices involve knowledge of linguistic and discoursal conventions in whole or in part. For example, in a religious service, one may need to know where to stand, kneel or sit as well as something of the verbal conventions (prayers, for example).
>
> The knowledge and skills required to engage in social practices are part of socially shared knowledge. They may have been "picked up" through experience or contact with other actors or they may have been learned via specific instruction within the home environment or as part of education or training. Although social practices are often well established and persistent within a particular culture, they are rarely "frozen" and unchanging.
>
> A single instance of a social practice is a *social event*, which when language-based (such as a writing center tutoring session) is also known as a *speech event*.

1) This activity invites you to engage in an (imaginary) social act and consider its relationship with language and discourse. Imagine you are dissatisfied with some devices you have purchased (for example, a laptop, an iPad, or a mobile phone), what means do you have for complaining?

2) Consider whom you would contact (participants in the potential exchange), how you would contact them (possible modes and genres), what responses you would expect, what your intended outcome would be, and how you would hope to achieve it. Consider how you feel with respect to your relationship with the company that produced the product in terms of power relationships. Do you feel in a position of power or weakness?

► Micro and macro level analysis

A critical approach to discourse seeks to link the text (micro level) with the underlying power structures in society (macro sociocultural practice level) through discursive practices upon which the text was drawn (meso or intermediate level) (Thompson, 2002).

A text, a description of something that is happening in a larger social context with a complex set of power relations, is interpreted and acted upon by readers or listeners depending on their rules, norms, and mental models of socially acceptable behavior. Prejudice, bias, and marginalization go unchallenged if the text is not critically analyzed to reveal power relations and dominance.

CDA focuses on how social relations, identity, knowledge, and power are constructed through written and spoken texts in communities, schools, the media, and the political arena. Discourse always involves power and ideologies, is connected to the past and the current context (is historical), and can be interpreted differently by people because they have different backgrounds, knowledge, and power positions— therefore, the "right" interpretation does not exist whereas a more or less plausible or adequate interpretation is likely.

► Discourse and power relations

Discourse and language can be used to make unbalanced power relations and portrayals of social groups appear to be commonsense, normal, and natural when in fact the reality is prejudice, injustice, and inequities. Using just words, those in power, or wishing to be so, can misdirect our concerns for persistent, larger systemic issues of class, gender, age, religion, and culture, making them seem petty or nonexistent. Unless we begin to debunk their words, we can be misled and duped into embracing the dominant worldview (ideology) at our expense and their gain. Although the term discourse is slippery, elusive, and difficult to define, we must try. When discourse is effective in practice, evidenced by its ability to organize and regulate relations of power, it is called a "regime of truth" (Foucault, 1980). It is this regime, a system by which a political system is controlled, that is revealed when we engage in critical discourse analysis. How can we say we "empower individuals" if we do not teach ourselves, and them, how to debunk and unveil the truth behind the regime?

▌• Task

♦ Selecting your topic and research questions

1. Individual work:

1) Read the following excerpt about the use of specific words or phrases in language. Then use it as a prompt for your own project, think about a specific topic, and list the issues or problems that you have about the selected topic. Next, write your problem statement as well as research questions.

Here is an example that relates not just to the use of a particular wording but to the grammar itself. From the middle of the nineteenth century until relatively recently, it was considered "correct" practice in English to use "he" and "him" as singular pronouns to stand in place of sex-indefinite nouns. So, if we were talking or writing about an author, artist, doctor, teacher, director, or bank manager and we did not know whether the person in question was a man or a woman, we would refer to that person with the pronoun "he" or "him." This usage was taught in schools and expounded by grammarians. But, even at that time, the use of "they" as a singular gender-free pronoun was fairly common in spoken English, but published written English followed the grammarian's prescriptive code. The only exceptions were when the job or activity involved was one that at that time was normally done only by a woman, such as *nurse*. For some women's jobs, even the nouns were marked for gender as in *maid*, *waitress*, *actress*. Although it was often observed by grammarians that "he" was gender-free in cases such as this (whimsically expressed as "male embraces female"), the pronoun system reflected a social situation where most of the powerful and creative jobs were done by men. For a long time some women objected to this pronoun use, but it was only as more and more women held jobs traditionally done by men, and vice versa, that there was a sufficiently large group of objectors for the situation to begin to change. Now, it has become generally acceptable for the gender-free "they" to be used as a singular as well as a plural pronoun, or as an alternative to the use of "he or she."

2) Areas of linguistic choices: Use the following questions to help you think about areas of choice. If you are interested in one of these, you can consider doing a critical discourse analysis of your own.

- How do pronouns help "position" speakers, addressees, and characters in discourse?
- What are the effects of negation?
- What are the effects of questions?
- How do choices about tense, aspect, and modality work?
- How do adjectives, adverbs, and other modifiers create systems of classification?

2. Group work: Ask around the classmates or peers who are interested in your topic, and invite three or four of them to join you for a team project. Then, start making the research plan for the project, and write a short passage including the topic, research questions, purpose of the research, and data to be collected, that is, kinds of text or discourse, spoken or written. You can also conduct the project by yourself, if it is necessary.

♦**Review of related studies**

3. Individual work: After you have defined the topic and research questions, search for relevant sources both print and web. When you have gathered enough primary and secondary sources, write literature review section of the project.

7.3 How to Conduct Critical Discourse Analysis

We need some skills to conduct a critical analysis of our own and other's discourse. CDA does not have a unitary theoretical framework or methodology because it is best viewed as a shared perspective encompassing a range of approaches instead of one school.

The following part will draw from these many approaches as it focuses on setting out some useful skills in critically analyzing written text. One key principle of CDA is that the way we write, and what we say, is not arbitrary—it is purposeful whether or not the choices are conscious or unconscious.

Also, while CDA can also focus on body language, utterances, symbols, visual images, and other forms of semiosis (signs and symbols) as means of discourse, this unit will be limited to analyzing written language.

► Techniques for macro level analysis

Ordinary and critical reading

Huckin (1997) recommends that one first approach a text in an uncritical manner, like an ordinary, undiscerning reader, and then come at it again in a critical manner. It is noted that engagement without estrangement is to submit to the power of the text, regardless on one's own position, thereby accepting the reading and offering unquestioning support of the status quo. To offset this "take," coming at it a second time with a critical eye involves revisiting the text at different levels, raising questions about it, imagining how it could have been constructed differently, mentally comparing it to related texts.

Local and global reading comprehension

Also, it is important that one does not start to decipher the text word by word; rather, one should place the text in its genre (type of text including a journal article, media piece, government position paper, public speech, manual, textbooks, conference paper). Each genre-orientation has a style of its own set of characteristics that identify it—a template of sorts.

We can all recognize an advertisement (well—it used to be easy until infomercials were invented), a journal article, a technical manual, a curriculum document, a government position paper—they all have different building blocks that make them unique from other types of documents. One simple example is a scientific journal article that typically includes a problem statement, hypotheses, literature review, theoretical underpinnings, sampling and method, results, analysis and discussion, and conclusions plus recommendations. Because these rules, for how to structure the genre, belong to the institution that owns the genre, the genre becomes a means through which the institution extends power.

◆**Data analysis—macro level**

1. Individual work:

1) Refer to the previous units on data collection and samples in qualitative research, collect the data for your independent or team project, and make sure there is an adequate amount of texts or materials collected for your analysis.

2) Then, conduct the macro level analysis by referring to the guidelines mentioned above, trying to understand the context or background of the materials.

3) Finally, write the first draft of the method section of your project, including research questions, data collection, data analysis and procedures if necessary.

2. Group work: In small groups share with each other the data you have collected, and discuss any problems you have encountered so far.

▶ Techniques for micro level analysis

Detecting the frame or perspective of the text

Still looking at the text as a whole, Huckin (1997) recommends, next, checking out what sort of perspective is being presented—what angle, slant, or point of view. This is called framing the details into a coherent whole and can be accomplished by several techniques, which, if understood, are incredibly revealing:

- Choosing and placing specific photographs, diagrams, sketches, and other embellishments to get the reader's attention
- Using headings and keywords to emphasize certain concepts by giving them textual prominence (called foregrounding if the text is emphasized and backgrounding if text is there but de-emphasized or minimized)
- Leaving certain things out completely, counting on if it is not mentioned, the average reader will not notice its absence, and thereby not scrutinize it
- Using certain words that take certain ideas for granted, as if there is no alternative (presupposition), begging the question, "what could have been said that wasn't, and why not"
- Manipulating the reader by using selective voices to convey the message that certain points of view are more correct, legitimate, reliable, and significant while leaving out other voices

Doing detailed textual level analysis

Having noticed the genre of text and how the message is framed, you are ready to move onto the more minute levels of analysis: sentence, phrases, and words. Several CDA techniques have been developed to facilitate this level of analysis. Examples are drawn from Huckin (1997):

- **Topicalization:** Just as text can be framed, so can a sentence, called topicalization. In choosing what to put in the topic position, the writer creates a perspective or slant that influences the reader's perception. For example, in a media piece about peace protestors, if 11 sentences refer to protestors and three refer to the officials, the text is clearly about the protestors' actions but not about the issue that prompted the rally.

- **Agency:** Sentences can also convey information about power relations. Who is depicted as in power and over whom? Who is depicted as powerless and passive? Who is exerting power and why? This property of the text is referred to as agency and can remain at the subconscious level unless made visible by the analyst or critical reader. For example, the passive voice is often used to portray the agents of an action as unknown ("I've been robbed"), obvious ("The suspect was arrested"), or unimportant ("Several experiments were conducted"). Choosing the passive voice over the active can also help create textual cohesion. But the passive voice can also be used to hide an agent who is known, or downplay the fact that an agent was involved.

- **Nominalization:** Again, as with the text in general, omission of information about agents of power can occur at the sentence level and is most often achieved by nominalization (converting a verb into a noun) and the use of passive verbs. We can see how this process works in the following example:

1 The instructor lost his lecture notes and was rather upset.

2 The instructor was upset about the loss of his lecture notes.

In the second case, the fact that the instructor was the person who lost the lecture notes is concealed by turning the verb "lose" into its noun form "loss." In cases like this, people are removed and therefore responsibility for the action has also been removed. This makes it seem as though events just happen.

- **Presupposition:** Many readers are reluctant to question statements that the author appears to be taking for granted; presupposition can also occur at the sentence level in the form of persuasive rhetoric that can be used to convey the impression that what an agent of power says carries more weight.

Still with the peace/conflict example, a demonstrator sign that reads "give peace a chance" presupposes that the government is presently not doing so. A government spokesperson who says, "some of the demonstrators were a bit more aggressive" conveys the impression that all demonstrators are aggressive to some degree.

- **Insinuation:** This tool is slyly suggestive, carrying double meanings. When the facts, or the way the facts are presented, are challenged, the originator of the discourse can readily deny any culpability. This ability to deny any intention to mislead gives the originator of the discourse a lot of power.

For example, imagine that a reporter writes that the turnout for the rally (2000 people) failed to match a former, larger turnout a few years earlier (5000). This wording conveys the message that the current rally failed somehow because the numbers are lower. This insinuation, suspicion, and unsuccessful undertone takes power away from those at the rally, when in fact the rally met all expectations of those who organized it, a success that could undermine the position of those they are demonstrating against.

- **Connotation:** Even one word can convey strong meaning—connotations. These connotations are not always, or seldom, in the dictionary, but often assigned on the basis of the cultural knowledge of the participants. Connotations associated with one word, or through metaphors and figures of speech, can turn the uncritical viewer's mind.

  As an example, the use of the word protestor instead of a demonstrator conveys a message. A protestor is against something while a demonstrator is trying to make something evident. The media conveys a negative image of those advocating for peace when it paints them as protesting against the government and corporate establishment.

- **Tone:** The tone of the text is set with the use of specific words to convey the degree of certainty and authority (called modality). The tone of doubt or surety is introduced by using words such as *may, might, could, will, can, must, it seems to me, without a doubt, it's possible that, maybe,* or *probably.*

  Moods of heavy-handed authority or deference can be created simply by choice of verb or modal phrases, which assert or deny the possibility, impossibility, contingency, or necessity of something.

- **Register:** Finally, as with the full body of the text, single words can convey register—do the words spoken ring true? Writers can deceive readers by affecting a phony register, one that induces mistrust and skepticism. Register can be affected by choice of person—first person (*I, me, my, we, our*), second (*you* and *your*), and third (*he, she, they, their, his, hers, him, her*).

  For example, quoting directly from university spokesperson using first person, while using third person to refer to a student challenging university policy, can convey the message that the university is more objective than the student, hence more legitimate.

▌• Task

◆Data analysis—micro level

1. Individual work: Examine your data again, and look for the specific words, phrases and sentences that may reveal various aspects of textual meaning listed above. Then, continue with the analysis section by adding the specific textual aspects you have identified and explored. When you have completed the analysis at different levels, write the analysis part of your project, describing the results of your analysis.

2. Group work: In small groups, discuss the types of analysis you have completed, pointing out any problems or issues you have about the analysis and trying to get suggestions or help from your peers or teachers.

7.4 **Value of Critical Discourse Analysis**

The critical approach holds that people need to think about improving their living conditions rather than accepting and coping with their present conditions. That improvement is contingent upon people being conscious of social realities that exploit or dominate them and then demanding liberation from these forces.

A critical perspective helps us gain personal freedom from internal constraints such as biases or lack of a skill or point of view and social freedom from external constraints such as oppression, exclusion, and abuse of power relations. CDA can be applied to reveal the hidden ideological meanings behind the written and oral word.

CDA does not provide answers to the problems but does enable one to understand the conditions behind the specific problem—the deep, ideological roots of the issue. It can be carried out in various institutional settings or on various social, political, and critical issues by paying attention to the details of what social members actually say and do. Starting with the full text, working down to the individual word level, one can examine the layers to reveal the "truth behind the regime"—the profoundly insidious, invisible power of the written and spoken word.

Task

◆**Writing up your research project**

1. Individual work: Write the discussion, if necessary, on the results of your analysis based on your reading of relevant studies and sources as well as any background or contextual knowledge and information that may support your explanation or analysis. Then, continue to write the conclusion of the research paper.

2. Group work: After you finish the draft of the project, work together with one of your classmates or peers, if you are not doing the team project, to check the important aspects of your research based on the rubric below. Then, make any revision or improvement based on the rubric given here as well as the peer's and teacher's suggestions to complete the final presentation draft.

Question	Excellent	Good	Fair	Poor	Missing
Does the topic proposal describe the area of intended research effectively?	5	4	3	2	1
Is the importance and/or significance of the research problem identified?	5	4	3	2	1

1) If you gave a score of 4 or 5, explain its strengths.

2) If you gave a score of 3 or below, explain its weaknesses. Inform the author where clarification or re-writes may be necessary.

3) In the author's draft, point out trends or themes you feel would be appropriate for their research. (List at least three areas)

4) Does the author make a convincing argument for the need to study this topic? (Indicate *yes* or *no* and explain your response.)

3. Classwork: Present your research project, either individual or collaborative, to the whole class, getting comment or feedback from your peers and instructors.

Sample Research

Please scan the QR code below to acquire the sample article. Read the article and think about its research methods.

Sample Article

Unit **8**

Case Study

A case study is fundamentally a qualitative approach used to look at a single case, a small group of participants, a class, or a program. Case studies are good for describing, comparing, evaluating and understanding different aspects of a research problem, and are commonly used in social, educational, clinical, and business research to make recommendations (Kinkead, 2015). For students, case studies are often a good choice in a research paper or thesis. They keep your project focused and manageable when you don't have the time or resources to do large-scale research.

This unit will focus on qualitative case studies, although case studies can also be quantitative or draw upon both qualitative and quantitative approaches in a mixed methods study. Qualitative case studies are preferred by researchers who believe that "reality" is multiple, contradictory, and changing, and that the researcher inevitably becomes part of the study. They are also better suited for exploring issues rich in context (for example, socialization of L2 students into a discourse community or the role of identity in language learning). In the field of applied linguistics, case studies are now usually associated with interpretive qualitative research.

8.1 Introduction

▶ What is a case (study)?

A simple definition of case study is not easy. For the leading case study theorists, the principle of boundedness is central. A case is a "bounded system," or a defined individual or entity (like a student, program, school, institution) that the researcher wishes to explore. A bounded system is composed of an individual (or institution) and a site, including the contextual features that inform the relationship between the two. And the boundaries of the case are firmly linked to the researcher's interests.

Once the boundaries have been determined (and it is important to note that boundaries may move as the study proceeds, as researchers' awareness of the individual and the context deepens or his interest changes), it is time to decide which tools to draw upon to examine the social phenomena of interest within those boundaries. The highly individualized and contextualized nature of the problems tackled by qualitative case study researchers makes it impossible to be prescriptive because they look first to the object of study and determine which methods and types of data are most likely to shed light upon it.

Chapelle and Duff define the case study specifically for language teaching research in the following terms,

"In TESOL, a case typically refers to a person, either a learner or a teacher, or an entity, such as a school, a university, or a classroom ... In language policy research, the case may be a country" (p. 164). Furthermore, they stress an important feature of qualitative case study that makes it a good choice for language teacher-researchers: "Acknowledging multiple realities in qualitative case studies, as is now commonly done, involves discerning the various perspectives of the researcher, the case/participant, and others, which may or may not converge" (Chapelle & Duff, 2003, p. 164, qtd. in Yin, 2003).

In short, for a qualitative case study, a "case" can be seen as a bounded system comprised of an individual, institution, or entity and the site and context in which social action takes place, the boundaries of which may not be clear and are determined by the scope of the researcher's interests. The "study" of a case requires the researcher to select methods and tools appropriate to the case. Some case studies may also include the "end product" of the process of analyzing the case (that is, the written report of the analysis and the findings). This is because the actual writing up of the case study report can be considered part of the analytical process—the researcher makes sense of the case himself while simultaneously making sense of it for the audience.

With this understanding of case study, this following section will proceed to a discussion of specific types of qualitative case study.

▶ Types of case studies

Stake's classification

The boundaries between types of case studies are not sharp, and a case study may fit under more than one type. Stake (1995), one of the leading case study researchers, defines three broad types of case study.

- First, he describes the intrinsic case study, in which interest lies purely in one particular case itself. There is no attempt at all to generalize from the case being studied, compare it to other cases, or claim that it illustrates a problem common to other, similar cases. The emphasis is on gaining a deep understanding of the case itself. The intrinsic case study requires a primarily descriptive approach, focusing on the particularity of the case at hand.

- The second type defined by Stake is the instrumental case study, in which a case is studied with the goal of illuminating a particular issue, problem, or theory. Unlike the intrinsic case study, the instrumental case study is more likely to require interpretation and evaluation, in addition to description. Instrumental case studies may be used to develop conceptual categories or illustrate, support, or challenge theoretical assumptions. In other words, case studies—both intrinsic and instrumental—may lay the groundwork for future studies by providing basic information about the realms in which little research has been conducted.

- The third type of case study identified by Stake is the collective or multiple case study. Again, one issue, problem, or theory is focused upon, but the researcher chooses to study more than one case to shed light on a particular issue if doing so will lead to a better understanding, and perhaps better theorizing, about a still larger collection of cases.

1 Kozol (1991) investigated the experiences of students in different school systems to gain a better understanding of the role of disparate school funding on the quality of education.

2 Norton (2000) looked at the experiences of several immigrant women in Canada to understand the role of identity in language acquisition.

Both Kozol and Norton look at multiple cases as a means of theorizing about a broader category of cases.

Yin's classification

Yin (2003) offers a different categorization of case studies, by describing them according to purpose: exploratory, descriptive, or explanatory.

- An **exploratory case study** is used when little is known about the case being examined. It is often used to lay the groundwork for subsequent, possibly more quantitative studies by defining questions and hypotheses. For example, based upon the findings, a researcher could later write and then administer a questionnaire to a larger sample of participants.

- A **descriptive case study** aims only to present a detailed, contextualized picture of a particular phenomenon. This is similar to Stake's definition of an intrinsic case study, where the emphasis is simply on gaining a deep understanding of the case itself.

- Finally, the purpose of an **explanatory case study** is to explain cause–effect relationships related to a phenomenon. An explanatory case study is frequently a long-term, or longitudinal case study, and may draw upon quantitative research approaches as well.

Regardless of the type of case study one chooses to conduct, cases are selected because they possess certain characteristics—psychological, linguistic, institutional, sociocultural, or biological—that the researcher wishes to explore.

▶ Reasons for using (qualitative) case study in applied linguistics

The researcher does not so much choose to conduct a case study; rather, the decision to conduct a qualitative case study is suggested by a careful consideration of the object of the study, what the researcher wishes to learn about it, and what he or she hopes to do with the findings. This section looks at these questions in turn (Hood, 2009, pp. 72–73).

- What is the object of study? As defined above, the object of study is a bounded system, comprised of an individual or entity and the context in which social action occurs. A case may be narrowly or broadly bounded, depending upon the scope of the researcher's interests. Still, it is obvious that some objects of study of interest in educational research are not bounded systems.

For example, a doctor may be a case. But his or her doctoring probably lacks the specificity, the boundedness, to be called a case. The prime referent in case study is the case, not the methods by which the case operates. And certain questions, though interesting, might fall outside of the scope of the case. The correlation between TOEFL scores and graduation rates, for example, is an issue best studied by surveying a large sample and conducting statistical analysis. At the same time, every bounded system does not necessarily make for a good case study. It depends on how you answer the next question.

- What does the researcher wish to learn about the case? Certain questions or interests will require the kind of in-depth, long-term study that qualitative case study affords. Other questions will not.

  Let's say you have a bounded system—a school district comprised of 1,000 students in an urban, professional, multicultural, and multilingual area. If you are interested in the efficacy of a particular language teaching technique, you might conduct a quantitative case study, complete with experimental and control groups, treatments, and statistical analysis of the results as measured by test scores. However, if you wanted to understand how the language is used at home and in public spaces in this community and how this affects L1 and L2 language use in the classroom, you will likely have to go into homes and schools and spend an extended period of time there. Home life is not the sort of reality easily or accurately measured by a questionnaire using a five-point scale; the actual and precise effects of home language use on classroom language use is not going to be revealed simply by test scores. For this question, you need to go into the community and the classroom, observe, talk to people, get a sense of the lived experience of these students, and deepen your understanding of that experience through extended contact.

- What does the researcher hope to achieve with the findings? The results of qualitative case studies do not "prove" anything in the positivist sense. They do not establish laws that will be confirmed or discarded through further study (though further study may deepen or change our understanding of a particular case). Rather, the results of case study are typically used in one of two ways.

First, they may be used to improve conditions or practice for that particular case. For example, the lessons drawn from language use in homes and in classrooms in the school district described above may suggest ways of improving the learning experiences of students throughout that particular school district.

Second, the results may be extended to other cases where the particulars are similar (that is, other urban school districts in professional, multicultural, and multilingual neighborhoods). This is the same sense in which lawyers and judges discuss case law—the applicability of a past court decision to a case under consideration is determined by the factual and legal similarities between the two.

There is a third possibility, when an intrinsic case study is conducted, that the researcher has no aim other than to understand a particular case very deeply. In any particular case, the qualitative case study will have limited goals for the use of the findings, compared to the quantitative research which aims for generalizability and theory testing.

Implicit in all of these questions is the researchers' belief system. Here it is important to note that the researcher may choose to conduct a case study if he believes there is value in the particular, and that objectivity, neutrality, and control of intervening factors is not always possible and not always desired.

> Terry is an instructor in an Intensive English Program (IEP) attached to a North American university. One goal of the IEP is to help international students improve their English proficiency—first to meet university entrance requirements, and then to go on and complete their degrees. Although Terry has helped many students enter the university, he is dismayed that some of them subsequently fail to graduate, and eventually withdraw.
>
> To understand the difficulties faced by his students once they leave the IEP and to see if there is any way IEP teachers could better prepare them for their university studies, Terry decides to conduct longitudinal case studies of two of his IEP students (one graduate and one undergraduate) currently working toward their degrees at the university. Here are the reasons for Terry's qualitative case studies:
>
> - First, he has determined that the students he wishes to study and the contexts in which they act comprise a bounded system.
>
> - Second, the rich data, deep analysis, and long-term contact with the cases afforded by case study is better suited to his research interests (the experiences of L2 students in the university community and the possible role of social networks in their success) than quantitative methods.
>
> - Third, his aim is not to generalize or test a hypothesis, but rather to improve support and training for other L2 students on the same campus. Recognizing the multi-perspectival nature of case studies and his own positionality within this case, he sets out to recruit two participants—one graduate and one undergraduate—whom he will observe closely and interview repeatedly over the next two years. (Hood, 2009, pp. 66–67)

8.2 Process of Conducting Case Study Research

The key to a case study is choosing or identifying a case that is worth to be studied. Choosing a case to investigate involves more than identifying (finding) the research problem. A case study encompasses a problem contextualized around the application of in-depth analysis, interpretation, and discussion, often resulting in specific recommendations for action or for improving existing conditions.

The case study approach mainly involves the following steps:

- Selecting a case in relation to research questions
- Building a theoretical framework
- Collecting your data
- Analyzing and interpreting your data
- Writing up the study

A detailed description of process involved in conducting a specific case study will be illustrated below, including different tasks designed for the actual research project, serving as the guidelines for the research.

▶ Step 1. Selecting a case in relation to research questions

Research questions

Where do research questions come from? It may come from complaints that students make about their instructors in the classroom or writing situation. Why does one assignment work better than another? This questioning attitude can be very helpful in finding a worthwhile topic.

Identifying the topic

To help you identify an interesting topic, think about possible answers to this question: what is the topic? It may come from literature response journals by English major students; frequency of grammar errors in college students; teacher feedback in writing instruction; the role of tutoring in the writing center, and other areas. Also, read the strategies for finding a research topic given below to help you decide on a topic:

- Review your course readings, particularly the suggested readings, for topic ideas. Don't just review what you've already read but jump ahead in the syllabus to readings that have not been covered yet.

- Search the university libraries catalog for a good, recently published book and, if appropriate, more specialized works related to the discipline area of the course.

- Browse through some current journals in your subject discipline. Even if most of the articles are not relevant, you can skim through the contents quickly. You only need one to be the spark that begins the process of wanting to learn more about a topic. Consult with your professor or instructors about the core journals within your subject discipline.

- Think about essays you have written for past classes, other courses you have taken, or academic lectures and programs you have attended. Thinking back, what interested you the most? What would you like to know more about? Place this in the context of the current course assignment.

- Search online media sources to see if your idea has been covered by the media. Use this coverage to refine your idea into something that you'd like to investigate further, but in a more deliberate, scholarly way based on a particular problem that needs to be researched.

Turn an idea or general thought into a topic that can be configured into a research problem. Don't begin by considering what to write about, but rather, ask yourself the question, "What do I want to know?" Treat the assignment as an opportunity to learn about something that's new or exciting to you.

Unlike quantitative designs, research questions in qualitative designs in general, and case studies in particular, are likely to evolve over the course of the study, as the researcher gains a deeper intimacy with the participants and the context. Case study research questions should be reexamined and revised throughout the study.

> Terry's question, "How does the university help or hinder international students' progress?," might be revised, as he becomes more aware of the problems faced by his participants, to something like, "How do particular professors view and fulfill their role as educators of international students, and how do the participants respond to their professors?"

In a purely intrinsic case study, a case may be selected before research questions are formulated—questions might grow out of the researcher's initial encounter with a case. Whether you select a case before or after formulating research questions, defining your case is not as simple as it may at first seem. Remember that the boundaries of a case and its context may not be fully understood at the outset. In fact, a major goal of case studies is to define those very boundaries. Identifying the case to be studied, in response to your initial exposure and curiosity, is relatively easy. But you will spend a lot of time and energy defining both case and context, and the interplay between the two, throughout your study. An effective way to start, once you have identified the case you wish to study, is to brainstorm all you know, suspect, and hope to discover about the case and the context. The picture that emerges will appear, initially, to be painted with broad strokes. As your project proceeds, take careful notes as your understanding changes; continually add definition and detail to that picture.

Once you have developed your problem statement and research questions, you should be ready to choose the specific case that you want to focus on and provide detailed contextual information about the case.

Several types of subjects are available: students in a class, yourself as a writer, mature writers, native and non-native writers. The participant(s) is/are then matched with a topic, such as coherence, errors, student-teacher conferences, revision, or technology.

Context: Provide sufficient contextual information about the case, including relevant biographical and social information (depending on the focus), such as ESL learning/teaching history, L1 background, years of residence in a new country, if necessary, data collection site(s), or other relevant descriptive information pertaining to the case and situation.

A good case study should have the potential to

- provide new or unexpected insights into the subject;
- challenge or complicate existing assumptions and theories;
- propose practical courses of action to resolve a problem; and
- open up new directions for future research.

> Terry has already taken two preliminary steps that might apply to all case study projects: he has identified a problem and framed it in terms of a very general research question, and he has selected two cases to study to shed light on the problem.
>
> Research questions for intrinsic, exploratory, and descriptive case studies are usually broadly stated; however, instrumental case study research questions, which might challenge a hypothesis by examining a disconfirming case, are often more narrowly defined. Though research questions may be more specific than "What's going on here?," they are typically built upon "how" and "why" type questions. Terry frames his research questions as:
>
> - Why do some former IEP students struggle to earn their degrees?
> - How are these students coping with difficulty?
> - How does the university help or hinder international students' progress?
> - How do social networks help or hinder their progress?

Strategies for selecting or identifying a specific case

- **If your subject of analysis is an incident or event,** the event or incident that represents the case to be studied is usually bounded by time and place, with a clear beginning and end and with an identifiable location or position relative to its surroundings. The subject of analysis can be a rare or critical event or it can focus on a typical or regular event. The purpose of studying a rare event is to illuminate new ways of thinking about the broader research problem or to test a hypothesis. Critical incident case studies must describe the method by which you identified the event and explain the process by which you determined the validity of this case to inform broader perspectives about the research problem or to reveal new findings. However, the event does not have to be rare or uniquely significant to support new thinking about the research problem or to challenge an existing hypothesis. Whether the event is rare or not, the methods section should include an explanation of the following characteristics of the event: (1) when did it take place; (2) what were the underlying circumstances leading to the event; and (3) what were the consequences of the event.

- **If your subject of analysis is a person,** explain why you selected this particular individual to be studied and describe what experience he or she has had that provides an opportunity to advance new understandings about the research problem. Mention any background about this person which might help the reader understand the significance of his/her experiences that make them worthy of study. This includes describing the relationships this person has had with other people, institutions, and/or events that support using him or her as the subject for a case study research paper. It is particularly important to differentiate the person as the subject of analysis from others and to succinctly explain how the person relates to examining the research problem.

- **If your subject of analysis is a place,** it must not only describe its various attributes relevant to the research problem (e.g., physical, social, cultural, economic, political, etc.), but you must state the method by which you have determined that this place will illuminate new understandings about the research problem. In general, a case study that investigates a place suggests a subject of analysis that is unique or special in some way and that this uniqueness can be used to build new understanding or knowledge about the research problem. It is also important to articulate why a particular place as the case for study is being used if similar places also exist. If applicable, describe what type of human activity involving this place makes it a good choice to study (e.g., prior research reveals the findings that can be used as the criteria).

- **If your subject of analysis is a phenomenon,** the phenomenon can encompass anything that can be observed or presumed to exist but is not fully understood. A phenomenon refers to a fact, occurrence, or circumstance that can be studied or observed but with the cause or explanation to be in question. In the humanities and social sciences, the case usually focuses on human interaction within a complex physical, social, economic, cultural, or political system. A case study of a phenomenon most often encompasses an in-depth analysis of a cause and effect that is grounded in an interactive relationship between people and their environment in some way.

The choice of a case or set of cases to study cannot appear random. Evidence that supports the method by which you identified and chose your subject of analysis should be linked to the findings from the literature review. Be sure to cite any prior studies that helped you determine that the case you chose was appropriate for investigating the research problem.

▌• Task

◆Identifying a case to be investigated

1. Group work/Classwork: Read the above strategies for identifying a specific case to study, and work in small groups or as whole class to share your ideas of subject of analysis with your classmates. Use your classmates' suggestions or questions to stimulate your thinking of a case that is worth some exploration. Your goal is to generate a wide range of possible cases you might like to investigate.

2. Individual work: When doing a case study, ask yourself the question: Who are my subjects/ participants? A single student, a group of students, a classroom, an administration, or yourself? Practical considerations such as time and access to information can influence case selection, but these issues should not be the sole factors used in describing the methodological justification for identifying a particular case to study.

A case typifies the sort of dilemma that many students may face during their school learning and they allow for a bridging of the gap between theory and practice. The following are examples of possible case studies that may help you to select a case:

- Information collected over a period of a semester concerning how two different students (one with high proficiency and one with low proficiency) performed during group activities
- An account of the problems a student experienced during her first few months of studying in the university
- An account of how a teacher implemented process writing instruction and the difficulties she encountered
- An account of observation of one high-achieving student and one low-achieving student over a semester in order to compare their patterns of classroom participation
- An account of how two students resolved a misunderstanding that occurred between them in relation to the goals of doing a task-based writing project
- A description of all the changes a student made in a composition she was working on over a three-week period, from the drafting stage to the final stage

Spend some time thinking of possible cases for your own research project. Try to identify a subject of analysis that can be investigated using a case study design, define the problems that the case presents, clarify particular issues, look at alternatives, and choose a particular course of action to follow.

⫸ Task

♦Considering research topics and questions

1. Group work/Classwork: Work in small groups or as the whole class and share your initial ideas, using your classmates' proposed research questions to stimulate more of your own thinking. Your goal is to generate a wide range of possible research questions you might like to investigate.

2. Individual work: Read the example* below, and based on the example, consider how to formulate your research question(s).

> Padula and Miller (1999) conducted a multiple case study that described the experiences of women who went back to school, after a time away, in a psychology doctoral program at a major midwestern research university. The intent was to document the women's experiences, providing a gendered and feminist perspective for women in the literature. The authors asked three central questions that guided the inquiry: (a) How do women in a psychology doctoral program describe their decision to return to school? (b) How do women in a psychology doctoral program describe their re-entry experiences? And (c) how does returning to graduate school change these women's lives?

---

*The example here shows the central research questions from a case study, selected from Creswell (2014, p. 243).

These three central questions all began with the word *how*; they included open-ended verbs, such as "describe," and they focused on three aspects of the doctoral experience—returning to school, reentering, and changing. They also mentioned the participants as women in a doctoral program at a midwestern research university.

▶ Step 2. Building a theoretical framework

While case studies focus more on concrete details than general theories, they should usually have some connection with theory in the field. This way the case study is not just an isolated description, but is integrated into existing knowledge about the topic. It might aim to

- **exemplify** a theory by showing how it explains the case under investigation;
- **expand** on a theory by uncovering new concepts and ideas that need to be incorporated; and
- **challenge** a theory by exploring an outlier case that doesn't fit with established assumptions.

To ensure that your analysis of the case has a solid academic grounding, you should conduct a literature review of sources related to the topic and develop a theoretical framework. This means identifying key concepts and theories to guide your analysis and interpretation.

Doing the literature review serves many purposes, primarily to find out where the holes are—areas where there are gaps in the knowledge base that a new case study may fill. A review also suggests methodology. Finally, the review of literature provides the foundation that can convince others of the findings of the final project.

▌• Task

♦Writing the literature review

Individual work:

1) Once the topic is defined, it's time to begin prewriting about the project, jotting thoughts in a journal or log. What do you know about the topic already? What is known from others? What are the major theories in the field?

2) Once you are certain about the scope of the study, doing a review of the scholarly literature to reveal the history of ideas and theories on the topic. Developing a list of key terms (e.g., peer editing, sentence length, feedback, digital writing) makes a search easier. It's important in the review to categorize different types of literature about the topic. Is it a research article? A textbook? A popular article? A website?

▶ Step 3. Collecting your data

Once you have selected a case and have defined general research questions, begin gathering data related to those questions. When it comes to data collection, you will have to decide the types of data that are most relevant for your research and then choose appropriate methods for collecting them.

> Terry collects a diverse set of data. Interviews with participants and, with their permission, their instructors are a primary source. Direct observation is conducted in the classroom and at other sites on campus, such as the writing center and the international student affairs office. Terry also asks participants to maintain a diary in which they document their experiences and feelings. In addition, he collects the preliminary and final drafts of written assignments, course syllabi and policy statements, and reading lists. To understand institutional policy, he collects documentation of the university's stated policies toward L2 students. (Hood, 2009, pp. 78–79)

There are many different research methods you can use to collect data on your subject. Case studies tend to focus on qualitative data using methods such as interviews, observations, and analysis of primary and secondary sources (e.g., newspaper articles, photographs, official records). Sometimes a case study will also collect quantitative data.

Data in second language acquisition (SLA) studies may be somewhat more restricted (either interviews, tests, writing samples, think-aloud protocols, or grammaticality judgments), and the analytic focus may be narrower and more technical as well, such as the development of linguistic or rhetorical structures in oral or written L2 production. Establishing a trusting relationship with research participants, using multiple elicitation tasks (data collection procedures), obtaining adequate relevant background information about case participants and sites, and having access to or contact with the case over a period of time are, in general, all highly desirable.

Data sources

The box below provides a brief overview of the most common data sources for case studies; other units in this book elaborate on how to use them.

Sources of Data

1. *Interviews:* Perhaps the most commonly used method of data elicitation in qualitative educational research, interviews may yield a wealth of valuable data. Interviews may be structured, semi-structured, or open, depending on the scope of inquiry and the role of individual interviewees. The interviewer can record the interview or take notes.

2. *Direct observation:* The investigator plays the role of observer, watching participants as they act in certain settings. Though positionality is still an issue, the investigator is not an active participant in the setting. He sits quietly on the fringe, taking notes. For many case study researchers, direct observation is a key source of data; countless hours may be spent at the research site, documenting in minute detail his or her observations.

3. *Participant observation:* Unlike direct observation, participant observation means that the investigator himself plays a key role in the setting. For example, a researcher conducting a case study

---

of an academic conference may attend sessions to gather data. He plays two roles—that of a researcher observing and that of a participant attending a session. Participant observation is, in a way, more difficult than direct observation because attention may be divided as the researcher participant tries to balance two roles.

4. *Diaries:* Participants' records of their own experiences, and their interpretations of those experiences, are particularly relevant to the case study researcher. They have the advantage of being recorded in proximity to the events themselves and may suggest follow up questions for interviews.

5. *Documents:* Wherever phenomena occur in the post-literate world, there is usually a paper trail. What can be gleaned from this record? Documents include letters, pamphlets, agendas, minutes, reports, other studies, and newspaper articles.

6. *Archival records:* Organizations keep records, and these records may shed light on various aspects of the case in question. These records may include client records, organizational charts, budgets, maps, census data, and even personal notes. All of these records may help you understand a case at a particular point in time.

7. *Artifacts:* Physical artifacts such as pictures, artwork, tools, or even technology may reveal much about the places where they were seen as necessary or desirable.

(adapted from Yin, 2003, p. 86)

1

A case study on a Chinese high school student writing English application letters*

The method used in this research was a single case study. Data from several sources were collected for the study. The focal point of analysis and point of orientation of the other sources were the drafts (with detailed comments from an English writing expert) and the final version of a writing task in the UW (University of Washington) application. The author of the application letters was a 12-grade Chinese senior high school student, referred to here as Tony (a pseudonym), who planned to pursue graduate study abroad. Other sources include: the in-depth interviews with Tony; email exchanges between Tony and Prof. X (a pseudonym), the writing expert; Tony's blogs; teaching reflections by some of Tony's teachers (a Chinese language teacher and an English writing teacher) on the web, and field notes. The aim is to gain as thorough an understanding as possible of the case and its context.

*The case study is adapted from Liqiu Wei, "Tracing Cultures behind the Struggling Experience of a Chinese High School Student Writing Application Letters in English," *Theory and Practice in Language Studies*, Vol. 2, No. 5, pp. 1048–1056, May 2012.

2

Terry has begun brainstorming a list of the types of data he believes will help him answer those questions:

- **Interviews with participants:** These could be conducted regularly, perhaps once a month, in Terry's office or via email. Early in the study, the interviews might be more open-ended, giving his participants an opportunity to raise the issues that they feel are most relevant. Later, they may become more structured as Terry identifies specific issues that he wishes to understand more deeply.

- **Interviews with participants' professors:** They may be able to shed light on issues that the participants themselves do not understand while adding an additional perspective on their experiences. Participants' permission is vital.

- **Classroom observation:** Terry would like to sit in on some of his participants' classes to better understand how they interact with professors and classmates during class. Participants' and professors' permission is essential.

- **Participant learning diaries:** Terry arranges for each participant to regularly write a learning diary, so he can keep track of and understand in their own words each participant's perspective on significant learning experiences and events.

- **Copies of participants' course syllabi, reading lists, assignment sheets, and policy statements:** These documents may help Terry better understand the demands being placed on his participants and help him frame questions about how they cope with particular demands.

- **Rules, policies, and resources for international students at the departmental and university level:** Such data will shed light on how his participants are viewed and supported at the institutional level. He may at some point seek to interview policy makers to better understand the rationale behind particular policies.

This is a preliminary list, to be altered as the study proceeds. Nevertheless, it provides Terry with a starting point for data collection. (Hood, 2009, pp. 75–76)

Methods for collecting the data

This section gives you suggestions for conducting your case study research through direct observation, interviews, or textual analysis, if needed.

Using observation to gather information

The key to successful observation of human behavior or other natural phenomena is having a clear sense of your purpose combined with preparation. The following practical strategies can be adopted for carrying out observational research (see Table 8.1).

Table 8.1 Strategies for using observations to collect data

Strategies	What to do	Comments
Determine the purpose and scope of your observation	Think ahead about the subject of your observation and the details, behavior, or processes involved. Make a list	Some phenomena can be observed only once; others can be observed regularly. If you plan on a series of observations, the first one can provide an overview or baseline, while subsequent observations can enable you to explore your subject in more detail or note changes over time
Make arrangements ahead of time	In making requests, state clearly who you are and what the purpose of your observation is. Be careful in your requests and in your thanks after your observation	If you need to ask permission or get clearance for your observation, be sure to do so long before you plan to start the observation
Take clear, usable notes while observing	Bring note—taking materials—either a laptop or plenty of paper, a clipboard or binder with a hard surface for writing, and good writing utensils. Document your notes with exact indications of location, time, and names and titles of people (if relevant)	Make sure that your notes are easy to read and well labeled with helpful headings
Go through your notes soon afterward	Fill in gaps and elaborate where necessary. You might then write a first draft while your observations are still fresh in your mind	Don't let too much time go by, or you will not be able to reconstruct details or recapture thoughts you had while observing

(Ramage, Bean & Johnson, 2009, p. 246)

Here are two examples of how students have used direct observation to conduct research.

1 A student intends to investigate how a revision approach developed by his teacher influences students' writing. Data were collected from the writing of three students, including a draft of each text, two journal entries concerning their reflections of their own writing; in addition, she kept notes on what the students said during writing conferences.

2 A student research team hypothesized that episodes of the cartoon *SpongeBob SquarePants* would contain fewer gender stereotypes than episodes of a 1930s Mickey Mouse cartoon. The researchers watched the cartoons in one-minute segments and for each segment recorded the presence of behaviors that they categorized as stereotypical or non-stereotypical male behavior and stereotypical or non-stereotypical female behavior.

Using interviews

Interviews can be an effective way to gather field research information. They can range from formal interviews lasting thirty or more minutes to quick, informal interviews, which only give brief answers to a few key questions. An interview might also be conducted over the telephone, without a face-to-face meeting. In some case studies, you might rely on longer, formal interviews with persons whose background or knowledge is relevant to your research question. To make interviews as useful as possible, learn to use the following strategies (see Table 8.2).

Table 8.2 Strategies for conducting an interview

Stages	Strategies	What to do	Comments
	Consider your purpose	Determine what you hope to learn from the interview. Think about your research question and the aim of the paper you are planning to write	This thinking will help you focus the interview
	Learn about your subject	Research important subjects related to your research question and the person you will be interviewing. Although you needn't become an expert, you should be familiar with your subject	Ideally, interviews should give you knowledge or perspective unavailable in books or articles
Before the Interview	Formulate your question	Develop a range of questions including short-answer questions like the following: How long have you been working in this field? What are the typical qualifications for this job? Create open-ended questions, which should be the heart of your interview. For example, What changes have you seen in this field? What solutions have you found to be the most successful in dealing with ...? What do you see as the causes of ...? Questions framed in this way will elicit the information you need but still allow the interviewee to answer freely	Be as thorough with your question as possible. Most likely you will have only one chance to interview this person. Avoid yes-or-no questions that can still stall conversation with a one-word answer. Avoid leading questions. The more you lead the interviewee to the answer you want, the less valid your research becomes

Stages	Strategies	What to do	Comments
	Gather your supplies	If you plan to record the interview, be sure to get your interviewee's permission, and spend time familiarizing yourself with recording equipment. Bring a laptop or pad of paper to take notes	Using a recorder allows you to focus your attention on the substance of the interview. Most likely, you will wan to take notes even if you are recording
During the Interview	Manage your time	Arrive on time. Also agree to a time limit for the interview and stick to it. (If necessary, you can request a second interview, or your interviewee may be willing to stay longer)	You will show a lack of professionalism if you are not particularly careful to respect the interviewee's time
	Be courteous	Thank the interviewee for his or her time. During the interview, listen attentively. Don't interrupt	Your attitude during the interview can help set up a cordial and comfortable relationship between you and the person you are interviewing
	Take notes	Take down all the main ideas and be accurate with quoted material. Don't hesitate to ask if you are unsure about a fact or statement or if you need to double-check what the person intended to say	If you are recording the interview, you can double-check quotations later
	Be flexible	Ask your questions in a logical order, but also be sensitive to the flow of the conversation. If the interviewee rambles away from the question, don't jump in too fast	You may learn something valuable from the seeming digression. You may even want to ask unanticipated questions if you have delved into new ideas
After the Interview	Go through your notes soon afterward	No matter how vivid the words are in your mind, take time very soon after the interview to go over your notes, filling in any gaps, or to transcribe your recordings	What may seem unforgettable at the moment is all too easy to forget later. Do not trust your memory alone

(Ramage, Bean & Johnson, 2009, pp. 247–248)

▌• Task

1. Group work: Before proceeding with the research itself, work in small groups to get preliminary feedback from peers or your instructor on the clarity of your research question and the design of your methods. You could create a set of interview questions and ask one or two of the group members—on a volunteer basis—to try responding to the questions. Your goal here is to discover whether the questions might be unclear or ambiguous.

2. Classwork: As a class, discuss problems that arose in creating and responding to interview questions or doing observations in your previous research projects. Were any questions unclear? How would you revise your interview questions or observation details based on the difficulties you encountered?

Textual analysis

Besides observing and interviewing, data collection can also involve testing, or analyzing writing samples. For example, reading transcripts of a peer-response group may employ the same kind of textual analysis as is found in literary criticism. Who are the characters? What is their motivation? Is there conflict? Based on your research question or purpose, textual analysis can take the form of rhetorical analysis, theme/idea analysis, critical analysis, or more linguistics-oriented analysis, which can be conducted at various levels, from micro to macro aspects, such as lexical, syntactical, or larger textual patterns. As for each type of analysis, refer to the unit of this textbook that discusses the text or discourse analysis approach.

▶ Task

◆Developing a research plan

1. Individual work: Based on the research question you have asked, write a draft of your introduction and your method section before you do the actual research. Drafting these sections first not only gets them out of the way but helps you think through your whole research process. Drafting your introduction section helps you understand your purpose more clearly and serves to clarify your research question and hypothesis. Drafting the method section helps you plan exactly the steps you will take to do the research.

2. Individual work/Group work: Consider ways that you might use one of the research methods presented above—observation, interview, or textual analysis—to answer your question. Begin designing your research plan, including procedures for observations or formulation of questions for your interviews. You can also work with your classmates.

3. Group work/Classwork: What is the time span of the study? A school term, a few days, or one year? Once you have formulated your research question, you need to develop a plan for collecting the data. Working in small groups or as a class, share your brainstorming. Your goal is to develop the beginnings of a research plan. Help each other talk through the stages of a possible investigation.

▶ Step 4. Analyzing and interpreting data

In qualitative case studies, data collection and analysis occur simultaneously and continuously, so it is somewhat misleading to mark them off as separate steps. At the outset, when data collection begins, case study designs can be quite tentative. With analysis from the very first interview, diary entry, or observation, research questions begin to take more solid form, the scope and direction of the inquiry emerges, and the boundaries of the case become clearer. It is also a cumulative process, whereby continual and recursive analysis of data adds shape and texture to the project and suggests direction for its own continuation. As you collect and analyze data, your task is to identify categories, themes, and patterns that help explain the phenomena under consideration and the contexts in which they occur.

Writing thick description in narrative style

A qualitative case study can be looked at as a good story, with characters (the participants), events, conflicts, resolutions, and conclusions. Furthermore, the narrative form allows the investigator to describe in fine detail the contexts in which the participants act, thus helping the reader of the report understand how the conclusions were drawn, adding to their trustworthiness.

Narrative also allows for a more personal tone. This is important for two reasons. First, the researcher is part of the story, interacting with the participants and being present in the research settings in a way that makes his story inseparable from the case. First-person *I* is entirely appropriate. Second, participants in qualitative case studies are real people, not mere statistical abstractions. The researcher seeks to understand them in terms of their own human complexity and particularity—he/she wishes to depict them as real people, deserving the reader's empathy. Nothing could be more personal than that.

In case study research, the profile of the single subject or certain participants is often written in "thick description." The term was expanded upon by Geertz (1973) as a way to describe the ethnographer's task of describing the "web of significance" (Geertz, 1973, p. 5) that forms culture and the individual's relation to it. In short, to understand how and why the participants act and react in particular ways, the investigator must describe the context and the participants in minute detail. This type of storytelling is important to case study.

> For Terry, what if one of Terry's participants is particularly silent and apparently detached from classroom activities? What is the significance of this silence? Is he indeed detached or alienated from the group, or is his silence a reflection of cultural differences or personality traits? If he is detached, is it because of a conflict with the professor or a classmate? Is it the result of dissatisfaction or frustration with the course? Whatever inference Terry draws, his audience will be skeptical. The only way to convince a reader of the validity of the inference is to make the web of significance explicit. Terry does this by describing the context as thoroughly as possible, putting the reader into that classroom with the participant, with the same understanding of the intervening factors that Terry has gleaned from a variety of sources. (Hood, 2009, p. 83)

Using thick description, the researcher paints a picture for the readers, renders visible the previously unseen forces that animate and motivate phenomena, and gains the readers' assent to the conclusions.

> The community in which Lynn lives is one of the few truly cross-cultural districts within Chicago. The local couplet, like the area, runs "From the mill/To Pill Hill." The mills are the steel mills of South Chicago; near them lie, often on relief, blacks and newly arrived Mexicans and Puerto Ricans. "Pill Hill" is the residential area where many Jewish doctors, dentists, and professors live. Between lie several miles of small brick bungalows owned by second generation Polish- and Serbian-Americans ....
>
> Lynn lives on "Pill Hill," the oldest of four children of a Jewish lawyer. Her mother is a high school history teacher at the same high school Lynn attends.

The profile of Lynn also includes texts she has written, essays, and poetry. In addition, the analysis also includes Lynn's comments on writing: "Yeah, I can sort of wrap it up here by saying, like, 'Throughout the interview which involved the math test blah, blah, blah.'" The analysis also includes behaviors she observes. In other words, the author assembles multiple data sources in order to draw conclusions. (qtd. in Kinkead, 2015, p.177)

Identification of significant patterns and speculations about causes

When analyzing and interpreting the various types of data collected, you should point out the significant patterns, that is, patterns that are directly related to your research question or hypothesis. The discovery of significant patterns leads naturally to speculation about causes. Understanding how a certain condition leads to other conditions contributes to our knowledge of the world and often may have practical consequences for improving our situation.

Analysis

- Case study data analysis generally involves an iterative, spiraling, or cyclical process that proceeds from more general to more specific observations.
- Data analysis may begin informally during interviews or observations and continue during transcription, when recurring themes, patterns, and categories become evident.
- Once written records are available, analysis involves the coding of data and the identification of salient points or structures.
- Having additional coders is highly desirable (but is less common in qualitative research than in quantitative research), especially in structural analyses of discourse, texts, syntactic structures, or interaction patterns involving high-inference categories leading ultimately to the quantification of types of items within categories.
- Data reduction may include quantification or other means of data aggregation and reduction, including the use of data matrices, tables, and figures.

Analysis occurs throughout the data collection and coding process. As you collect, code, and review your data, certain patterns, themes, and issues begin to emerge. These emerging ideas may refocus your study, or it may send you in a new direction. It is impossible to be prescriptive, to offer a step-by-step data analysis procedure, because of the particularistic nature of case study—the case and the investigator's questions about it will determine both the data to be collected and the means of analyzing it.

Richards (2003), while resisting the temptation to be prescriptive, lists some general procedures—what he calls "aspects" (p. 272)—performed by the investigator (see the box below).

---

1. Collect data.
2. Think about the data in relation to the research project.
3. Categorize (code) the data.
4. Reflect on the data (write notes, memos, comments, etc.).
5. Organize the data in different ways to find previously unseen patterns and connections.
6. Connect the emerging issues and themes to concepts and theories that may help explain them.
7. Collect more data, based on the directions suggested by previous analysis.

(adapted from Richards, 2003, p. 272)

Interpretation

- Establishing the significance or importance of themes or findings is crucial; the discussion should ideally link these themes explicitly to larger theoretical and practical issues.
- However, generalization to populations is not appropriate or desirable in most case studies.
- Be cautious about drawing unwarranted inferences because of the small sample size, particularly if the case is not typical of others in the same set.
- L2 researchers frequently propose models or principles based on their results to be supported, tested, compared, or refuted by themselves or others in subsequent research.

Data may be analyzed and interpreted through a variety of ideological lenses (e.g., positivist, poststructuralist, feminist, or critical), although descriptive/interpretive approaches are still the most common in second language teaching. Provide sufficient evidence for your claims or interpretations to make them clear, credible, and convincing to others. Consider alternate explanations, and account for results that run contrary to the themes that emerge or for differences among triangulated sources. It may be worthwhile to consult case participants for their interpretation of (nontechnical) data or findings. L2 learners or others who are not highly proficient in their L2 may not have the maturity or the linguistic competence to convey their perspectives easily; in some cases, an assistant who can speak the participant's L1 to explain the research purposes and elicit the participant's views in their L1 may be helpful, depending on the focus of the study.

In summary, case studies are intended to explain, describe, and explore. It is believed that case-study research lays the foundation for the question or issue to be studied further through empirical designs and that case-study research may not be an end in itself, but is often used to study innovations (Kinkead, 2015, p.182).

Having decided to collect data from a range of sources, Terry has set up the study so that his findings will likely be strengthened through triangulation. He begins his analysis immediately after the first round of interviews with his participants. Certain themes emerge from those interviews, so he codes them and keeps his eyes open for more data on the same themes. As the study progresses, he accumulates a well-organized, easily accessible mountain of data. The accumulating data continually reaffirm the inferences he begins to draw—first tentatively, then with more confidence with each confirmation. (Hood, 2009, p. 82)

▸ Task

1. Individual work: Based on your understanding of this step in a case study, continue with your own case study project, focusing on the case description and analysis.

2. Individual and group work: Read the following sample of case description and analysis by yourself, paying special attention to how the case is presented and described in detail as well as the analysis made. Then, in small groups, discuss with your classmates any problems or issues that you think may arise in your own case study. You can also share with each other the case study you are engaged in at present and how you will describe and analyze the selected case.

Sample: Case description and analysis*

The case study

The case study described in this section focuses on the development of socio-pragmatic competence by one ESL learner in the area of making requests. Helena is an accountant who was born in Hong Kong of China and brought up with Cantonese as her mother tongue. She learnt English at school and her IELTS score was 6.5. She had been in New Zealand for two years when she enrolled in the workplace communication skills course and she was highly motivated to obtain work. We focus on the development of Helena's socio-pragmatic proficiency in making requests in a way considered appropriate to the New Zealand sociocultural context. In particular, we illustrate her developing awareness of the effectiveness of certain relatively indirect request strategies in many New Zealand social contexts.

---

*The excerpt is taken from a research paper "From classroom to workplace: tracking socio-pragmatic development" by Janet Holmes and Nicky Riddiford, published in *ELT Journal*, Volume 65/4, October 2011. This paper reports on a collaborative study that tracks the development of skilled migrants' socio-pragmatic performance over a period of 12 weeks, from their entry into the classroom, through six weeks of instruction and then into the workplace context. Using a detailed case study, this paper examines the effects of conscious learning, as well as opportunities for social interaction, in the acquisition of appropriate ways of negotiating workplace requests. The excerpt, part of the case study in the paper, is used here as a sample to illustrate how to describe and analyze the case.

Stage 1

At the beginning of the programme, students were presented with a number of scenarios which included requirements that they refuse, request, or produce small talk; they were asked to role play one of the two participants. The scenarios systematically varied social factors, such as relative status, degree of familiarity, or social distance, and the size of the imposition of the speech act. The request scenario which is our focus was presented as follows:

Staying late tonight

An unexpected and urgent request from the CEO means that you would like your secretary, Mrs Jenny Smith, to stay late tonight to help you prepare a report. You have worked with your secretary for three years. Discuss with your secretary if she can stay on at work for two extra hours.

In this scenario, the student is allocated a managerial role, making a high stakes demand of a subordinate with whom she has worked for some time. Note that the scenario does not explicitly ask participants to use a request, rather they are instructed to "discuss" the issue with their secretary. This allows the possibility of choosing speech acts of different degrees of illocutionary force ranging from directive through request to hint.

In her first rendition of her role in this scenario, Helena produced the following.

Excerpt from role play

Helena: Do you have plans tonight?
Secretary: Yes, I do actually.
Helena: Oh okay, so do you think you can work a little bit late tonight?

Helena's approach is not as direct as that of some other students in that she does not baldly make the request for the secretary to work late in her first turn. She begins with a pre-request, "Do you have plans tonight?," which is an appropriate lead-in to the planned request. However, she then gives no indication that she has processed the secretary's response, "Yes I do actually," which serves as a pre-refusal. Rather, Helena ignores the signal that the secretary is not available and goes ahead with the request in a relatively direct form. She uses two appropriate mitigating phrases, namely the hedges "do you think ..." and "a little bit," indicating some degree of awareness that the request needs attenuation in the New Zealand context. Nevertheless, overall, her rendition of the request would be regarded as inappropriately authoritarian in most New Zealand workplaces.

► Step 5. Writing up the study

How will results be reported? What theory informs the study? Writing up the study involves providing contextual background, a review of literature, a summary of data used (e.g., samples of student writing, tables, figures, summaries, or descriptions), and interpretation. While the case study uses a qualitative approach, quantitative analysis may also be included. Recommendations can be made based on the results. Any problems or limitations to the study are also included. And suggestions for future research are put forward as well. Specifically, consider the aspects described in the following box.

---

1. *Implication and significance of the study*: This is concerned with the "So what?" question. What is important about this research? How does it advance our knowledge? What, if any, are its practical applications?

2. *Limitations of the study*: As a general rule, authors often explicitly point out problems with their own research. This honesty is part of the scientific ethos aimed at advancing knowledge. Typically, authors go out of their way to mention possible flaws and other limitations of their studies and to caution other scholars against overgeneralizing form their research. They might refer to problems in selecting the subject of analysis or duration of the study, flaws in the research design that might contaminate results, possible differences between the participants or respondents, or lack of analysis or interpretation of the data.

   You own research project here will probably exhibit a number of problems that would limit readers' confidence in your findings. To increase your own ethos as a scientific writer, you should make these objections yourself as part of the analysis or discussion section.

3. *Suggestions for Further Research*: At the conclusion of the analysis or discussion sections, avenues for future research are often suggested. Typically, it shows how your own research raises new questions that could be profitably explored. You might try this approach at the conclusion of your analysis or discussion that you think might be the logical next steps for other researchers interested in your area of study.

   (Ramage, Bean & Johnson, 2009, p. 259)

As mentioned previously, for a case study, it is hard to be prescriptive, so there is often great variation in how they are organized and developed. Student researchers are encouraged to turn to exemplars in the field to see how more experienced researchers have approached the task. Stake's outline of a case study report may provide a helpful model for you (see the box below); reading a range of published case studies would also be instructive.

Case study presentation of findings—example outline

1. *Entry vignette:* to help the reader get a feel for the place and time of the case.

---

2. *Issue identification:* to introduce the researcher, how the case came to be an object of study and what he hopes to learn.

3. *Extensive narrative:* to present the most significant data to describe the case and its context as clearly as possible.

4. *Issue development:* not to generalize beyond the present case but to try to understand its complexity. Here understanding of other cases and other research may be drawn upon.

5. *Descriptive detail and integration:* to elaborate on and confirm the most relevant issues that have been raised in the report so far.

6. *Assertions:* to summarize what the researcher has come to understand about the case.

7. *Closing vignette:* to remind the reader that the report is the researcher's encounter with the case.

(adapted from Stake, 1995, p. 123)

For inexperienced student researchers, the best thing to ensure that their first attempt in case studies yields high-quality results is to read exemplars in the field. Every major journal that publishes case studies usually establishes specific guidelines for reporting case study findings on its website.

▶ Task

♦ Writing up your project

Individual work: Write the draft of your project by checking the specific elements of a case study report given below. When you finish, revise your paper. Because an academic paper follows a conventional structure, you should check your draft against the required format. Make sure you have put the right type of material in the appropriate section. Inside each section, revise for effective transitions, conciseness, and clarity.

Reports of case studies should include the following elements:

- a statement of the study's purpose and the theoretical context;
- the problem or issue being addressed;
- central research questions;
- a detailed description of the case(s) and explanation of decisions related to sampling and selection;
- context of the study and case history, where relevant;
- issues of access to the site/participants and the relationship between you and the research participant (case);
- the duration of the study;
- evidence that you obtained informed consent, that the participants' identities and privacy are protected, and, ideally, that participants benefited in some way from taking part in the study;

- methods of data collection and analysis, either manual or computer-based data management and analysis, or other equipment and procedures used;

- findings, which may take the form of major emergent themes, developmental stages, or an in-depth discussion of each case in relation to the research questions; and illustrative quotations or excerpts and sufficient amounts of other data to establish the validity and credibility of the analysis and interpretations;

- a discussion of factors that might have influenced the interpretation of data in undesired, unanticipated, or conflicting ways; and

- a consideration of the connection between the case study and larger theoretical and practical issues in the field.

8.3 Improving the Quality of Case Study

A case study is an appropriate research design when you want to gain concrete, contextual, in-depth knowledge about a specific real-world subject. It allows you to explore the key characteristics, meanings, and implications of the case. You might use just one complex case study where you explore a single subject in depth, or conduct multiple case studies to compare and illuminate different aspects of your research problem.

▶ Factors to be considered

When conducting a case study, consider the following aspects for factors involved in the research:

- **Does the case represent an unusual or atypical example of a research problem that requires more in-depth analysis?** Cases often represent a topic that rests on the fringes of prior investigations because the case may provide new ways of understanding the research problem.

- **Does the case provide important insight or illuminate a previously hidden problem?** In-depth analysis of a case can be based on the hypothesis that the case study will reveal trends or issues that have not been exposed in prior research or will reveal new and important implications for practice. Note that it is important to conduct a thorough literature review to ensure that your assumption about the need to reveal new insights or previously hidden problems is valid and evidence-based.

- **Does the case challenge and offer a counterpoint to prevailing assumptions?** Over time, research on any given topic can fall into a trap of developing assumptions based on outdated studies that are still applied to new or changing conditions or the idea that something should simply be accepted as "common sense," even though the issue has not been thoroughly tested in practice. A case may offer you an opportunity to gather evidence that challenges prevailing assumptions about a research problem and provide a new set of recommendations applied to practice that have not been tested previously. For example, perhaps there has been a long practice among scholars to apply a particular theory in explaining the relationship between two subjects of analysis. Your case could challenge this assumption by applying an innovative theoretical framework (perhaps borrowed from another discipline) to the study of a case in order to explore whether this approach offers new ways of understanding the research problem. Taking a contrarian stance is one of the most important ways that new knowledge and understanding develops from existing literature.

- **Does the case provide an opportunity to pursue action leading to the resolution of a problem?** Another way to think about choosing a case to study is to consider how the results from investigating a particular case may result in findings that reveal ways in which to resolve an existing or emerging problem.

- **Does the case offer a new direction in future research?** A case study can be used as a tool for exploratory research that points to a need for further examination of the research problem. A case can be used when there are few studies that help predict an outcome or that establish a clear understanding about how best to proceed in addressing a problem. For example, after conducting a thorough literature review, you discover that little research exists showing the ways in which elementary school teachers contribute to promoting student English writing in China. A case study of how these teachers contribute to teaching children to write in English in a particular school can lay the foundation for understanding the need for more thorough research that documents how elementary school teachers think about writing for cartoons as a valuable means for developing children's basic English writing. The case could also point to the need for scholars to apply mind-body alignment theories of learning to the issue of lack of writing practices in school education.

▶ Ethical issues

While doing the case study research, you should adhere to the following guidelines:

- **Obtain informed consent.** Explain to potential participants the purpose of your research, your methods for collecting data, and the way your data will be used. In the case of interviews or observations, reach agreement on whether the respondent will be named or anonymous. Obtain direct permission from recording the session or noting down the details.

- **Explain that participation in your study is voluntary.** Do not apply any kind of personal or social pressures that would make it difficult for a respondent to say no.

(Ramage, Bean & Johnson, 2009, p. 260)

▌• Task

Classwork: Discuss the ethics of your study. Might some students feel embarrassed or even harmed by your study if their answers were made public? How might safeguards be built into the study to minimize the chances of any person's being made to feel uncomfortable?

Sample Research

Please scan the QR code below to acquire the sample article. Read the article and think about its research methods.

Sample Article

Unit ⑨

Survey Research

Almost all of us are familiar with survey research. We are constantly surveyed about our buying habits, political views, personal beliefs and just about everything else, and the results of this type of research are published and consumed constantly in newspapers, magazines, on television and on the Internet. In the field of ESL writing, survey research has long had an important role, and is used to investigate the characteristics, attitudes and opinions of language learners. Such survey research has provided valuable insights in the areas of learner beliefs, learning strategies, learner motivation and language learning anxiety, among others. These notions (i.e. beliefs, strategies, motivation, anxiety) are psychological constructs, abstract notions that are assumed to exist, although they cannot be observed directly. Therefore, survey research instruments allow researchers to operationalize (and consequently, measure) these constructs, and can involve both qualitative and quantitative components (Wagner, 2015).

9.1 Introduction

▶ What is survey research?

The word *survey* literally means to look at or to see over or beyond or, in other words, to observe. However, **observations** made during the course of a survey are not limited to those of the physical type. Survey research involves a critical observation of events, objects, subjects and ideas without attempt to control the condition of such phenomena. It is a method of obtaining large amounts of data, usually in a statistical form, from a large number of people in a relatively short time using closed-ended questions. It describes a given state of affairs which exists at a particular time and requires a direct contact with individual whose characteristic, behaviours and attitudes are relevant to the investigation.

A key strength of survey research is that, if properly done, it allows one to generalize from a smaller group to a larger group from which the subgroup has been selected. The subgroup is referred to as the **sample**, and techniques for drawing samples will be treated later. The larger group is known as the **population**; it must be clearly defined, specifically delimited, and carefully chosen. The observations or measurements made during survey research, or any other kind of research, generate **data** or information. These data are particularly susceptible to bias introduced as a result of the research design (and at other stages in the research process), so that problem will be considered in research.

The basic assumption of most survey research is that, by carefully following certain scientific procedures, one can make inferences about a large group of elements by studying a relatively small number selected from the larger group. For example, if one wanted to learn the opinions of all university teachers in China regarding information literacy, one could study a sample of several hundred teachers and use their responses as the basis for estimating the opinion of all of them. Thus, survey research is the process of collecting data from a sample group so as to determine the status of that group as per that time with respect to one or more variables. It is concerned with the present and attempts to determine the status of the phenomena being investigated.

In this sense, it differs from experimental research in that the researcher does not manipulate the setting or environment in order to investigate how this affects particular variables or the relationship between variables. Instead, the goal of survey research is to get information about learners' characteristics, beliefs or attitudes; information that is usually not available from production data, such as performance or observational data (Creswell, 2014).

Survey research can be done at one point in time or carried out at different points in time, i.e., longitudinal. The former is mainly descriptive, exploratory and explanatory while the longitudinal survey focuses on trend analysis. Survey research either uses questionnaires or structured interviews for data collection with the intention of generalizing the sampled data to a population.

A variety of methods are available for administering surveys; however, the most popular are face-to-face, telephone, Internet survey and mail. This is a good method to use to get data about *what*, *why*, and *how many*. It deals with questions that seek to find out about the nature of the target population and is best utilized when control of dependent and independent variables is not easily achievable or desirable. It is instrumental when the sample has to be studied in its natural setting and occur in the current time or the recent past.

▶ Use of surveys

Surveys are one of the most frequent modes of observation and measurement. They are used to determine the behavior or opinions of a particular population (e.g. students or teachers in a school) and to measure the degree to which an individual exhibits the characteristic of interest (e.g. use of a writing center).

The use of surveys is a commonly employed nonexperimental research design. That is, surveys are most commonly used in quantitative research, where the responses are statistically analyzed in order to draw conclusions about the population being studied. Survey research seems straightforward, i.e., ask questions, get answers and tabulate the results. Everyone is used to filling out questionnaires and, therefore, generally feels comfortable with their use. It seems to be a simple and easy form of research to perform, but the reality is that it is not simple or easy to do correctly.

Surveys are used as a method of gathering data in many different fields. They are a good choice when you want to find out about the characteristics, preferences, opinions, or beliefs of a group of people. Common uses of survey research are as follows:

- Social research: investigating the experiences and characteristics of different social groups
- Market research: finding out what customers think about products, services, and companies
- Health research: collecting data from patients about symptoms and treatments
- Politics: measuring public opinion about parties and policies
- Psychology: researching personality traits, preferences and behaviors

▶ Advantages and disadvantages of survey research

Advantages

The principal advantage of survey studies is that they provide information on large groups of people, with very little effort, and in a cost-effective manner. Surveys allow researchers to assess a wider variety of behaviors and other phenomena than can be studied in a typical naturalistic observation study.

Survey research is better suited than experimental research to studying a large number of cases, including those that are geographically dispersed. Also, survey research is generally considered to be more appropriate for studying personal factors and for exploratory analysis of relationships.

Disadvantages

The major drawbacks of survey design are (1) controlling against sample bias which can greatly compromise generalization of the findings to the population; and (2) its dependency on the cooperation of the respondents which in the long run determines the degree of the results' reliability. Information that is not known by the respondents can hardly by detected and the information that is personal or secretive may easily be inaccurate.

Unlike experimental research, survey research does not enable the researcher to manipulate the independent variable, provides less control of the research environment, and therefore is not considered capable of definitely establishing causal relationships. In other words, survey research is considered to be less rigorous than experimental research (Creswell, 2014).

9.2 Steps in Doing Survey Research

Survey research means collecting information about a group of people by asking them questions and analyzing the results. To conduct an effective survey, follow these six steps:

- Defining the survey purpose in initial planning
- Determining the sample
- Designing the survey instruments
- Distributing/Administering the survey
- Analyzing the responses
- Writing up the survey results

▶ Step 1: Defining the survey purpose in initial planning

Survey research tends to require a higher degree of planning than other research approaches.

When doing the initial planning of the project, you must consider what you want to investigate (reviewing the literature and formulating the research questions), why you want to investigate this topic (identifying the gap in the literature) and who you want to investigate (the population and the sampling techniques that will be used). Based on this planning and research, you then must decide how you are going to investigate this topic (the methodology that will be used; the instruments that will be used for the data collection; whether the data will be qualitative, quantitative or both; and how the data will be analyzed).

A key first step in conducting a survey is often overlooked. This is the need to define in specific terms the purpose for a survey. Determining the purpose of the survey will also determine the survey scope. Survey scope refers to the methodological requirements that are driven by the chosen purpose of the survey, such as the number and type of respondents needed, the content areas to be covered, practical requirements such as language translation, and the timing of data collection.

You should ask five important questions before considering using a survey for research:

- Is research feasible at all in these circumstances?
- Is survey research the right way to approach the problem, to obtain the kind of answers that are required?
- Is a survey feasible—would it yield valid conclusions?
- Is it ethically appropriate to use survey methods rather than some other approach?
- Is it ethically appropriate to carry out any form of research, given the research questions and the social context?

A survey can serve a range of purposes, reflecting the variety of intended uses to which the data collected will be applied. Examples include pinpointing areas of concern, measuring learners' attitudes, monitoring program impact, and providing input for future decision making. The specific research problem or question(s) should play a major role in determining the purpose and objectives for the survey.

▶ Task

Individual work: Here are two possible survey research projects for your reference. If you are interested in such research projects, you can select one as your own survey research.

1) Conduct a survey of the students in your class to compile raw data about the ways present-day college students spend their leisure time. Choose one of these forms of leisure to examine further. Once you have narrowed your topic, conduct a more thorough and detailed survey of students at your school (for example, if you choose watching television, ask students when they watch it, what kinds of shows they watch, and why they watch them). The results of your second survey may help you narrow the focus of your research even further (for example, to situation comedies, or even more specifically to a particular show). Once you have sufficiently narrowed your topic, conduct a library

search both on the specific topic and on leisure in general. For the final paper, write a research paper on how the particular form of leisure that you have chosen meets college students' recreational needs.

2) Survey 30 students in your class to find out their opinions about a current event or a controversial issue, asking them five specific questions. Then, in about 2,000 words, compare and evaluate the responses you received, organizing and classifying responses around either the characteristics of the respondents or the nature of the responses.

▶ Step 2: Determining the sample

The second major step of survey research is determining and selecting who will complete the survey. In some instances, a census maybe preferable if data are needed from every individual in a population. However, usually a sample, a small subset of a population selected to be representative of the whole population, is chosen.

Survey research involves trying to find out information about a particular population, e.g. all university EFL (English as a foreign language) learners in China; all of the EFL learners in a particular language program in China. Rarely is an entire population surveyed (an obvious exception is a national census, where a government seeks to obtain information from every member of the population). Because of the huge amount of resources needed to actually complete a census, most research utilizes surveys, in which information is obtained from a sample of the population. While it might be possible for a government to attempt to survey all L2 language users in a country, it is much more feasible (and often useful) to sample from this population. The notion of sampling is a very important consideration in survey research, because the quality and representativeness of the sampling determines the extent of the generalizability of the results of the research of the sample to the larger population.

Populations

The target population is the specific group of people that you want to find out about. This group can be very broad or relatively narrow. For example:

- The population of a country
- College students in China
- Second-generation immigrants in the U.S.
- Students of a specific high school aged 16–18

Your survey should aim to produce results that can be generalized to the whole population. That means you need to carefully define exactly who you want to draw conclusions about.

Sample and sample size

It's rarely possible to survey the entire population of your research—it would be very difficult to get a response from every person in a country or every college student in a university. Instead, you will usually survey a sample from the population. It's called a sample because it only represents part of the group of people (or target population) whose opinions or behavior you care about. In general, though, the sample should aim to be representative of the population as a whole. The larger and more representative your sample, the more valid your conclusions.

The sample size depends on how big the population is. Deciding the size of the sample to be sent a survey can be challenging for the beginning survey researcher.

- A statistical calculation can be made given a predetermined margin of error and a table of sample sizes for confidence ranges (Creswell, 2014). These tables of calculating sample sizes can be found in most introductory-level research texts. However, for a more pragmatic approach, the size of the sample should be based on the purpose and objectives of the survey.

- An online sample calculator can be used to work out how many responses you need.

The underlying aim in selecting a sample size is to focus more on accuracy than the need for a large sample size.

Sampling procedures

There are many sampling methods that allow you to generalize to broad populations. For example, one way of sampling is to use a "random sample," where respondents are chosen entirely by chance from the population at large. Sampling methods are usually divided into two broad types: probability and nonprobability.

Probability sampling

Probability sampling provides a statistical basis for reporting that the sample drawn is representative of the entire population. Using probability sampling means that every individual in an organizational survey would have a known, nonzero probability of being included in the sample. Probability sampling uses random selection to eliminate any form of subjectivity in choosing who will be surveyed and who will not. Examples of probability sampling techniques include simple random, stratified random, systematic, and cluster sampling. These techniques can be utilized according to the needs, resources, size of the population and quest for generalizability of the individual research projects (Wagner, 2015).

- **Random sampling** is a variety of sampling in which the researcher seeks to include a truly representative sample of the population in the study. The goal is to assure that every member of the population has an equal chance of being included in the sample. Unfortunately, it is actually very difficult to obtain a truly random sample, and the representativeness of the sample will always be affected by sampling error.

- A **stratified random sample** is a version of random sampling in which subgroups are selected from within a particular population, and samples are then generated for each of these subgroups.

- **Systematic sampling**, a more widely used technique, is a sampling technique in which every *n*th person is selected.

- **Cluster sampling** is a technique in which natural subgroups (clusters) within a population can be identified, and then random samples are generated for each of the clusters.

An example might serve to make the notion of sampling clearer. Say that a researcher is hoping to explore why students at a particular university are studying English as a foreign language. If a list of all the EFL students existed, the researcher could survey each of these learners (in essence, conduct a census) about their motivation for learning English. However, this list might include 1,000 learners, and surveying 1,000 participants would require huge amounts of resources, so the researcher instead chooses to survey a random sampling of these learners. She could have a computer randomly choose 100 participants from the list. If the researcher were interested in comparing particular groups within this population of EFL learners (e.g. to compare the motivation of English majors with non-English majors), she might choose instead to perform stratified random sampling by having a computer randomly choose fifty English majors and fifty non-English majors). She could also perform systematic sampling by generating a list of the 1,000 EFL learners in alphabetical order, randomly choosing one of the first ten names on the list and then selecting every tenth learner to survey (Wagner, 2015, p. 77).

Random sampling, stratified random sampling and systematic sampling all assume that a "list" of all the learners in the population exists (in this example, all of the EFL students in this particular university). In reality, however, for many researchers, no such list of all the individuals in a chosen population exists or else the researcher does not have access to this list. If this is the case, then cluster sampling is an option. Again, using the example of our university EFL students, it is possible or even probable that a list of all the current EFL students does not exist (or is out of date or the researcher does not have access to the list). But the researcher does know that there are eight different levels of EFL classes offered at the university. The researcher might then choose to sample eight different classes of students, randomly choosing one class from each of the eight different levels. She could also randomly choose twelve students within each class to survey.

Nonprobability sampling

Using appropriate probability sampling helps support the generalizability of the results of survey research. Nevertheless, much of the survey research conducted in applied linguistics utilizes nonprobability sampling—convenience samples.

Convenience sampling involves surveying individuals who are readily available and who the researcher has access to. The use of convenience samples can be informative and can yield interesting and useful results. However, the drawback is that it is not possible to generalize the results to a larger population.

Nonprobability sampling provides the advantage of being relatively convenient and economical to construct. The main drawback is that it does not guarantee that all eligible members of a population will have an equal chance of being included in the sample. Nonprobability sampling is often used for surveys of hard-to-identify populations and also for pilot tests of questionnaires.

> Returning to the EFL university student example, if a researcher surveyed the students in her own two classes (a convenience sample) about their motivation for learning English, she might find useful information about the students in these classes, but she could not generalize her results to the rest of the population (all of the university EFL students). The survey researcher must also be concerned with other sampling issues, including nonresponse bias, sampling error, self-selection and sampling with replacement.

Before you start conducting survey research, you should already have a clear research question that defines what you want to find out. Based on this question, you need to determine exactly who you will target to participate in the survey.

Task

◆Research questions and samples

1. Individual work: Review the criteria for a good research question mentioned in the previous parts, think about the topic that interests you and try to ask one or two questions that you want to explore about the topic. Then, based on the clear question, decide the type of participants you want to investigate.

2. Group work: Work in small groups, share with each other the topic, research questions, and participants for the project, discussing any problems or difficulties involved and offering suggestions or solutions to your peer. Then, decide on the type of project you are planning to do, individual or team work.

◆Review of related studies

3. Individual work: After you have defined the topic and research questions, search for relevant sources both print and web. When you have gathered enough primary and secondary sources, read, summarize and evaluate the source materials in detail. Then, write the literature review for your project.

▶ Step 3: Designing the survey instruments

At this stage, the researcher needs to design the survey instruments that will be used in the data collection. The design process includes selecting the instruments to be used (see the section below for the different types of survey instruments), creating the instruments (or adapting instruments used by other researchers), piloting the instruments and revising the instruments based on the piloting process.

There are two different types of survey data collection instruments: questionnaires and interviews. The self-administered questionnaire is commonly used because respondents can complete the survey themselves (e.g., mail survey or Internet survey). The other most frequent type of survey research is the interview in which researchers ask the questions and record respondents' answers (e.g., face-to-face interview or telephone interview). As with the selection of the sample, the determination of the type of instrument to be used is driven by the purpose and objectives of the survey.

Questionnaires and interviews are differentiated by the modes in which they are administered and the type of information that each are designed to elicit. Modes of survey administration vary and include face-to-face, computer-assisted, telephone, interactive voice response, mail, and the Internet. The choice of mode is often determined by the research topic, characteristics of the population targeted, types of questions, question topic, and available resources (i.e., participants, time, costs, etc.).

Typically, questionnaires are given in written form and are used in order to get information from or about a large number of individuals, while interviews are administered orally and are used to get more in-depth information from a smaller sample of individuals. A questionnaire is a written instrument in which respondents read questions or statements and respond to these questions by selecting a choice offered or writing their own response. Interviews are conducted orally by a researcher in order to elicit oral responses from a participant. An interview schedule refers to the list of questions that the interviewer will ask the participant and serves to ensure that all participants will be asked all of the same questions, in the same order.

In many ways, questionnaires and interviews reflect the larger quantitative versus qualitative data analysis continuum. Questionnaires are designed for efficiency; they can be administered to a large number of participants easily, they can be objectively scored, and the data can be analyzed quantitatively. The shortcomings of questionnaires, however, are also readily apparent. The data derived from questionnaires often provide only a superficial assessment of sometimes very complex constructs. Conversely, the data derived from interviews can be quite rich and in-depth. However, this richness comes at a cost of efficiency, in that the researcher (usually) has to meet individually with the participant to administer the interview. The data elicited must then be transcribed and then analyzed qualitatively (Wagner, 2015).

Questionnaires and interviews are not mutually exclusive—many survey research projects will employ both instrument types in order to get richer interview data that complement the broader questionnaire data. The purpose of the study and the research questions investigated will dictate the type of data collection instruments used. Because of space constraints, the focus of this section here will be mainly on the design of questionnaires.

Questionnaires

Types of questionnaires

A questionnaire with a list of questions is distributed by mail, online or in person, and respondents fill it out themselves. In general, there are three types of questionnaires: mail, online and in-person, each with its own benefits and disadvantages, as illustrated below.

Mail

Sending out a paper survey by mail is a common method of gathering demographic information (for example, in a government census of the population).

- [✓] You can easily access a large sample.
- [✓] You have some control over who is included in the sample (e.g. residents of a specific region).
- [✗] The response rate is often low.

Online

Online surveys are a popular choice for students doing research, due to the low cost and flexibility of this method. There are many online tools available for constructing surveys, such as SurveyMonkey, Wenjuanxing, etc.

- [✓] You can quickly access a large sample without constraints on time or location.
- [✓] The data is easy to process and analyze.
- [✗] The anonymity and accessibility of online surveys mean you have less control over who responds.

In-person

If your research focuses on a specific location, you can distribute a written questionnaire to be completed by respondents on the spot. For example, you could approach the customers of a shopping mall or ask all students to complete a questionnaire at the end of a class.

- [✓] You can screen respondents to make sure only people in the target population are included in the sample.
- [✓] You can collect time- and location-specific data (e.g. the opinions of a store's weekday customers).
- [✗] The sample size will be smaller, so this method is less suitable for collecting data on broad populations.

(Creswell, 2014; Wagner, 2015)

Adapting available questionnaires

When writing questions for a survey, there is no need to reinvent the wheel. If the topic to be surveyed already appears in published studies, it may be possible to use or modify existing items or questions. That is, you should refer to existing instruments and surveys designed to measure the same concept or area of study when possible. Other sources for generating questions include experts, literature (a review can often find templates for question phrasing), and interviews (i.e., gathering more formative information from members of your targeted population). In fact, it is recommended that researchers use questions with known and acceptable validity and reliability measures from other studies whenever possible.

Creating questionnaires

If no appropriate items exist, then questions need to be written. The goal of writing a survey question is to develop a query that every potential respondent will interpret in the same way, be able to respond to accurately, and be willing to answer.

Question items in questionnaires

Questions can be either closed or open-ended (Wagner, 2015):

- Closed-ended questionnaires have a stimulus (these can be questions or statements, but here all these will be regarded as questions) that the participants read and then choose the most appropriate response from a list of possible responses. These possible responses can be in a variety of formats. They can be dichotomous choices (e.g. yes/no, true/false, agree/disagree); they can be in multiple-choice format where all of the possible answers are listed; or they can be Likert scale items, in which the respondents have a number of possible responses to choose from.

- Open-ended questionnaires require the participant to write an answer in response to the stimulus question. The responses elicited with open-ended questionnaires can vary from one word (in response to "What is your native language?") to extensive written texts (e.g. in response to "What is your motivation for learning English?").

Choosing question wording

- Define the issue in terms of *who, what, when, where, why,* and *way* (the six Ws).
- Use ordinary words. Words should match the vocabulary level of the respondents.
- Avoid ambiguous words: *usually, normally, frequently, often, regularly, occasionally, sometimes,* and so on.
- Avoid leading questions that clue the respondent to what the answer should be.
- Avoid implicit alternatives that are not explicitly expressed in the options.
- Avoid implicit assumptions.
- Respondent should not have to make generalizations or compute estimates.
- Use positive and negative statements.

Principles for writing survey questions

- Choose simple over specialized words.
- Choose as few words as possible to pose the question.
- Use complete sentences to ask questions.
- Avoid specificity that exceeds the respondent's potential for having an accurate, ready-made answer.
- Develop mutually exclusive response categories.
- Avoid double-barreled questions.

Suggestions for question ordering

- The opening questions should be interesting, simple, and nonthreatening.
- Qualifying questions should serve as the opening questions.
- Basic information should be obtained first, followed by classification, and, finally, identification information.
- Difficult, sensitive, or complex questions should be placed late in the sequence.
- General questions should precede specific questions.

Types of information elicited

Questionnaires (closed and open-ended) can be designed to elicit objective data—information about the characteristics of the participants such as age, length of residence in an English speaking country, years of English study, etc., and they can elicit subjective data—information about the beliefs, attitudes and values of the participants. Often, a particular survey will elicit both types of information, such as the background characteristics of the participants as well as their attitudes about learning English (Wagner, 2015).

Three types of information are obtained from a questionnaire: (1) basic information, (2) classification information, and (3) identification information.

- Basic information relates directly to the research problem.
- Classification information consists of socioeconomic and demographic characteristics. It is used to classify the respondents in order to analyze results across different groups.
- Identification information includes name, address, and telephone number. Identification information may be obtained for a variety of purposes, including verifying that the respondents listed were actually interviewed, remitting promised incentives, and so on.

Because basic information is the most important aspect of a study, it should be obtained first, followed by classification and then identification information. Classification and identification information is of a more personal nature. Respondents may resist answering a series of personal questions. Therefore, these types of questions should appear at the end of the questionnaire. Ensure that the information obtained fully addresses all the components of the problem, and have a clear idea of the target population.

So, you need to decide which questions you will ask and how you will ask them. It's important to consider

- the type of questions;
- the content of the questions;
- the phrasing of the questions; and
- the ordering and layout of the questions.

Likert scale question items

One of the most commonly used items in survey research is the Likert scale item. First developed by Rensis Likert for measuring attitudes, this type of item usually includes a statement and then generally has four or five response options, typically including *strongly agree*, *agree*, *don't know (or no opinion or neutral)*, *disagree* and *strongly disagree* or some variation of these. These response options are then assigned a number by the researcher (typically 5 for strongly agree and 1 for strongly disagree), which can be used for quantitative analysis. Some researchers prefer to use more than five categories, with response options such as somewhat agree, slightly agree, somewhat disagree, etc. Including a larger range of response options can serve to improve the psychometric properties of the questionnaire but can also serve to make it more difficult for participants to respond in that they might have difficulty differentiating between the different degrees of agreement or disagreement (Wagner, 2015).

There is no consensus among researchers about the use of the *no opinion* or *don't know* response. Some researchers suggest not giving the survey takers this option, because participants who do not have strong feelings about the material in the survey tend to select this category, and if many of the participants choose this category, the results of the overall survey often will not reach statistical significance. Thus, not giving the participants this option can lead to more interpretable results. However, some argue that respondents choose this neutral response because it most accurately describes their response to the statement and that it is inappropriate to not offer this response simply because it is inconvenient for the researcher.

One of the reasons that these Likert scale items are particularly useful is that a number of items can be used to try and assess the same construct.

> So, to return to the motivation example, the researcher might want to investigate a particular population's motivation for learning English. Based on her personal experience and the review of the literature conducted in planning the project, she might want to investigate a number of possible external motivators (e.g. needed for a good job, desire to communicate with English speakers, desire to live or travel in an English speaking country). The researcher can then create a number of Likert scale items to assess the participants' attitudes for each of these different components of the motivation construct. Then, the items measuring a particular component can be summed or averaged to form a composite scale (Wagner, 2015, p. 78).

Generally speaking, the more items that are used to measure a particular concept, the more reliable and accurate is the overall scale. Often, items that are measuring the same construct will include reverse-coded items. So, for example, one item in the "job" motivation scale might state "Speaking English is necessary for my job," while the reverse coded item would be something like, "Learning English is not important for my occupation."

Scoring issues

When using this approach to determine the total score for each respondent on each score, it is important to use a consistent scoring procedure so that a high (or low) score consistently reflects a favorable response. This requires that the categories assigned to the negative statements by the respondents be scored by reversing the scale. Note that for a negative statement, an agreement reflects an unfavorable response, whereas for a positive statement, agreement represents a favorable response. Accordingly, a "strongly agree" response to a favorable statement and a "strongly disagree" response to an unfavorable statement would both receive scores of five.

Advantages and disadvantages

The Likert scale has several advantages. It is easy for the researcher to construct and administer this scale, and it is easy for the respondent to understand. Therefore, it is suitable for mail, telephone, personal, or electronic interviews. Several variants of the Likert scale are commonly used that vary the number of scale points (for example, 7 or 9 points) as well as the descriptors (for example, importance, familiarity) and other characteristics. The major disadvantage of the Likert scale is that it takes longer to complete than other itemized rating scales. Respondents have to read the entire statement rather than a short phrase.

Questionnaire formatting

After the individual items have been created, the questionnaire is then compiled and formatted. The format of a survey is a key in both the clarity of design and visual impact. Construction of the survey should commence after the questions are developed. The goal is to order and group questions and response choices to use space most efficiently and effectively.

For reliability purposes, the goal for the researcher is to standardize the questionnaire so that every one of the respondents gets the exact same items, in the same order. Questions should be ordered from shortest and easiest to answer to longest and most difficult to answer. Also, keep together all questions of a single type, of a single function, of a single response format and question form and all questions on a given topic (Wagner, 2015).

The format should be spread out and uncluttered. To facilitate design and improve efficiency of survey completion, contingency questions can be used to create visual skip patterns, jumping a respondent over a group of questions that is not relevant to them. Contingency questions prompt the respondent with a preliminary question to determine if subsequent questions will apply. For example, "Does your school currently provide writing center help to students? If NO, Go to #10" (skipping questions on writing center practices, if not applicable).

When constructing a survey, instructions are to be included with appropriate placement of transitions (e.g., between alternating question types) as needed.

It is important to create a questionnaire that looks professional, with no typographical errors or formatting inconsistencies. The respondents will automatically make a number of assumptions about a questionnaire based on its appearance. If the questionnaire looks professional, participants are more likely to respond to it seriously. For more information on formatting issues, consult more.

▌• Task

♦**Questionnaire design**

1. Group work: Work in small groups, talk about the survey research, especially the questionnaires you want to use for your project, pointing any problems or issue you have and giving help or suggestions to your peers.

2. Individual work: Based on the previous work, design the items or aspects for your questionnaire survey, following the steps described above, and with the help of the online tools provided on some websites, create your questionnaire.

▶ Step 4. Distributing/Administering the questionnaires

Pilot testing

After the initial questionnaire has been created, it is important to pilot or prestest the questionnaire to see how it performs. Ideally, the questionnaire can be piloted on participants that are members of the target population and then analyzed statistically. Based on this analysis of which items seem to be working well and which items are problematic, you can revise or delete certain items and add different items if necessary. Then you can do another pilot administration of the questionnaire, analyze the results and revise as needed.

Note that no matter how well you design a survey or questionnaire, there are always potential misunderstandings that will occur. Pretesting the survey also can assist in minimizing measurement error and is an essential part of ensuring that the survey will deliver the data it was intended to once it is deployed.

Also, it is vital that someone other than the questionnaire designer/writer actually take the questionnaire. At the very least, the researcher can trial the questionnaire on friends or colleagues and get their feedback about the questionnaire. Even if these respondents are not part of the population for which the questionnaire is intended, they can give the researcher valuable information that will assist in the revision process. Often the developer is too close to the questionnaire—he or she cannot see the problems or issues that might be obvious to someone who has not spent many hours researching and developing this survey instrument (Wagner, 2015).

Therefore, it is best to pilot test the questions and revise, revise, revise before general circulation of the final survey forms. The pilot test should be used with a sample as similar as possible to that of the main study.

Process of polite testing

Below is a four stage process for pilot testing (Dillman, 2000):

- Stage 1: Reviewing by knowledgeable instructors or advisors
- Stage 2: Interviewing with potential survey respondents to evaluate the cognitive and motivational qualities of each question
- Stage 3: A small pilot test in which participants should be informed that they are taking part in a try-out study with encouragements made for respondents to be critical, to ask about things that they don't understand, and to help make the survey better
- Stage 4: A final check from a small group of people who have had no role in the development or revisions of the survey to catch the inevitable "silly mistakes" that a new pair of eyes usually catch

During the creating and testing stages, efforts must be paid to assess, and improve if necessary, the validity and reliability of the survey. Read resources available to help you determine the quality of the survey.

Administering the survey

Only after the instrument has been piloted and revised should it be administered to actual participants. For questionnaire administration, which often includes larger groups of participants, if at all possible, the researcher should attend the administration in person. While it might be possible for a classroom teacher to administer the questionnaires to his or her class of students, the classroom teacher will invariably not be as invested in the research as the primary researcher nor will he or she be as knowledgeable about the research or able to answer all the questions participants might have. Administering the questionnaire in person, in a polite and professional manner, generally leads to a higher response rate and better results (Wagner, 2015).

It is very important that the researcher anticipate issues that might arise during the administration. Again, the process of piloting the questionnaire should help the researcher anticipate possible problems. A useful suggestion is, as much as possible, to prepare the participants for the questionnaire before they appear for the large-scale administration. This can be accomplished by providing participants in advance with information about the study and its purpose (email is often useful for this) and about the questionnaire procedure itself. The researcher should check out the space where the administration will occur, making sure that there is adequate and comfortable space for the respondents. While it may seem obvious to mention that the researcher should double-check that she has enough copies of the questionnaire, and that these copies are collated and in the appropriate order, numerous questionnaire administrations have been scuttled by photocopying problems. When the participants arrive for the administration, the researcher should welcome them, make them feel as comfortable as possible and explain the purpose of the research, the instructions for responding to the questionnaire and answer any questions respondents might have. Again, this might seem obvious, but large-scale administrations can be quite stressful, and if not adequately prepared, the researcher can forget to make the respondents as comfortable as possible. The goal, of course, is to make participants want to respond to the interview or questionnaire as fully and truthfully as possible. Respondents who feel unwanted or unwelcome are much less likely to devote their time and attention to the survey, and the results will be of dubious value. After the administration is completed, the researcher should thank the respondents for their participation (Wagner, 2015).

Sampling issues were mentioned previously, but sampling is also an administration issue. Appropriate sampling procedures necessitate that the researcher try to get everyone that was targeted in the sampling procedure to actually perform the interview or complete the questionnaire. Even the most conscientious researcher can end up with an unrepresentative sample if not everyone in the targeted sample completes the survey. This is called nonresponse bias. For example, if a researcher is exploring students' motivation for learning English and uses a sampling procedure that randomly chooses four classes in a language program to be surveyed, it is important that every student in those four classes be surveyed. If the researcher administers the questionnaire in the four classes in which seventy-five of the eighty students are present, it is very important that the researcher follow up and try to get the remaining five students who were not present in their classes that day to complete the questionnaire. This might sound trivial, but these missing five students could represent serious nonresponse bias. Perhaps these five students often skip class because they are not motivated to learn English. By not getting these students' input, the results of the study are of questionable value (Wagner, 2015).

Questionnaires can also be conducted on the Internet or via email. This type of survey research has a number of advantages, the most obvious being the lower costs involved. Rather than having to create and administer physical questionnaires (either in person or via postal mail), the questionnaires can be presented on a website or emailed to potential participants, allowing the participants to respond to the questionnaires when it is convenient for them. The other major advantage is that much of the data entry can be done automatically.

When using a web-based survey service, the participants usually complete the questionnaires online, the data is entered automatically, and the results are immediately available for the researcher. Web-based surveys do pose special research problems that have to be addressed, however. Like all other surveys, it is important that adequate sampling procedures be followed, and the researcher must endeavour to follow up with potential participants who did not respond to the initial solicitation. Web-based surveys might be especially prone to bias issues like self-selection bias. Another issue is the need to make online surveys password protected. When participants are solicited for participation in the survey, they should be given a special password that is only able to be used once or else participants might skew the results of the survey by responding multiple times. Web-based surveys also present security issues, and special care should be taken to ensure that secure connections be used so that anonymity can be ensured, especially if the survey is of a sensitive nature (Wagner, 2015).

▌• Task

◆Questionnaire distribution

1. Group work: Work in small groups, present your questionnaire to the peers, asking for their suggestions or comments, and then revise if necessary. When the questionnaire is finalized, ask the group members to help send it to the targeted participants via the Wechat moments or other online interactive platforms.

2. Individual work: After completing your questionnaire design, think about how you will administer the survey, following the guidelines mentioned in this section.

▶ Step 5. Analyzing the responses

After the questionnaires have been administered, it is necessary to analyze the data. Questionnaire data usually entails larger sample sizes and generally necessitate inputting the data into a spreadsheet such as Excel or a statistical program such as SPSS, so that the data can be analyzed statistically. First you have to process the data, usually with the help of a computer program to sort all the responses. You should also clean the data by removing incomplete or incorrectly completed responses. One of the most important things to consider is the issue of reverse-coded items. Although it might seem obvious, it is imperative that the researcher remember to reverse-code these items when inputting the data. That is, if a Likert scale was used with 5 for strongly agree and 1 for strongly disagree, when inputting the values for the reverse-coded items, it is necessary to input 1 for strongly agree, 2 for agree, etc. (Wagner, 2015, p. 82).

After the data are inputted, descriptive statistics (mean, standard deviations, skewness and kurtosis) can be computed. If statistical procedures that require a normal distribution are going to be used in the analysis, these descriptive statistics can be consulted to check that the assumptions regarding normality are met. For further types of statistical texts, readers are referred to statistics methods books, such as Gravetter and Wallnau (2009). The same set of survey data can be subject to many analyses.

There are some useful resources for conducting survey research:

- Brown, J.D. 2001, *Using Surveys in Language Programs*, Cambridge University Press, Cambridge. This book provides in-depth coverage of issues related to survey research. It is organized according to the steps involved in conducting survey research (*planning*, *designing the instrument*, *gathering data*, *analyzing data statistically*, *analyzing data qualitatively* and *reporting*). The chapter devoted to statistical analysis is especially thorough and useful for those interested in using survey methodology.

- Dörnyei, Z. & Taguchi, T. 2010, *Questionnaires in Second Language Research: Construction, Administration, and Processing*, 2nd edition, Routledge, New York, NY. This book is a very practical guide to the construction and administration of questionnaires in L2 research. The book gives specific instructions and suggestions for creating reliable, valid and useful questionnaires.

Reliability of the questionnaire

It is also important to examine (and report) the reliability of the questionnaire. Usually, the **internal consistency reliability** will be estimated using Cronbach's alpha. Internal consistency reliability is used to estimate the extent to which scores on the different items correlate with each other, and Cronbach's alpha is a coefficient (ranging from 0 to 1) that indicates the extent to which the items are measuring a single (unidimensional) construct. The closer this coefficient is to 1, the more consistently the items are measuring the same thing. Depending on what the questionnaire is intended to assess, the reliability can be estimated for the overall questionnaire, for each subsection of the questionnaire or for the individual scales (Wagner, 2015).

Reliability for the overall questionnaire

If the questionnaire is narrow in scope, composed of ten items that are all intended to assess the unidimensional construct "learners' motivation in their English classroom," for example, then the reliability should be assessed for the overall questionnaire.

Reliability for subsections

If the questionnaire is broader in scope, with three subsections, all designed to measure different components of motivation for learning English (e.g. "English in the classroom," "English on the job" and "English for tourism"), then it would be appropriate to estimate reliability for each of the distinct subsections.

Reliability for each scale

If the questionnaire is very broad in scope, with numerous scales all designed to measure different components of motivation, then it would be most appropriate to estimate reliability for each scale.

Internal consistency reliability is an estimate of the degree to which the different items are consistently measuring a single construct. In general, an alpha of 0.70 is the minimum acceptable. A reliability coefficient much below 0.70 indicates that the items are not consistently measuring the same unidimensional construct but may in fact be measuring a number of different things (Wagner, 2015).

⁞• Task

◆Data analysis

1. Individual work: Analyze the results of the survey, try using statistical analysis discussed above, if necessary, or follow the steps or guidelines suggested in relevant sources.

2. Group work: For the individual project, ask one or two peers to help check the analysis, and for team work, the members can match and compare their work, to find out any discrepancies, and then discuss or negotiate with each other to solve the problem. Note that this work is mainly to ensure the reliability of your analysis.

▶ Step 6. Writing up the survey results

Finally, when you have collected and analyzed all the necessary data, you will write it up as part of your research paper.

In the methodology section, you describe exactly how you conducted the survey. You should explain the types of questions you used, the sampling method, when and where the survey took place, and the response rate. You can include the full questionnaire as an appendix if relevant.

Then introduce the analysis by describing how you prepared the data and the statistical methods you used to analyze it. In the results section, you summarize the key results from your analysis.

In the discussion and conclusion, you give your explanations and interpretations of these results, answer your research question, and reflect on the implications and limitations of the research.

⏵Task

◆**Writing up the project**

1. Individual work: Complete your writing by combining the separate parts you have written based on the work in each stage.

2. Classwork: Present your final project in class, getting feedback and comments. Then, revise accordingly.

⑨.③ Internet Surveys

In recent years, Internet and intranet surveys have experienced an explosive increase in usage to perhaps challenge the dominance of paper-and-pencil surveys in educational settings. While e-mail was explored as a survey mode during the late 1980s and early 1990s, the rapid growth of the Internet has seen Web-based surveys emerge as one of the most dramatic changes in survey research.

▶ Benefits of Internet surveys

This technology allows researchers to collect data from participants all over the world 24 hours a day and 7 days per week. Surveys can be delivered quickly to anyone connected to the Web, and data can be saved automatically in electronic form, reducing costs in space, dedicated equipment, paper, mailing, and labor.

Once a survey is properly programmed, data can be stored in a form ready for analysis, saving costs of data coding and entry that used to be an expensive and time-consuming part of the research process.

Additional advantages of Internet surveys including flexibility in design and implementation. It is also possible that Internet surveys provide a less threatening approach for collecting sensitive data and offer a novel medium for participation to avoid the "survey fatigue" reported with paper-and-pencil modes.

⏵ Drawbacks

Yet, a number of disadvantages of Internet surveys also exist, of which the three most important relate to sources of error, ethical issues, and the expertise required.

- Sources of error: All survey researchers are concerned with minimizing sources of error but coverage error (sample is not equal to intended target population), sampling error, and measurement error introduced by the Internet delivery mode remain potential limitations. Although the percentage of the population with the hardware, access, and skills needed to respond to Internet surveys is continually increasing, the general population coverage still does not equal that achieved by using conventional survey modes.

- Ethical issues: Internet surveys also raise potential ethical issues regarding invading privacy to contact respondents then protecting participant privacy and confidentiality.

- The expertise required: While significant advances have been made in the hardware and software needed for creating and hosting Internet surveys, a level of technical expertise far greater than for traditional survey modes remains a necessity for developing and administering a survey on the Web.

To sum up, fundamental difference exists between the design of paper and Internet surveys. In a paper survey, the designer completes the questionnaire that is then viewed by the respondent so that both see the same visual image. In an Internet survey, the designer and respondent may see different images of the same survey because of different computer operating systems, browsers, network connections, screen configurations, and individual designer decisions such as the use of color and text wraparound. The technology associated with the Internet does offer some exciting options for survey designers. Multimedia surveys can now be developed that incorporate audio and video. Advances in mobile computing and wireless technology are allowing investigations of surveys delivered to personal digital assistants (PDAs) and cell phones. Internet surveys also offer the opportunity to improve on skip patterns where respondents can be presented with questions based on previous answers. Expertise as well as literature on Internet survey layout and design should be consulted for a researcher new to this delivery mode.

There are numerous websites and software packages devoted to the creation and administration of surveys and questionnaires. Most of these websites allow users to try out the service for free.

- www.surveymonkey.com
- www.questionpro.com
- www.KeySurvey.com
- www.polldaddy.com
- http://freeonlinesurveys.com

9.4 Improving the Quality of Survey Research

▶ Steps to improve the quality

There are a number of steps that can be taken to improve the survey research quality.

First, keep the survey as simple, short and focused as possible. The longer and more complex the survey becomes, the lower the response rate. One of the important goals of any survey is to maximize the response rate, thereby increasing the potential validity of the findings. As a general rule, any survey with a response rate less than 75% is highly suspect. The goal should be a response rate of more than 85%, if at all possible.

When considering the results of a survey study, ask the question, "If everyone who did not respond to the survey had responded with answers that were the opposite of the study findings, would it substantially change the study conclusions?" If the answer to that is yes, then the results of the survey are at least suspect, if not invalid. A target response rate of 85% is a desirable goal because even if the remaining 15% had entirely different responses, they would be unlikely to change the overall conclusions substantially.

Second, use existing validated-measurement instruments whenever possible. Rather than developing a new scoring system or a new measurement scale for a parameter (e.g., anxiety or motivation), it is much better to use something that already has been validated through other studies. This can increase the validity of survey-based studies.

Third, use a polite test. No matter how well you design a survey or questionnaire, there are always potential misunderstandings that will occur. It is best to pilot test the questions and revise continuously before general circulation of the final survey forms.

Measurement error

Measurement error can cause the results of a survey to deviate from the truth, thereby reducing the reliability and/or validity of a survey. A truly perfect measurement process does not exist, but the amount of measurement error can be minimized.

Error types

There are 2 types of measurement error that directly influence survey research.

- **Random error**, in which chance factors influence the measurement of a variable (e.g., guessing an answer correctly). It has its greatest effect on reliability because it reduces consistency of the results.
- **Systematic error**, which affects all responses or scores in a similar way across all occasions of use (e.g., an incorrect skip pattern placement). Systematic error has its greatest effect on the validity of a survey.

There are a variety of purposes and procedures for assessing the validity of a survey ranging from content validity to construct validity, each with differing meanings, uses, and limitations depending on what is being measured. Gathering empirical evidence for the validity of a survey is a continual process with errors in measurement arising from several potential sources.

Error sources

Sources of measurement error are numerous and include those related to the respondent and the actual survey instrument.

- As all surveys inherently are self-report, respondent errors include but are not limited to overreporting of events, underreporting of events, partial answers, inconsistent responses, and incorrect placement of responses.
- Instrument errors (which can be greatly reduced by careful survey construction) include inadequate instructions, use of vague or unfamiliar terms, poor ordering of questions, poor overall format of the instrument, and response options that do not fit the question.

Strategies to minimize measurement error

Measurement error can be reduced if basic cognitive design principles of simplicity, consistency, organization, natural order, and clarity are used.

- Simple designs help to reduce error. One way to simplify the design is to emphasize selected terms using underline or bold text as appropriate.
- Footnotes can be used for information not directly relevant to completing the survey such as copyrights.
- Grouping questions by related concepts also assists in reducing measurement error.
- Formatting a survey to create a natural reading flow, using left justification and adequate spacing, can also help a respondent distinguish between sections.

Well-designed surveys can make for a more efficient and effective experience for both respondent and researcher, minimizing measurement error and potentially improving the response rate. Pay attention to the following to minimize measurement errors:

- Don't reinvent the wheel (other instruments may exist and experts should be consulted).
- Don't start your survey without a title and introduction that includes the purpose (and answers the question "Why is this important [for me] to complete?").
- Don't be vague, use jargon, or include terms that are ambiguous.
- Don't use leading or value-laden terms.
- Don't include abbreviations or acronyms without spelling them out first.
- Don't be too lengthy—less is more.
- Don't forget that response choices should be mutually exclusive and exhaustive.
- Don't ask double-barreled questions (those that contain more than 1 construct).
- Don't omit a specific time frame and period of reference for recall.
- Don't conduct your survey without a pilot or pre-test.

▶ Ethical considerations

When conducting a survey, ethical issues ranging from anonymity and confidentiality to informed consent should be considered.

- The need for data should be balanced with the individual respondent's right to privacy. Respondents should be adequately informed about the survey's nature and purpose, comprehend the information they have received, and be competent to make a decision to participate.
- Maintaining confidentiality of responses and identifying information is important (unless respondent waives confidentiality for specified uses). When possible, the responses should be anonymous.
- However, there are some circumstances when identifiers are needed. In this case, the results should be presented in ways that cannot be used for the identification of individual respondents.
- An institutional review board should be consulted to assist in assuring that the interests of subjects are protected.

Sample Research

Please scan the QR code below to acquire the sample articles. Read the articles and think about their research methods.

Sample Articles

Unit ⑩

Experimental Research

Experimental research is often used to investigate the language behavior of sample groups under controlled conditions. While experiments have largely fallen from popularity in writing research in favor of more qualitative, natural, and "thicker" data-collection techniques, there are contexts in which they may be appropriate. Experimental techniques explore the strength of a causal relationship between two variable features of a situation such as test scores, proficiency, instruction, and so on. The idea is that the researcher seeks to discover if one variable is able to influence another by holding other factors constant and varying the treatment given to two groups. The experiment is set up so that data is collected to minimize threats to the reliability and validity of the research. Statistical tests are then carried out on the data to find out if differences between the control and the experimental groups are significant.

10.1 Introduction

▶ What is experimental research?

An experiment is a type of research that aims to isolate a particular event so that it can be investigated without disturbance from its surroundings. It is primarily aimed at gaining data about causes and effects—to find out what happens if you make a change, why and when it happens and how. So, experimental research is a way of determining the effect of something on something else. In other words, a researcher begins with an idea of why something happens and manipulates at least one variable, controls others, to determine the effect on some other variable.

Let's assume that we want to know whether focusing a learner's attention on some aspect of language increases that individual's learning of that aspect of language. One way to do this is to find two groups of learners which are matched on their preexperiment knowledge of this aspect of language. There is then a treatment session in which the experimental group receives focused attention on the particular part of language under investigation, while the control group receives exposure to the same part of language, but their attention is not intentionally directed. A post-test measures improvement from the pre-test. In sum, experimental research involves the manipulation of at least one variable, known as an independent variable, while keeping other relevant variables constant, and observing the effect of the manipulation on some other variable (known as a dependent variable), for example, a test score (Gass, 2015).

Experimental research belongs to highly quantitative studies that attempt to empirically test a hypothesis by using "hard" data and statistical techniques. This methodology is especially attractive in examining social and educational issues, because it seeks to produce definitive conclusions and measurable results. Results from experimental research are primarily concerned with whether or not a treatment works.

Experiments are used in many different subject areas, whether these are primarily to do with how things (objects, substances, systems, etc.) interact with each other, or how people interact with things, and even how people interact with other people. Although experiments are commonly associated with work in laboratories where it is easiest to impose control, they can be carried out in almost any other location.

Data and findings produced by experimental research provide the most definitive conclusions possible and thus are very appealing to policymakers, researchers, and stakeholders. Experimental or "true" designs are the gold standard for research because these studies attempt to establish causal relationships between two or more factors. A well-designed experimental study allows the researchers to answer a research question with a high degree of certainty because their conclusions are backed up by concrete data.

⑩.2 Basic Concepts/Terminology in Experimental Research Design

▶ Treatment and control groups

The group in an experiment which receives the specified treatment is called the **treatment group** or the **experimental group**. The term **control group** refers to another group assigned to the experiment, but not for the purpose of being exposed to the treatment. Thus, the performance of the control group usually serves as a baseline against which to measure the effect of the full treatment on the treatment group.

▶ Variable

A **variable** refers to almost any concept, or thing, or event that researchers are interested in, that varies or can be made to vary, and that is related to the research can be called a variable. Researchers pay particular attention to variables that may influence the results (this is of MUCH concern to researchers). The variables in a study of a cause-and-effect relationship are called the independent and dependent variables. There are three important variables that apply to all designs:

- **Independent variable** is the cause. Its value is independent of other variables in your study.
- **Dependent variable** is the effect. Its value depends on changes in the independent variable.
- Extraneous or confounding variables (external to the experiment) are variables that may influence or affect the results of the treatment on the subject. A **confounding variable**,

also called a confounder or confounding factor, is a third variable in a study examining a potential cause-and-effect relationship. In your research design, it's important to identify potential confounding variables and plan how you will reduce their impact. Failing to account for confounding variables can cause you to wrongly estimate the relationship between your independent and dependent variables. For instance, you may find a cause-and-effect relationship that does not actually exist, because the effect you measure is caused by the confounding variable (and not by your independent variable).

A variable of specific experimental interest is sometimes referred to as a **factor**. Ordinarily, the term is used when an experiment involves more than one variable. These variables are often identified as factors and are labeled "Factor A" and "Factor B," etc. **Level** refers to the degree or intensity of a factor. Any factor may be presented in one or more of several levels, including a zero level.

▶ Hypothesis

Experimental design means planning a set of procedures to investigate a relationship between variables. To design a controlled experiment, you need a testable **hypothesis**, a statement that can be tested by scientific research, that is, at least one independent variable that can be precisely manipulated and at least one dependent variable that can be precisely measured. A hypothesis states your predictions about what your research will find. It is a tentative answer to your research question that has not yet been tested. A hypothesis is not just a guess—it should be based on existing theories and knowledge.

▶ Manipulation, control, and randomization

Research designs also have three primary elements: **manipulation** (the ability to influence the independent variable), **control** (the ability to minimize potential extraneous variables), and **randomization** (unbiased or random study subject assignments).

Randomization, or random assignment, refers to how subjects are assigned to study groups. Designs where randomization is used provide each subject with a known probability of being assigned to each of the study groups (e.g., experimental or control). In most studies the probability of assignment to the two groups is equal.

Typically, researchers frequently resort to simple counting off and other short cuts. Another way of selecting subjects is simply to use intact groups: such as all the students in a given classroom. Researchers are usually worried whether the students were assigned to the classroom in a non-random way. The problem is whether some subtle factors were operating to exert a bias of selection factors in the assignment to groups.

▶ Variance

Variance refers to the variability of any event. If one uses a fine enough measuring device, one can find differences between any two objects or events.

▶ Validity

The inside logic of an experiment is referred to as **internal validity**. It is the degree of confidence that the causal relationship you are testing is not influenced by other factors or variables. Primarily, it asks the question: does it seem reasonable to assume that the treatment has really produced the measured effect? Extraneous variables which might have produced the effect with or without the treatment are often called "threats to validity."

External validity, on the other hand, refers to the proposed interpretation of the results of the study. It is the extent to which your results can be generalized to other contexts. For example, you can ask the question: with what other groups could we reasonably expect to get the same results if we used the same treatment? If Treatment X resulted in lowered anxiety in adult male students, could you logically claim that it will produce the same effect in adult female students?

Questions can arise from our need to generalize from a limited set of observations. No one is interested in observations that in no way extend beyond this particular restricted set of data. Generalizability depends on whether the observed behavior measurement [O] is representative of the people, the surrounding conditions and the treatments to which we now wish to extend it. Types of questions include:

- Did some of the early procedure in the research affect the subjects so that their later measurements were, in part a result of that?
- Were the subjects themselves a representative sample of the general population of people to which it is desired to extend the research findings?
- Was there something in the research or setting that would cause or influence the measurement of the variable of interest?
- Was the treatment accompanied by any personal interaction that may be somewhat peculiar to the research or to the subjects or the experimenter involved?

The important thing is to clarify where the results of your observations may be legitimately extended and where they can not yet be legitimately extended. Helpful in this regard is a comprehensive description of the demographic characteristics of the subjects of the research and a complete and comprehensive description of the methodology used so that the reader of the research can judge for himself or herself whether the results can be generalized to his or her situation.

▶ Blocks

Blocks usually refer to categories of subjects with a treatment group. For example, we might divide the group into younger, adult and old learners and further divide the groups into a group treated with Teaching Method A and another treated with Teaching Method B. The advantage is to enable us to discover how the treatment affects each of the age groups. For example, we might find that overall, Teaching Method B outperforms Teaching Method A, except for old learners, where Method A outperforms Method B. This phenomenon is known as an interaction between treatment (the teaching method) and subject characteristics (age).

▶ Interaction

Interaction refers to variables in the treatment which may interact with each other. It may make a difference whether a variable is used by itself, with another, or with different levels or degrees of another. Higher order interactions are possible. One factor may depend on the presence or absence of two other factors; termed a second-order interaction.

10.3 Types of Data Yielded

There are six major classes of information with which an experimental design must cope. They include

- post-treatment behavior or physical measurement [P1];
- pre-treatment behavior or physical measurement [P2];
- internal threats to validity [I];
- comparable groups [C];
- experiment errors [E]; and
- relationship to treatment [R].

▶ [P1] Post-treatment behavior or physical measurement

In a typical experiment, this is the data, the class of information of primary interest. What was the physical measurement or behavior of the subject after treatment? All designs shed some light on this class of information. Usually only immediate or short-range results are obtained. More complicated kinds of information derive from, and concern questions of comparing post-treatment behavior between groups who have had various kinds, levels, or even absences of treatment. Five categories of post-treatment behavior or physical measurement can be identified:

- P1-1: behavior or measurement immediately after treatment
- P1-2: a comparison of post-treatment behavior between experimental and control groups
- P1-3: a comparison of the post-treatment behavior between experimental groups or blocks
- P1-4: long-term effects with continuing treatment and periodic observations
- P1-5: long-term effects without continuing treatment but with observation(s)

▶ [P2] Pre-treatment behavior or physical measurement

Information concerning pre-treatment behavior or condition requires some observation, a test, or measurement, to be administered before the experimental manipulation. Without such observations, the design itself will not answer any questions about the subjects before the experimental conditions have been introduced. Such information, however, may be accrued from general knowledge or other studies. Direct acquisition of this information adds to the cost of an experiment. Furthermore, it may have a confounding effect, that is, sometimes the pre-treatment observation or measurement influences the subsequent behavior of the subject. When it is over, it may not be clear whether the behavior was due to the treatment, the pre-treatment observation or measurement, or both. Several classes of pre-treatment information can be acquired:

- P2-1: behavior or measurement immediately before treatment
- P2-2: comparing pre-treatment to post-treatment behavior or measurement
- P2-3: a comparison of pre-treatment behavior or measurement between different pairs of subjects
- P2-4: a comparison of the differences between pre-treatment and post-treatment behavior among groups of subjects
- P2-5: the effect of the pre-treatment observation or measurement on subsequent behavior or measurement of the subject

▶ [I] Internal threats to validity

This class of information refers to some rival hypothesis that threatens clear interpretation of the experiment. A common group of rivals threatens most experiments, particularly those using human subjects. Typically, the rival hypothesis asserts that something outside of the experiment proper produced the behavior or measurement of interest. To discover whether or not such rival events exert an influence, the designer must usually provide for one or more control groups. Typically, internal threats to validity include:

- I-1: the subjects exhibited behavior because of some event other than the treatment.
- I-2: the subject could or would perform the behavior, or would have exhibited the measurement without the treatment.

▶ [C] Comparable groups

This class of information, available only when two or more experimental units or groups of subjects are used, deals with whether the subjects in the different units were about the same in relevant attributes before the treatment, and during the treatment, except for the treatment condition itself. If the experimental designer cannot provide information as to the comparability of groups, he/she must be prepared to admit the possibility that the groups differed in some essential aspect which produced the results observed.

Equating the groups by some pre-test or measurement or random assignment are the two major techniques of providing this information. Thus, there are two types of comparability information:

- C-1: were the groups (either experimental or control) comparable before the treatment?
- C-2: did the groups receive a comparable degree of experiences during the time of the study (except for differences in treatment)?

▶ [E] Experiment errors

Experiment errors refer to some unwanted side effects of the experiment itself which may be producing effect rather than the treatment.

▶ [R] Relationship to treatment

This class of information deals with the possible interaction of the treatment effects with different kinds of subjects, other treatments, different factors within a complicated treatment, different degrees of intensity, repeated applications or continuation of the treatment, and different sequences or orders of the treatment or several treatments. Typically, information of this type is acquired from blocking, from factorial designs, and various repeated measures designs.

- R-1: did the treatment interact with subject characteristics so that subjects with different characteristics behaved or reacted differently?
- R-2: how does the treatment interact when combined with other sorts of treatment?
- R-3: does the treatment contain different factors which may operate differentially on the subjects?
- R-4: what is the effect of different levels or degrees of the treatment?
- R-5: what is the effect of different orders or sequences of various treatments?

10.4 Experimental Design

▶ What is experimental design

Experimental design is a planned interference in the natural order of events by researchers. They do something more than carefully observe and measure what is occurring. A selected condition or a change (treatment) is introduced. Observations or measurements are planned to illuminate the effect of any change in conditions.

Experimental design focuses on quest for inference about causes or relationships as opposed to simply description. Researchers are rarely satisfied to simply describe the events they observe. They want to make inferences about what produced, contributed to, or caused events. To gain such information without ambiguity, some form of experimental design is ordinarily required. As a consequence, the need for using rather elaborate designs ensues from the possibility of alternative relationships, consequences or causes. The purpose of the design is to rule out these alternative causes, leaving only the actual factor that is the real cause. For example, Treatment A may have caused observed Consequences O, but possibly the consequence may have derived from Event E instead of the treatment or from Event E combined with the treatment. It is this pursuit of clear and unambiguous relationships that leads to the need for carefully planned designs.

The design is an essential part of research strategies, and entails

- selecting or assigning subjects to experimental units;
- selecting or assigning units for specific treatments or conditions of the experiment (experimental manipulation);
- specifying the order or arrangement of the treatment or treatments; and
- specifying the sequence of observations or measurements to be taken.

▶ Types of experimental design

Broad categories of experimental designs

- **Pre-experimental design** is where the researcher studies a single group and provides an intervention during the experiment. In this case, there is no control group to compare with the experimental group.
- **Quasi-experiment design** is where the researcher uses control and experimental groups but does not randomly assign participants to groups.
- **True experiment** is where the researcher randomly assigns the participants to treatment groups.
- **Single-subject design** involves observing the behavior of a single individual or a small number of individuals over time.

(Creswell, 2014).

One procedure to have control over experiments is using **covariates**, for instance pre-test scores as moderating variables and controlling for their effects statistically, selecting homogeneous samples, or blocking the participants into subgroups or categories and analyzing the impact of each subgroup on the outcome (Creswell, 2014).

The selection of a specific type of design depends primarily on both the nature and the extent of the information we want to obtain. Complex designs, usually involving a number of "control groups," offer more information than a simple group design. However, not all of the relevant information needed can be derived from any given design.

Specific experimental designs

Some commonly used experimental designs are described here. They include

- one-shot (including one-shot repeated measures);
- one-group, pre-post;
- static group;
- random group;
- pre-post randomized group;
- randomized block; and
- factorial.

The following letters will be used to describe the various experimental design activities:

- GP: selection of the group or experimental unit ...
- R: random assignment to a group ...
- BK: blocking subjects, or other variables, into sets ...
- T: administering a treatment to a group ...
- O: observing (measuring) results ...

One-shot

The one-shot is a design in which a group of subjects are administered a treatment and then measured (or observed). In experimental research, an experimental treatment should be given to the subjects, and then the measurement or observation made. Usually, with this design, an intact group of subjects is given the treatment and then measured or observed. No attempt is made to randomly assign subjects to the groups, nor does the design provide for any additional groups as comparisons. Thus, one group will be given one treatment and one "observation." This design is diagrammed as follows:

GP–T–O

The one-shot design is highly useful as an easy measure of a new treatment of the group in question. If there is some question as to whether any expected effects will result from the treatment, then a one-shot may be an economical route. In cases where other studies, or the cumulative knowledge in the field provide information about either pre-treatment baseline measurements or behavior, the effects of other kinds of treatments, etc., the experimenter might sensibly decide that it is not necessary to undertake a more extensive design. Simplicity, ease, and low cost represent strong potential advantages in the oft-despised one-shot.

This design answers only one question and that is in reference to post-treatment behavior, P1-1. It will describe the information about the behavior of the subjects shortly after treatment.

One variation of it, the one-shot repeated measures design is used to assess the effects of a treatment with the same group or the same individual over a period of time. A measure, or an observation is made more than once to assess the effects of the treatment. This design can be diagrammed as:

GP–T–O–T–O–T–O

This design is an extension of the simple one-shot and adds only information regarding the effects of repeated or continued treatment. Often the design can acquire high yield when other extra-design sources of knowledge can be related to it.

This design handles only the questions related to class P1 or post-treatment behavior, questions P1-1 and P1-4. It answers questions about behavior or effect shortly after treatment and the longer-term effects related to subsequent treatments. It might handle class R questions, R-5 relationships of the treatment in that the effect of the repeated treatments may be observed. It will not answer questions P1-2, P1-3, P1-5 nor any class P2, I, C, E, or R-1 through R-4 questions.

One-group, pre-post

In this design, one group is given a pre-treatment measurement or observation, the experimental treatment, and a post-treatment measurement or observation. The post-treatment measures are compared with their pre-treatment measures. This design is diagrammed as follows:

GP–O–T–O

The usefulness of this design is similar to that of the one-shot, except that an additional class of information is provided, i.e., pre-treatment condition or behavior. This design is frequently used in education research to determine if changes occurred. It is typically analyzed with a matched pairs t-test.

This design will answer the same question as the one-shot design P1-1, so that not only the post-treatment behavior of the subjects is answered, but it will also answer some questions in pre-treatment condition or behavior, namely P2-1 and P2-2.

Static group

In this design, two intact groups are used, but only one of them is given the experimental treatment. At the end of the treatment, both groups are observed or measured to see if there is a difference between them as a result of the treatment. The design is diagrammed as follows:

GP–T–O

GP——O

This design may provide information on some rival hypotheses. Whether it does or not depends on the initial comparability of the two groups and whether their experience during the experiment differs in relevant ways only by the treatment itself.

Whether the groups were comparable or not is crucial in determining the extent of information yielded by this design. The design could be used to compare the value of a writing portfolio. If a researcher cannot, on the basis of information outside the experiment itself, assume the comparability of the groups, the design will yield only information regarding P1-1 and P1-2. However, If additional information is available to equate the two groups initially, it may handle some of the class I questions. Without additional information, on the basis of the design alone, it cannot.

Random group

This design is similar to the static group design except that an attempt is made to insure similarity of the groups before treatment begins. Since it is difficult to have exactly similar subjects in each of two groups, the design works toward a guarantee of comparability between groups by assigning subjects to groups at random. If the researcher does this, there is likely to be reasonable comparability between the two groups. This design can be diagrammed as:

R–GP–T–O

R–GP——O

This design has long been a primary experimental design. It provides fairly clear-cut information as to the relationship between treatment and post-treatment measurement or behaviors.

Since this is often the sole reason for the research, the randomized group design is frequently the appropriate selection. However, it does not provide information about pre-treatment behavior. This design will answer questions P1-1 and P1-2. Since the groups are randomized, the design will cope with the internal threats to validity. Subject changes due to other causes should affect the control group so that a comparison of the post-treatment behavior should reveal any differential effects of the treatment. Class C, comparable group questions C-1 and C-2 are also answered in the randomization provided that there are no probable differences between the groups entering the experiment except for the treatment. The design will not cope with questions of class P1-3, P1-4, P1-5, P2 of pre-treatment behavior, class E questions, or class R questions. It is frequently analyzed with a two-sample *t*-test assuming equal variances of the groups.

Pre-post randomized group

This design adds a pre-test to the previous design as a check on the degree of comparability of the control and experimental groups before the treatment is given. This experimental design could be diagrammed as:

R–GP–O–T–O

R–GP–O——O

This yields information of P1-1, P1-2 as to post-treatment behavior and a comparison of post-treatment behavior between groups. It also answers most P2 questions on pre-treatment behavior, and questions P2-1 through P2-4. It answers most of the class I questions, that is, threats to internal validity. It handles class C questions, the groups are comparable because they are randomized.

The design does not answer P1-3, P1-4, or P1-5; nor the class E questions relating to experiment errors. It does not answer the class R questions regarding the relationship of the treatment nor P2-5, the effect of the pre-treatment observations on the subsequent behavior or measurements of the subjects.

Randomized block

This design is of particular value when the experiment wants to determine the effect of a treatment on different types of subjects within a group. This design can be diagrammed as:

————BLK–T–O

R–GP

————BLK–T–O

————BLK——O

R–GP

————BLK——O

Typically, this design refers to blocking or grouping of subjects with similar characteristics into treatment subgroups. The group to be used in an experiment is usually given some pre-treatment measures, or previous records are examined, and the entire group is blocked or sorted into categories. Then equal numbers from each category are assigned to the various treatment and/or control groups. While blocking according to subject characteristics is most typical of this design, blocking could be based on other relevant attributes. For example, if subjects are to be treated during different times of the day, such as morning and afternoon, we might block a morning and an afternoon group within each treatment condition.

Factorial

As you see above in the blocking design, the subjects are assigned to different groups on the basis of some of their own characteristics such as age, gender, or some other physical characteristics. Sometimes we wish to assign different variations of the treatment as well, and the procedure is similar. For example, we may wish to try two kinds of treatments varied in two ways (called a 2×2 factorial design). Some factorial designs include both assignment of subjects (blocking) and several types of experimental treatment in the same experiment. When this is done it is considered to be a factorial design. A diagram of a 2×2 factorial design would look like:

R–GP–T————O

A1 B1

R–GP–T————O

A1 B2

R–GP–T————O

A2 B1

R–GP–T————O

A2 B2

The factorial design as described here is really a complete factorial design, rather than an incomplete factorial, of which there are several variations. The factorial is used when we wish information concerning the effects of different kinds or intensities of treatments. The factorial provides relatively economical/practical/adequate information not only about the effects of each treatment, level or kind, but also about interaction effects of the treatment. In a single 2×2 factorial design similar to the one diagrammed above, information can be gained about the effects of each of the two treatments and the effect of the two levels within each treatment, and the interaction of the treatments. If all these are questions of interest, the factorial design is much more economical/efficient than running separate experiments.

The factorial handles some of the same classes of information as the previously described randomized group design: P1-1, P1-3 and class C questions. It provides little support for class I questions, but some weak inferences might be drawn. The design also answers class R questions, R-2, R-3 and R-4 concerning relationships among treatments, factors, or levels. It does not answer questions P1-2, P1-4, P1-5, or P2 questions, nor does it answer either class E or questions R-1 or R-5.

⓾.❺ Process of Experimental Research

For the novice or student researcher, it is often difficult to get started in designing and conducting experimental studies. When designing the experiment, you should think about your topic, your research question(s) as well as one or more hypotheses, and decide how you will manipulate the variable(s). Following this initial stage are some other issues you need to consider: how many subjects or samples will be included in the study, and how subjects will be assigned to treatment levels.

▶ Step 1. Defining your research question and variables

This step is probably the most critical part of the planning process. Once stated, the research questions provide the basis for planning all other parts of the study: design, materials, and data analysis. In particular, this step will guide the researcher's decision as to whether an experimental design or some other orientation is the best choice.

Research questions

Research questions must be stated explicitly and must have some basis in previous literature. For example (Gass, 2015):

> *1* Prior research (Gass, Svetics & Lemelin 2003) argued that focused attention promoted learning in some parts of the grammar and not in others and differentially affected learners at different proficiency levels. Does focused attention on noun–adjective agreement in Italian promote learning to a greater extent than focused attention on wh-movement in Italian for beginning learners of Italian?

The first question is explicitly stated, although as we will see below, there are variables that are in need of further elaboration and greater explicitness. The second question, while interesting and one which school districts are constantly debating, is not researchable given the vagueness as well as the word should which implies some sort of right or wrong and which, as a result, cannot be empirically evaluated.

Strategies for a proper research question

To state a specific research question, you need to first think about the topic, which simply involves identifying a general area that is of personal interest, and then narrowing the focus to a researchable problem. This will lead to an appropriate research question.

English Technical Writing Computer-Based Instruction (CBI)

In our situation, the students intended to develop and evaluate interactive technical writing units. They thus had the interest in investigating or assessing how the completed CBI units operated, that is, the "effectiveness" of the units.

- The research topic was "CBI usage in teaching college technical writing courses."

- The research problem was "how effectively interactive CBI units on different technical writing skills would teach those skills." Later, this "problem" was narrowed to an examination of the influences on student learning and attitudes of selected features of a specific CBI unit, Writing Style.

- The questions of greatest interest to the students concerned the effects on learning of (1) animated vs static graphics, (2) learners predicting outcomes of group work vs not making predictions, and (3) learner control vs program control.

In general, if a research question involves determining the "effects" or "influences" of one variable (independent) on another (dependent), use of an experimental design is implied. The variables concerned are expected to operate in certain ways based on theoretical assumptions and prior empirical support.

In sum, in experimental research, there need to be answerable questions. There are a number of characteristics that one can think of when determining whether a question is answerable or researchable. Given the limited resources (time and money) of most research, questions must be feasible in relation to the time and budget of the problem. This often entails scaling back on the level of complexity of the research question. As is implied from the discussion above, the question needs to be significant in relation to current research in the field of inquiry. And, of course, ethics must play a role in the questions that are asked. This topic is dealt with in greater detail below. Question 2 above fails in that it would probably not be feasible given the never-ending number of **variables** involved, even though it is significant in that it is an important question for all school districts (Gass, 2015).

Manipulating variables

Variables are characteristics of a class of objects that vary, as in the variable of eye color or height or weight for humans. In experimental research, variables need to be made explicit. This is actually one of the most difficult parts of a research project.

> For Research Question 1 above, there are a few variables about which decisions need to be made to render those variables sufficiently explicit, so that research can be conducted. For example: How will focused attention be operationalized? By coloring instances of noun–adjective agreement in a written text? By providing an explicit grammatical description? By frequency—that is by introducing numerous instances of noun–adjective agreement in a passage?
>
> When conducting and reporting experimental research, researchers must be clear on how they are defining their terms.
>
> A second variable in the research question under consideration is the notion of learning. In the history of SLA, different definitions have been used and here too numerous decisions have to be made.
>
> - Is learning measured by a paper/pencil (or computer) test or by spontaneous use? If by a paper/pencil or computer test, what kind of test? If the latter, how does one elicit spontaneous use? And, what does it mean if a form is not used? Does it mean that the learner does not know it or does it mean that the learner does not think she or he needs to use it? If the latter, then learning may have taken place as a result of the treatment, but there may be extraneous reasons for it not being used.
>
> - Further, if spontaneous use is the criterion for learning, how many instances of the structure/sound/lexical item need to occur? Mackey (1999), for example, required the presence of at least two examples of structures in two different post-tests. Is learning being operationalized only through a test given immediately following the treatment, or will the test be given one week later, or a month later?
>
> - Other variables relate specifically to the question being considered. For example, investigating noun–adjective agreement in Italian requires further decisions. Are only feminine nouns to be included, only masculine nouns or both? Because nouns that end in -*a* or in -*o* almost invariably indicate what the gender of the noun is, will nouns that do not obviously indicate gender be included?

In sum, variables are characteristics that vary. As mentioned earlier, in experimental research, there are essentially two primary variables of concern: **independent variables** and **dependent variables**.

- **Independent variables** are the object of investigation. They are those variables that the researcher is investigating in order to determine their effect on something else. In the above example, focused attention on the two grammatical structures is the independent variable.

- **Dependent variables** are those variables that the independent variable is having an effect on. Thus, learning is the dependent variable in the above example.
- In addition to these two variables, there are **extraneous variables.** These variables are independent variables that the researcher has not controlled for. In essence, they can seriously interfere with the results of a study. In the above example of focused attention, let's assume that a researcher has operationalized focused attention by coloring red all instances of noun–adjective agreement in a reading passage. Let's also assume that the researcher did not test for possible color-blindness of the participants. Then, color-blindness is an uncontrolled variable that could have interfered with the interpretation of the results.

Note that in a controlled experiment, you must be able to

- systematically and precisely manipulate the independent variable(s);
- precisely measure the dependent variable(s); and
- control any potential extraneous variables.

If your study design doesn't match these criteria, there are other types of research you can use to answer your research question.

▌• Task

1. Group work: Work in small groups. Share with each other the topics and related research questions you want to explore, referring to the criteria of a good research questions we have learned and discussed in the previous unit. Then, based on your discussion, decide on the topic, research questions, and the variables for the individual or group project you intend to do.

2. Individual work:

1) This section shows that in experimental research you should begin with a specific research question in mind. You may need to spend time reading about your field of study to identify knowledge gaps and to find questions that interest you.

2) Read carefully the above sections on variables, and think about the variables involved in your research project. Finally, write a clear and specific research questions, showing the variables in your investigation.

▶ Step 2. Writing your research hypothesis

Now that you have a strong understanding of the subject you are studying, you should be able to write a specific, testable hypothesis that addresses your research question.

In experimental research, there are not only research questions, but also hypotheses. Hypotheses are predictions based on the research question.

If you want to test a relationship between two or more things, you need to write hypotheses before you start your experiment or data collection. A hypothesis states your predictions about what your research will find, giving a tentative answer to your research question. So, you need to develop or state a hypothesis based on the research question.

Strategies for developing a hypothesis

Asking a question

Writing a hypothesis begins with a research question that you want to answer. The question should be focused, specific, and researchable within the constraints of your project. For example:

> *Do students who attend more lectures get better exam results?*

Doing some preliminary research

Your initial answer to the question should be based on what is already known about the topic. Look for theories and previous studies to help you form educated assumptions about what your research will find.

At this stage, you might construct a conceptual framework to identify which variables you will study and what you think the relationships are between them.

Formulating your hypothesis

Now you should have some idea of what you expect to find. Write your initial answer to the question in a clear, concise sentence. For example:

> *Attending more lectures leads to better exam results.*

Refining your hypothesis

You need to make sure your hypothesis is specific and testable. There are various ways of phrasing a hypothesis, but all the terms you use should have clear definitions, and the hypothesis should contain

- the relevant variables;
- the specific group being studied; and
- the predicted outcome of the experiment or analysis.

Your hypothesis can be phrased in three ways:

- To identify the variables, you can write a simple prediction in *if...then* form. The first part of the sentence states the independent variable and the second part states the dependent variable. For example:

> *If a first-year student starts attending more lectures, then their exam scores will improve.*

- Hypotheses can be more commonly phrased in terms of correlations or effects, where you directly state the predicted relationship between variables. For example:

> *The number of lectures attended by first-year students has a positive effect on their exam scores.*

- If you are comparing two groups, the hypothesis can state what difference you expect to find between them. For example:

> *First-year students who attended most lectures will have better exam scores than those who attended few lectures.*

Writing a null hypothesis

If your research involves statistical hypothesis testing, you will also have to write a null hypothesis. The null hypothesis is the default position that there is no association between the variables. The null hypothesis is written as H_0, while the alternative hypothesis is H_1 or H_a. For example:

> The number of lectures attended by first-year students has no effect on their final exam scores. (H_0)
>
> The number of lectures attended by first-year students has a positive effect on their final exam scores. (H_1)

The research goal is to reject the null hypothesis (Gass, 2015).

For example, in research question 1 above, the following hypothesis might obtain:

> Focused attention on noun–adjective agreement in Italian will promote learning to a greater extent than focused attention on wh-movement in Italian for beginning learners of Italian.

Alternatively, if there is no reason to expect anything other than a difference, the hypothesis might be phrased as follows:

> Focused attention on noun–adjective agreement in Italian will promote learning to a different degree than focused attention on wh-questions in Italian for beginning learners of Italian.

▐• Task

♦Working on the hypothesis

1. Group work: Read the following research questions, and write a null hypothesis (H_0) and an alternative hypothesis (H_1) for each of the questions based on what you have learned in the above section. In a small group, discuss the hypotheses you have written, focusing on any weaknesses or problems, and then give constructive ideas to each other.

1) What effect does daily use of social media have on the attention span of under-16s?

2) Can flexible online teaching arrangements improve learning satisfaction?

2. Individual Work: Based on the group work, think about the research topic and research questions you have chosen for your project, and write the finalized hypotheses for your project.

▶ Step 3. Assigning your subjects to treatment groups

How you apply your experimental treatments to your test subjects is crucial for obtaining valid and reliable results.

As mentioned earlier, reliability and validity are both about how well a method measures something: **Reliability** refers to the consistency of a measure (whether the results can be reproduced under the same conditions). **Validity** refers to the accuracy of a measure (whether the results really do represent what they are supposed to measure). The validity of your experiment depends on your experimental design.

First, you need to consider the study size: how many individuals will be included in the experiment? In general, the more subjects you include, the greater your experiment's statistical power, which determines how much confidence you can have in your results.

Then you need to randomly assign your subjects to treatment groups. Each group receives a different level of the treatment (e.g. no phone use, low phone use, high phone use).

You should also include a control group, which receives no treatment. The control group tells us what would have happened to your test subjects without any experimental intervention.

Random assignment

Another important step in experimental research is the random assignment of participants to one group or another. Random assignment of individuals means that each individual has an equal chance of being assigned to any of the conditions of the study (experimental or control). That is, the process of assignment is random. Randomization is intended to eliminate the possibility that extraneous variables will creep into the research design.

To take the above example of question 1, had there been randomization, there would have been an equal chance of having color-blind individuals in both the adjective–noun group and the *wh*-question group.

In general, in educational settings, we cannot always have random assignment of individuals and we are more often dependent on the contexts that already exist (e.g. intact classes) for our research. This is known as **quasi-experimental research** (as opposed to true experimental research) because not all variables can be completely controlled; in particular, we are dependent on assignment of participants based on class placement rather than on random assignment. But, in such instances, there should be random assignment of the group/class to one condition or another (randomized block design) (Gass, 2015).

Note that an experiment can be completely randomized or randomized within blocks:

- In a completely randomized design, every subject is assigned to a treatment group at random.
- In a randomized block design (stratified random design), subjects are first grouped according to a characteristic they share, and then randomly assigned to treatments within those groups.

Experiments are always context-dependent, and a good experimental design will take into account all of the unique considerations of your study system to produce information that is both valid and relevant to your research question.

In sum, by first considering the variables and how they are related, you can make hypotheses or predictions that are specific and testable. How widely and finely you vary your independent variable will determine the level of detail and the external validity of your results. Your decisions about randomization, experimental controls, and measures will determine the internal validity of your experiment.

▌• Task

◆ Research design

Individual work: The following sample describes the research design of an experimental study. First, read the brief introduction of the research, including research questions and hypotheses, to get a big picture of what the research is about. Then, read the research design carefully, paying special attention to the experiment treatments and different aspects involved in the research design. Finally, based on your own selected topic and research questions, think about the research design for your own experimental study.

A Brief Introduction

This experimental research "Undergraduates Arguing a Case" is an instructional study conducted by Susheela Varghese and Sunita Abraham, and published in *Journal of Second Language Writing* 7(3): 287–306 (1998). In the study students were trained in two key aspects of argumentation, namely, the structural and interpersonal components. The structural aspects were taught and measured in terms of Toulmin's framework of argument analysis (i.e., the quality of claims, grounds and warrants used). The interpersonal aspects in turn were measured in terms of the creation of a clear persona, audience adaptiveness (the appropriate use of rational and emotional appeals), and stance towards the unique discourse of argumentation. Students performed a pre-instruction writing task, underwent eight weeks of explicit instruction in argumentation, then performed the task again. Findings contrasting pre- and post-test results reveal statistically significant improvement in students' abilities to formulate claims, to offer specific and developed grounds, and to use more reliable warrants. Students also showed improvement in the interpersonal aspects of argument, building better writer credibility, developing fuller rational and emotional appeals, and conveying both sides of an argument in order to resolve the problem at hand.

- **Research question:** What concrete changes in argument skills do students display after having received explicit instruction in the Toulmin analysis of argument as a means of refining their argumentation skills?

- **Hypotheses:** In keeping with the focus of prior definitions of argument on both the substance and goal of argument, both the structure and purpose of argument were developed into hypotheses for this study as follows:

H_1: *Students will use the various components of argument (namely, claim, data and warrant) with greater specificity in the post-test. Specifically, they will produce more explicit claims, more specific and developed grounds, and more reliable warrants in the post-test than in the pre-test.*

H_2: *Students will reflect a higher degree of competence in the interpersonal aspects of argumentation, namely, the representation of self (persona), audience adaptiveness (use of rational and emotional appeals), and stance towards argumentative discourse (the ability to convey more than one side of an argument) in the post-test.*

The first hypothesis thus focuses on the components of argument structure, using three measures (quality of claim, quality of grounds, and quality of warrants) to assess improvement in this area. The second hypothesis in turn predicts that subjects will improve at the interpersonal level of argument, and uses the measures of persona (representation of self), audience adaptiveness (rational and emotional appeals), and stance towards discourse to evaluate growth.

Sample: Research Design

As mentioned above, this study was designed to determine the effectiveness of instruction in argument by course participants within the Academic Reading and Writing module offered at the National University of Singapore. The ideal experimental design would have been to divide all subjects into an instructional condition (those who received training in argument) and a control condition consisting of those within the course not receiving specific training on argument. It was not, however, pedagogically viable to deprive any of the students in the course of preferred modes of instruction, since administrative regulations at the University require parity of instruction for all students registered within the module. Altenatively, a control group could have been obtained by drawing upon second-year undergraduates taking a module in reading/writing which did not offer explicit training in argumentation. Unfortunately, however, all the other course options offered in the same semester were courses on the structure of the English language (phonetics and phonological analysis, syntactic analysis, semantic analysis). So, while the lack of a control group was recognized as a limitation of the current study, the authors nevertheless felt that the possible benefit of quantifying progress in argumentation was pressing enough to proceed with the study in its current form. A pre-test was administered to gauge baseline skills in argumentation in Week 1 of the twelve-week module. Students were subsequently given eight weeks of instruction about argumentation. All students participated in the instructional condition (thus meeting curricular requirements set by administration). A post-test was administered in Week 10 of the twelve-week semester to assess the development of students' skills in argumentation.

Profile of Subjects

The subjects in this study comprise 30 randomly selected students from the Academic Reading and Writing module. All 30 subjects were second-year undergraduates, with a major in English Language. Of the 30 subjects, 17 were female, aged 21, and 13 were male, aged 23. (It is customary for Singaporean male undergraduates to be two years older than their female counterparts since all males customarily complete 2½ years of national service before commencing their tertiary education.)

All 30 subjects could also be more accurately described as "English-knowing bilingual" (Pakir, 1995) rather than EFL or ESL students since the medium of instruction in all schools and colleges in Singapore is English. (The educational language policy also requires all students to pass a second language, usually their mother tongue, at all levels.) All 30 subjects in this study thus have at least 13 years of English-medium schooling. Moreover, as English-language majors, these subjects are considered high-proficiency as all 30 obtained A's and B's on their Singapore-Cambridge 'A' Level General Paper examinations as part of the entry requirement into the Department of English Language & Literature. The data analysed in this study thus comprise the 30 pre-test and 30 post-test scripts, written by these 30 randomly selected subjects.

Instructional Content

The instructional content of the Academic Reading and Writing module drew upon Toulmin's (1958) well-established fundamentals in argumentation, namely the presence of claim, evidence and warrant for its working terminology. For those unfamiliar with Toulmin's terminology, the **claim** is the statement or proposition that the arguer wants the audience to accept and/or act upon. The **grounds** comprise the facts, examples, data, etc. offered in support of a claim, and the **warrant** is the (often unstated) assumption which justifies using the grounds offered as a basis for the claim being argued.

For example, a simple claim might be: "Janice is a good student." A writer could then substantiate this assertion with instances of Janice completing her assignments in a timely fashion, clarifying doubts with classmates or a teacher, demonstrating an ability to research interesting topics independently and so forth. For such an argument to be accepted by the reader, the writer and reader must share basic assumptions or warrants that these various behaviors constitute characteristics of a good student.

Once students were familiar with this basic terminology, they were taught to evaluate the soundness of the arguments they read. Toulmin, Rieke, and Janik (1979) suggest that readers begin evaluating an argument by establishing the presence and quality of argument components. They rightly suggest that readers quickly lose faith in an argument if, for example, the claim is ambiguous or evidence is missing. In reading both good and bad examples of arguments, students recognized the presence or absence of the various argument components and then reached their own decisions, in discussion or in writing, about the effectiveness of various arguments. They then proceeded to write their own arguments. In doing so, they were specifically advised not to write to the formula of claim, data and warrant, since the result would be stilted prose that might not achieve its persuasive aim. Rather, they were counseled to apply Toulmin's terminology to evaluate their arguments.

In short, then, in the eight weeks of instruction, students were taught the Toulmin model of argument structure as a means by which they could evaluate arguments that they read as well as arguments which they wrote. Instruction about the interpersonal aspects of argument, however, was a little more piecemeal in that students were not provided with a schema akin to the Toulmin model. Rather, students learned about the need to consider the audience's motivation and emotional response to an argument in relation to comments made by the instructor about texts read and written by students.

In all, students read and orally critiqued an average of three to four short arguments per week over the eight weeks of instruction. Their writing load in turn comprised a mixture of shorter (500-word) and longer (1000-word) arguments, written and re-drafted in fortnightly cycles. Students also did some writing under timed conditions as rehearsal for the two-hour long end-of-semester examination.

Designing the Argumentative Task

On the basis of prior experience in teaching and evaluating argumentation, the authors identified two key aspects of argumentation—the structure of argument as clarified in Toulmin (1958) and the interpersonal aspects of argument—for instruction and assessment. They then designed an argumentative task which would elicit the sub-skills associated with the two key aspects of argumentation above. For structure of argument, these were the formulation of explicit claims, the use of specific and adequately developed grounds, and more reliable warrants. For the interpersonal aspects of argumentation, in turn, the sub-skills identified were the representation of self (persona), audience adaptiveness (appropriate use of rational and emotional appeals), and stance towards argumentative discourse (the ability to convey more than one side of an argument). The task consisted of a short writing prompt, taken from *The Straits Times*, Singapore's largest-circulating English daily, which students were asked to respond to:

> **BG Yeo on getting female grads to marry sooner**
>
> For women now in university and who plan to get married, I think we should encourage them to settle down earlier and have children earlier. You know all those sum goo **lok pors** (matchmakers of old) should come along and matchmake you and get you to get married and so on. I think we should bring them back.

The task instructions were as follows:

> Write a "letter to the editor" response to BG Yeo's suggestion about reintroducing matchmakers. You may argue FOR or AGAINST his position, but your text should not exceed one page (two sides of one sheet of paper).

The selection of the topic was based on two main criteria: authenticity and familiarity.

...

Students were given 45 minutes (the duration of the class period) in which to write their essays. While a longer writing time would have been desirable, it is worth highlighting that tertiary students in Singapore are required regularly to produce a three to four page essay in just 45 minutes during University examinations, and that the present task called for a much shorter text, viz. a one-page response.

The post-tests were written on the same topic with the same time limit to control for topic and time effects respectively. Students did not have access to pre-test essays and had not seen them in 10 weeks. Most students reported that they were surprised when asked to do the post-test task, since they had not given the pre-test or the topic it dealt with any further thought during the intervening ten-week period. Many also said that they could not remember what they had written in the pre-test essay. However, the researchers' observation is that most students did use arguments similar to those they had raised in their pre-test scripts. Such tendencies have been reported elsewhere, such as in Clark and Delia (1976) where students used similar persuasive strategies across tasks and audiences.

Scoring Procedure

Ten scripts (not included in the final sample) were used as a pre-coding sample to establish criteria for scoring. Both authors then rated the 60 texts randomly selected for this study. All data were coded blind. Inter-rater reliabilities were .91 for the task as a whole, ranging from a low of .87 for the rational and emotional appeals measures to .95 for the measures of persona and stance.

Step 4. Statistical analysis–interpretation

Interpretation of results is done as a first step through statistical analyses. A discussion of different kinds of statistics and designs is beyond the scope of this unit, but there are numerous books that deal with these topics (Gass, 2015).

Significance level

In general, for most research in the field of second language writing (SLW) or applied linguistics more generally, the significance level (α level) is generally set at 0.05. This means that when we look at statistical results, there is a 95 per cent chance that our results are due to the experimental treatment and only 5 per cent chance that the results are due to chance alone. In many studies, researchers will talk about the results approaching significance when the statistical analysis is slightly about 0.05 (e.g. 0.06–0.09). In disciplines where the consequences of a chance finding are greater (e.g. life-altering medical treatment), different α levels are required. In other words, the α level is a generally accepted guide that is used by researchers in a discipline. When we are accepting or rejecting hypotheses, we want to avoid any errors in interpretation.

Error types

There are two noteworthy error types, known as Type I (also known as an α error) and Type II (also known as a β error). The former refers to the rejection of a (null) hypothesis when it should not be rejected, and the latter refers to the acceptance of a (null) hypothesis when it should be rejected.

Both of these errors are minimized through rigorous and appropriate use of statistics. Statistical significance gives us a "yes/no" indication of the significance of one's results. In most cases, a dichotomous decision is insufficient; one wants to know instead how strong findings are. Effect sizes, because they are not dependent on sample size, are frequently used. Probability levels are highly dependent on sample size, whereas effect sizes are not (Creswell, 2014).

Elimination of other factors

As part of the interpretation process, one has to be able to eliminate with a reasonable degree of confidence that other factors did not enter into the picture. There are ways to minimize this possibility. One already discussed is randomization. Another is by testing for the extraneous variable and eliminating the participants who have that characteristic.

The research could also include that variable into the design by including it as a variable and then testing for its influence. And, a variation like the latter one is to match participants, so that one has a particular characteristic and another does not (Creswell, 2014).

▶ Step 5. Writing up the research

Based on the tasks completed in each stage, you can get ready for the writing task. While writing up your research report, follow the guidelines and the typical **IMRD** pattern given below, that is, the four major sections of a research paper: **Introduction**, **Method**, **Results**, and **Discussion**.

Introduction

Explain the purpose of the study. What problem is being addressed? Why is it interesting or important from a theoretical perspective? Briefly review the literature, emphasizing pertinent and relevant findings, methodological issues, and gaps in understanding. Conclude the introduction with a statement of purpose, your research questions, and, where relevant, your hypotheses; clearly explain the rationale for each hypothesis.

Method

Explain your study in enough detail so that it could be replicated. Include the following details in this section.

Participants

Clearly state whether there is a population that you would ideally want to generalize to; explain the characteristics of that population. Explain your sampling procedure. If you are using a convenience sample, be sure to say so. Arguments for representativeness can be strengthened by comparing characteristics of the sample with that of the population on a range of variables. Describe the characteristics and the size of the sample. When appropriate, describe how participants were assigned to groups.

Measures

Summarize all instruments in terms of both descriptions and measurement properties (i.e., reliability and validity). Provide estimates of the reliability of the scores in your sample in addition to reliability estimates provided by test publishers, other researchers, or both; when you make judgments about performance or when language samples are coded for linguistic characteristics, include estimates of classification dependability or coder agreement.

Procedure

Describe the conditions under which you administered your instruments.

- **Design.** Make clear what type of study you have done—was your study evaluating a priori hypotheses, or was it exploratory in order to generate hypotheses? Explain your design, and state whether your comparisons were within subjects, between subjects, or both. Describe the methods used to deal with experimenter bias if you collected the data yourself. If you assigned participants to subgroups, explain how you did so. If you used random assignment, tell the readers how the randomization was done (e.g., coin toss, random numbers table, computerized random numbers generation). If you did not use random assignment, explain relevant covariates and the way you measured and adjusted for them, either statistically or by design. Describe the characteristics and the size of the subgroups. In place of the terms experimental group and control group, use treatment group and contrast group.

- **Variables.** Define the variables in the study. Make explicit the link between the theoretical constructs and the way(s) they have been operationalized in your study. Define the role of each variable in your study (e.g., dependent, independent, moderating, control). Explain how you measured or otherwise observed the variables.

- **Sample size.** Provide information on the sample size and the process that led to the decision to use that size. Provide information on the anticipated effect size as you have estimated it from previous research.

Results

- Explain the data collected and their statistical treatment as well as all relevant results in relation to your research questions. Interpretation of results is not appropriate in this section.

- Describe the assumptions for each procedure and the steps you took to ensure that they were not violated.

- When using inferential statistics, provide descriptive statistics (including mean, mode, median and standard deviation), confidence intervals, and sample sizes for each variable as well as the value of the test statistic, its direction, the degrees of freedom, and the significance level (report the actual p-value).

- Avoid inferring causality, particularly in nonrandomized designs or without further experimentation.

- Use tables to provide exact values; present all values with two places to the right of the decimal point.

- Use figures to convey global effects. Keep figures small in size; include graphic representations of confidence intervals whenever possible.

- Always tell the readers what to look for in tables and figures.

Discussion

- **Interpretation.** Clearly state your findings for each of your research questions and their associated hypotheses. State similarities and differences with effect sizes reported in the literature. Indicate whether the results or findings of your research are consistent or inconsistent to those of previous studies in the field, and explain the reasons behind this. Discuss whether features of the methodology and analysis are strong enough to support strong conclusions.

- **Conclusions.** Note the weaknesses of your study. Identify theoretical and practical implications of your study. Discuss limitations and suggest improvements to your study. Provide recommendations for future research that are thoughtful and grounded both in terms of your results and in the literature.

⊩ Task

♦Writing and presenting your research project

1. Individual work: Read the guidelines given above, and try to write up your research project by including each component or section described.

2. Classwork: If possible, present your completed draft in class, trying to get feedback and suggestions from your peers or instructor, if possible. Then, spend some time revising your writing.

10.6 Other Issues

▶ Validity and reliability

As mentioned earlier, **validity** refers to the correctness and appropriateness of the interpretations that a researcher makes of his/her study. **Reliability** refers to score consistency across administrations of one's instrument. For both concepts, accurate and appropriate instruments are at the core. Thus, if our hypothesis involves learning, we need to have an accurate and appropriate instrument to measure learning. For example, if we are looking at knowledge representation, we need to have a measure that appropriately reflects that and not something that just measures an ability to use the language. In many instances, part of the theoretical discussions in the literature involve how best to represent particular constructs.

Often variables cannot be measured directly. In these instances, we come up with a working definition that allows us to identify the variable in question with something that is understandable and measurable. This is known as an **operationalization**. Thus, in the example presented earlier of focused attention, we cannot directly measure this construct, but we can come up with a reasonable surrogate (e.g. coloring or highlighting in some way). Once we have operationalized a variable, we can more easily work with it (Gass, 2015).

Both validity and reliability are ways of ensuring quality in research. As noted, experimental research is a way of finding answers to questions in a disciplined way. These results may have farreaching impact (including decisions relating to educational practices), and it is incumbent on the research community to ensure that research (experimental and other) is carried out in as careful a way as possible, ensuring quality at each step of the way.

▶ Ethical considerations

As with all research, ethical considerations abound. The most obvious concerns the protection of human subjects, usually elaborated on by each institution's ethical review board.

In brief, in most educational settings, one must obtain permission from a human research committee before conducting any research or before recruiting volunteers for a research project. The overriding concern is that no harm comes to participants with the ideal being that there be benefits.

As researchers design studies, there is often a control group against which to measure the effects of a particular treatment. But, here too, there is an ethical question. If we have reason to believe that our treatment is beneficial, then we have recruited volunteers who will not receive the treatment. One possibility is to provide the treatment to the control group after all data have been collected.

Polio and Gass (2007) designed a study in just this way, although even in this study, there were limitations to equal treatment.

The main research question was: can a brief intervention study in which preservice teachers are instructed on how to interact with learners promote learning in a subsequent interaction?

The design involved an experimental and a control group. The experimental group received a 15–20 minute session with a researcher who went over ways to increase student output (e.g. asking open-ended questions rather than yes/no questions). This was followed by an interactive session with an ESL learner in which they were asked to put into practice what they had learned. So as not to disadvantage the control group and maintain the integrity of the study, the training session with the control group was conducted following the interactive session. Thus, all preservice teachers had the benefit of a training session which had been hypothesized to be beneficial in the promotion of learning. Yet, the control group's training was conducted after the experiment so as not to influence the research results. This, of course, does not take into account the benefits that the ESL students in the experimental group had over those in the control group. Unfortunately, the complete balancing of benefits would have required the control group of ESL students to return for a second round, and this was not logistically possible (Gass, 2015, pp. 95–96).

In general, it is important to strictly follow the guidelines established by one's institution regarding all aspects of a study, including modes of recruiting, actual treatment and assessment details and the reporting of information in such a way as to respect privacy and anonymity issues.

In addition to local review boards, the American Psychological Association (2010) has important guidelines for many aspects of the research process.

A final point to be made which has ethical ramifications has to do with honesty in reporting, and in particular with the elimination of participants. When elimination takes place, it has to be done judiciously and with justification. For example, in studies which measure reaction time, it may be the case that a participant is not focused on the task. This may be determined by inordinately fast reaction times which make it clear that she or he is just pushing a response button without processing the required material. Often, in such studies, a cut-off point will be determined, such as two standard deviations above or below the mean, with individuals falling on the outside limits of this cut-off point being eliminated from analysis. Whatever criteria are used, it is important that a detailed and principled justification be provided to avoid any question of impropriety (Gass, 2015).

Sample Research

Please scan the QR code below to acquire the sample article. Read the article and think about its research methods.

Sample Article

Unit ⑪

Mixed Methods Research

The mixed methods research uses both qualitative and quantitative data collection and analysis methods to answer research questions, providing a depth and breadth that a single approach may lack by itself. Research using both methods aims to gain a complete and holistic understanding of the subject's needs, challenges, wants, willingness to take action, and more. Over the last few decades, the practice of collecting and analyzing both quantitative and qualitative data within one study has become quite popular in applied linguistics, However, the right time to use either method or both can vary depending on your research goals and needs. Also, such integration can pose some challenges to student researchers.

⓫⓵ Introduction

▶ What is mixed methods research?

There are three broad research traditions in applied linguistics: quantitative, qualitative, and mixed methods.

Quantitative research

Quantitative research is expressed in numbers and graphs. It is used to test or confirm theories and assumptions. This type of research can be used to establish generalizable facts about a topic from a large amount of data. Typical kinds of quantitative research are surveys and experimental research.

In quantitative research, researchers gather numeric data, for example, proficiency test scores or multiple choice question (or "closed-response item") responses on questionnaires; they then try to objectively analyze this data using a variety of statistical techniques, and let the numeric results prove or disprove a hypothesis so that those results can be generalized from a sample to a larger population.

Qualitative research

Qualitative research is expressed in words. It is used to understand concepts, thoughts or experiences for detailed information. This type of research enables you to gather in-depth insights on topics that are not well understood. Examples of such research include interviews, focus groups, case studies, and discourse analysis.

In qualitative research, researchers try to understand participants' experiences with the central phenomenon (the focus of the study) in a natural setting, using research approaches such as ethnography or case study. Instead of numbers, researchers collect words (text, such as interviews or observation notes), and images (pictures or audio-visual footage) about the phenomenon of the study. Without preconceived hypotheses or ideas, they analyze the data for common patterns (themes) in order to allow multiple interpretations of participants' individual experiences. In this type of research, the goal is not to try to prove or disprove something; rather, the aim is to explore and then describe in rich detail the phenomenon that is being investigated.

Quantitative and qualitative research use different research methods to collect and analyze data, and they allow you to answer different kinds of research questions.

Mixed methods research

In mixed methods research, a researcher collects both numeric information (for example, through closed-response items on questionnaires) and text (from face-to-face interviews, picture descriptions, and so on) to better answer a study's research questions.

As compared with quantitative and qualitative research, mixed methods research is often recognized as less conventional research traditions. It is defined as a procedure for collecting, analyzing, and mixing quantitative and qualitative data at some stage of the research process within a single study in order to understand a research problem more completely (Creswell, 2008). The term "mixing" implies that the data or the findings are integrated and/or connected at one or several points within the study.

Research question: *How satisfied are students with their studies?*

Quantitative research approach

You survey 300 students at your university and ask them questions such as, "On a scale from 1–5, how satisfied are you with your professors?"

You can perform statistical analysis on the data and draw conclusions such as, "On average students rated their professors 4.4."

Qualitative research approach

You conduct in-depth interviews with 15 students and ask them open-ended questions such as, "How satisfied are you with your studies?," "What is the most positive aspect of your study program?" and "What can be done to improve the study program?"

Based on the answers you get you can ask follow-up questions to clarify things. You transcribe all interviews using transcription software and try to find commonalities and patterns.

Mixed methods approach

You conduct interviews to find out how satisfied students are with their studies. Through open-ended questions you learn things you never thought about before and gain new insights. Later, you use a survey to test these insights on a larger scale.

It's also possible to start with a survey to find out the overall trends, followed by interviews to better understand the reasons behind the trends.

It is ideal to use a mix of both quantitative and qualitative methods to supplement gaps in data. These methods can be iterative and conducted at different points throughout a research project to follow up and verify different insights gathered from either method. Using both quantitative and qualitative survey questions is the best way to holistically understand audience segments.

▌• Task

Pair work: Discuss the following with your peer.

1) What is mixed methods research? Give a definition using your own words. Explain how it is different from quantitative and qualitative research approaches.

2) Quantitative research emphasizes the importance of measuring outcomes, while qualitative research focuses on understanding the process of what's going on in a setting. Read the following paragraph, and share with each other some English or Chinese writing experiences or practices where qualitative research can be used to explore what happened.

In applied linguistics, quantitative researchers often measure gains in proficiency over a period of time—the outcomes of learning. However, qualitative researchers focus on the process, by trying to understand how those gains were made, what the participants thought about improving their proficiency, and how the setting—and the other people there—influenced them. This kind of research is often longitudinal, and a lot of qualitative inquiry requires researchers to spend a relatively prolonged period of time in the research setting to develop deep and comprehensive understandings of what goes on there. With a more detailed and intensive focus on each participant, working even in one setting is very time and labor intensive so the number of participants is usually small and they are carefully chosen.

▶ Characteristics of mixed methods research

Mixed methods research has defined procedures for collecting, analyzing, and mixing quantitative and qualitative data in a study, based upon three main characteristics: (1) timing, or the sequence or order of collecting and analyzing quantitative and qualitative data in a study; (2) weighting, or the priority given to one type of data in the study; and (3) mixing, or the way quantitative and qualitative data and results are integrated during the research process (Ivankova & Creswell, 2009).

- **Timing:** Timing refers to the sequence or order of the implementation of the quantitative and qualitative data collection and analysis procedures in the study when one phase builds on another. The two possible timing options include: (1) sequentially—collecting and analyzing the data one after the other (quantitative→qualitative, or qualitative→quantitative); or (2) concurrently—collecting and analyzing both quantitative and qualitative data at the same time (quantitative + qualitative).

- **Weighting:** Weighting refers to the relative importance or priority given to each type of data. The two possible weighting options include giving equal weight to the quantitative (QUAN) and qualitative (QUAL) data, or giving one type greater emphasis—to quantitative data (QUAN vs qual) or qualitative data (QUAL vs quan). When making the weighting decision, there are a number of things to consider: What is more strongly emphasized in the purpose statement, exploration (qualitative) or prediction (quantitative)? Which data collection process, quantitative or qualitative, is most central to the study? Which data analysis procedures, quantitative or qualitative, are more sophisticated, complex, and discussed more extensively when the study is presented?

- **Mixing:** Mixing refers to how the two methods, quantitative or qualitative, are integrated within the study. It is an essential component of mixed methods research. Mixing quantitative and qualitative data can occur at different stages in the study: during the data collection, the data analysis, or the interpretation of results. Deciding on how to mix depends on the purpose of the study, its design, and the strategies used for data collection and analysis.

If the purpose of the study is to explain quantitative results that were obtained first, qualitative data can be collected after quantitative data by interviewing (or administering an open-response questionnaire) to a small number of participants, based on these quantitative results (see "Explanatory Design" below). Mixing here occurs at two points: when selecting participants for interview and creating interview questions grounded in the statistical results (connecting the quantitative and qualitative phases), and at the interpretation stage of the study, when discussing the results from the two phases. If the purpose of the study is to develop a closed-response questionnaire or survey grounded in the views of the participants, first qualitative data is collected through interviews and then the questionnaire is developed; then quantitative data is collected using this questionnaire. Mixing here occurs while analyzing the qualitative data for codes and themes and transforming them into questionnaire items and scales (see "Exploratory Design" below). If the purpose of the study is to compare the quantitative and qualitative results, both quantitative and qualitative data are collected and analyzed separately. Mixing here occurs at the data interpretation stage, when the results from two data sets are compared (see "Triangulation Design" and "Embedded Design" below). (Ivankova & Creswell, 2009)

▶ Major types of mixed methods designs

There are four mixed methods designs that are most frequently used by researchers. These are explanatory design, exploratory design, triangulation design, and embedded design. The following sections will describe and illustrate each design, using Creswell's (2003) widely used notation: large and small letters in the labels (QUAL/quan or qual/QUAN) indicate weight of the quantitative and/or qualitative approaches, and the symbols "→" indicate timing in the data collection and analysis. This part is mainly adapted from

"Mix Methods" in *Qualitative Research in Applied Linguistics: A Practical Introduction* (Ivankova & Creswell, 2009, pp. 139–145).

Explanatory design

The explanatory design is the most straightforward mixed methods design, and it is used extensively in applied linguistics research. The word "explanatory" in the design name suggests explanation: qualitative findings are used to help explain, refine, clarify, or extend quantitative results. Quantitative and qualitative data are collected and analyzed in sequence: first quantitative data is collected and analyzed, and then qualitative data. A typical example would include conducting follow-up qualitative interviews of representative or extreme cases to more deeply explore quantitative results.

Saito and Ebsworth's (2004) exploration of Japanese ESL students' perceptions of the classroom activities and classroom-related behaviors of their English teachers in the United States and in Japan

- They first surveyed a large sample of Japanese ESL learners in both countries using a 49-item questionnaire.

- Then they conducted follow-up interviews with three students to help interpret and elaborate the results obtained from the survey. The figure below presents the visual diagram of the explanatory design procedures in this study.

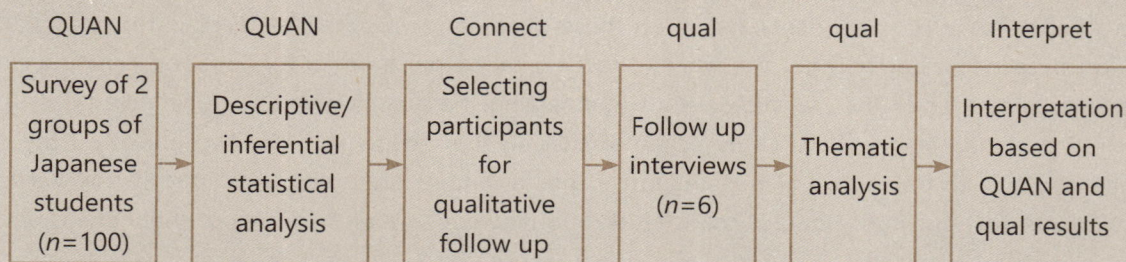

QUAN	QUAN	Connect	qual	qual	Interpret
Survey of 2 groups of Japanese students (n=100)	Descriptive/ inferential statistical analysis	Selecting participants for qualitative follow up	Follow up interviews (n=6)	Thematic analysis	Interpretation based on QUAN and qual results

The weight in this design is typically placed on quantitative data because the quantitative data collection represents the major aspect of this mixed methods data collection process; it also comes first in the sequence. The mixing of the two methods occurs at two stages in the research process: first, while developing the qualitative interview protocol and choosing the participants for in-depth exploration of the quantitative results; and second, while integrating the results from both quantitative and qualitative phases at the interpretation and discussion stage of the study.

The data analysis typically involves several options. A researcher might choose to follow up on extreme or representative cases from the quantitative analysis, or seek to explain the quantitative results in more depth. The structure of an explanatory design report typically follows the sequential character of the design: the quantitative data collection and analysis is described first, followed by the description of the qualitative data collection and analysis. A separate section in the report might discuss how the two phases were connected in the research process. During the discussion of the study results, a researcher explains how the qualitative findings helped elaborate or extend the quantitative results.

An advantage of the explanatory design is that its two separate phases make it straightforward and reasonably easy to implement for novice researchers. This sequential nature also makes it simple to describe and report on. However, compared to a straightforward quantitative study, an explanatory design study may take longer to complete.

Exploratory design

The exploratory design is used when a researcher needs first to explore a topic using qualitative data before measuring or testing it quantitatively. This design is particularly appropriate when studying a topic which has been little explored, so there is little information about the relevant constructs (ways of conceptualizing the topic) and how to measure important variables. In this design, the qualitative data is collected and analyzed first, followed by the collection and analysis of the quantitative data.

As the name suggests, this design allows a researcher first to explore a topic by collecting qualitative data to help identify principal themes and possibly generate a theory. Then, the researcher collects quantitative data to examine the initial qualitative results, such as to test a theory or to develop a measurement instrument such as a questionnaire or survey.

Daud's (1995) application of the exploratory design to investigate teachers' attitudes toward computer-assisted language learning (CALL)

- In the first phase, five case studies were conducted in four schools and a university to explore teachers' attitudes toward CALL.

- Next the qualitative findings from these studies were used to develop a 56-item questionnaire to measure those attitudes, which was then tested for reliability and validity with a larger sample of school and university teachers. The figure below presents the visual diagram of the exploratory design procedures in this study.

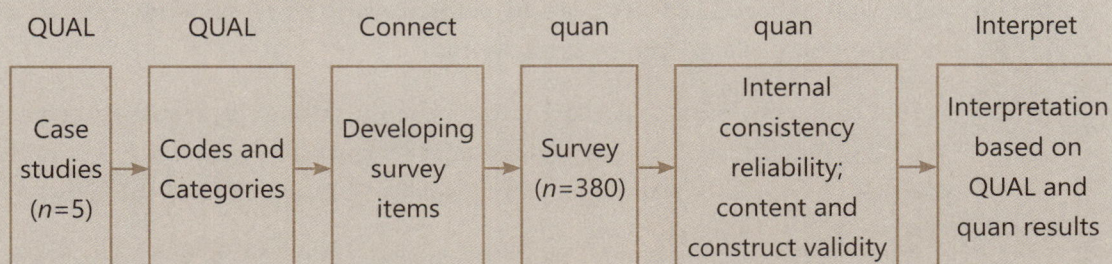

QUAL	QUAL	Connect	quan	quan	Interpret
Case studies (*n*=5)	Codes and Categories	Developing survey items	Survey (*n*=380)	Internal consistency reliability; content and construct validity	Interpretation based on QUAL and quan results

The weight in the exploratory design is typically given to the qualitative data, because it provides the foundation for the quantitative exploration of the topic. The mixing of the two methods occurs while developing the quantitative survey items based on the qualitative data analysis and also while comparing the quantitative results with initial qualitative findings.

The most popular approach for data analysis is to use the qualitative themes and categories to develop the quantitative measurement instrument (Creswell, 2008). In writing up the research, a researcher first reports the qualitative data collection and analysis and then explains the development of the instrument. Next, the quantitative data collection and analysis are discussed, and finally the overall results of the study are presented.

Like the explanatory design, the two-phase nature of the exploratory design makes it straightforward for a researcher to design, implement, and report on. However, like in the explanatory design, implementing the two separate phases of the study can be time consuming. In addition, developing a measurement instrument is not easy. A researcher must use careful procedures to ensure that it is grounded in the qualitative results—that it is not constructed from common sense or theory, but based upon the qualitative data collected—and that it is tested for reliability and validity.

Triangulation design

The triangulation design is the most common mixed methods design, and also the most complex. The name "triangulation" comes from the same term used in surveying and in ship navigation in which multiple measurements are used to provide the best estimate of the location at a specific point, like the point at the top of a triangle. The explanatory and exploratory designs are straightforward to implement because of the sequential order of each data collection and analysis phase; however in the triangulation design, quantitative and qualitative data are collected simultaneously. For instance, both a questionnaire and focus group interviews are conducted at the same time with the same participants, and then a researcher compares the quantitative and qualitative results. Often quantitative and qualitative data are collected using a questionnaire that contains closed-ended (quantitative) and open-ended (qualitative) response items. The triangulation design is best suited when a researcher wants to collect both types of data at the same time about a single phenomenon, in order to compare and contrast the different findings to produce well-validated conclusions.

> **Lopez and Tashakkori's (2006) application of the triangulation design to investigate the effects of two types of bilingual programs (two-way and transitional) on the academic performance and attitudes of fifth grade students who entered kindergarten or first grade with different levels of English proficiency**
>
> - They collected both quantitative data, such as students' academic achievement scores, Spanish reading skills, and attitudes toward bilingualism, and qualitative data, including interviews with the randomly selected subsample of 32 students.
>
> - Both quantitative and qualitative data were collected, analyzed, and reported separately. Quantitative data analysis revealed no significant differences in standardized measures of English achievement between the two programs, although significant differences were found among students in oral language acquisition in English, Spanish-reading ability, their attitudes, and perceived levels of proficiency in English and Spanish. Qualitative data indicated that students in the two-way

bilingual education program had more positive attitudes toward bilingualism.

- Based on the quantitative and qualitative results of the study, Lopez and Tashakkori concluded that despite some similarities in the outcomes, each bilingual education program also has its unique effects.

The figure below presents the visual diagram of the triangulation design procedures in this study.

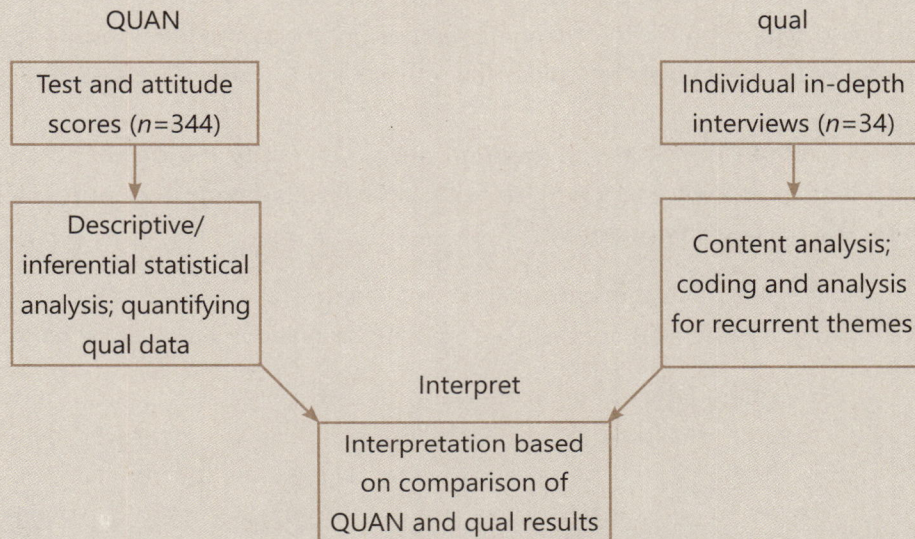

```
        QUAN                                                  qual

  ┌─────────────────┐                              ┌─────────────────┐
  │ Test and attitude│                              │ Individual in-depth│
  │  scores (n=344) │                              │ interviews (n=34) │
  └────────┬────────┘                              └────────┬────────┘
           │                                                │
           ▼                                                ▼
  ┌─────────────────┐                              ┌─────────────────┐
  │   Descriptive/  │                              │ Content analysis;│
  │inferential statistical│                         │ coding and analysis│
  │ analysis; quantifying│                          │ for recurrent themes│
  │    qual data    │                              └────────┬────────┘
  └────────┬────────┘          Interpret                    │
           │              ┌─────────────────┐               │
           └─────────────▶│ Interpretation based│◀──────────┘
                          │  on comparison of │
                          │QUAN and qual results│
                          └─────────────────┘
```

The weight in this design can be given to either quantitative or qualitative data, or equally to both. The mixing of the two methods occurs either at the data analysis stage or during the interpretation of the results from the two components of the study. As for data analysis, there are a lot of options. The most popular approach is to compare the quantitative results and qualitative findings to confirm or cross-validate the findings from the entire study. Another commonly used strategy is to transform qualitative data into quantitative data by counting codes, categories, and themes (called quantifying), or quantitative data into qualitative data through cluster or factor analysis (called qualifying) in order to compare it directly with another data set or include it in the overall analysis. The reporting structure of the triangulation design differs from the sequential explanatory and exploratory designs. A researcher presents the quantitative and qualitative data collection and analysis in separate sections, but combines the interpretation of the quantitative and qualitative findings into the same section, to discuss whether the results from both study components converge or show divergence.

An advantage of the triangulation design is that it typically takes less time to complete than the sequential explanatory and exploratory designs. It can also result in well-validated and substantiated findings because it offsets the weaknesses of one method with the strengths of another method (Creswell et al., 2003). There are, however, two significant challenges: first, it requires a lot of effort, as well as expertise, to collect and analyze two separate sets of data simultaneously; and second, it is sometimes technically difficult to compare different quantitative and qualitative data sets, especially if the two sets of results do not converge.

Embedded design

The embedded design is used when a researcher needs to answer a secondary research question that requires the use of different types of data within a traditional quantitative or qualitative design. To accomplish this, one type of data collection and analysis is embedded or nested within the design associated with another type of data. For example, a researcher may need to embed qualitative data within a quantitative experimental design and will conduct qualitative interviews during the research study to understand the reasons for certain participants' behaviors. Less frequently, a researcher may embed quantitative survey data within a traditionally qualitative case study to help describe the broader context in which a case is situated. Unlike the triangulation design, the embedded design has a predominant method (quantitative or qualitative) that guides the research study (Creswell et al., 2003).

Andrews's (2006) use of the embedded design to study the development of teachers' second language awareness with specific reference to cognitive processes of teaching English and particularly grammar

- The study was primarily qualitative by nature, as the data was collected in the form of interviews with teachers, classroom observations, and teacher narratives.

- The quantitative data, in the form of test scores, was used to answer one study research question, "What is the present level (as measured by a test) of each teacher's subject-matter knowledge as it relates to grammar?," and inform the discussion of the teachers' past and present subject-matter knowledge.

- The analysis of the test scores over time indicated that teachers' language awareness and grammar-related cognition had changed very little, while the overall study described teachers' underlying beliefs about grammar pedagogy and the role of explicit grammar teaching.

The figure below presents the visual diagram of the embedded design procedures in this study.

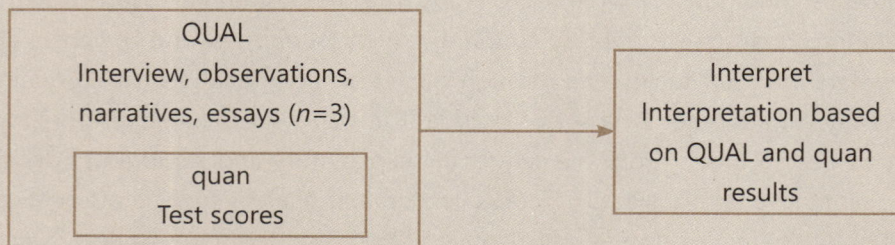

The weight in this design is given to the predominant method, quantitative or qualitative, that guides the project (Creswell et al., 2003) and within which another method is embedded. The mixing of the quantitative and qualitative data occurs either at the data analysis stage if the data is collected concurrently (like in the triangulation design), or at the interpretation stage if the two types of data are collected sequentially (like in the explanatory and exploratory designs). The quantitative and qualitative data analysis in this design is conducted separately because they seek to answer different research questions. Depending on the timing of the data collection, the structure of the report could follow either a sequential or concurrent design model.

The main advantage of the embedded design is that a researcher builds the study on a design that is well known (for example, a case study). Another advantage is that a researcher can collect the two types of data at the same time. However, it might sometimes be challenging to integrate the quantitative and qualitative results because the two methods are used to answer different research questions. Nevertheless, due to the nature of the questions, researchers can present the two sets of results separately.

▌• Task

Group work: Discuss the following questions in groups.

1) What are the four major mixed methods research designs? Explain each using your own words.

2) How do researchers decide which of the four designs to use? What characteristics should they consider?

▶ Reasons for using mixed methods approach

Creswell et al. (2003) identified four main reasons for combining quantitative and qualitative methods within one study. Each of these objectives is addressed by a specific mixed methods design discussed above:

- Explain or elaborate on quantitative results with subsequent qualitative data (the explanatory design).
- Use qualitative data to develop a new measurement instrument or theory that is subsequently tested (the exploratory design).
- Compare quantitative and qualitative data sets to produce well-validated conclusions (the triangulation design).
- Enhance a study with a supplemental data set, either quantitative or qualitative (the embedded design).

Li and Qin's (2006) use of a mixed methods approach to study the relationship between Chinese students' learning styles and learning strategies to English language learning success

- Using both quantitative and qualitative research approaches help them to obtain an overall picture of the learning style distributions of the students and the relationship between learning styles and learning strategies.

- Collecting and analyzing both quantitative and qualitative data gave them an opportunity to gain in-depth understanding of the trends and patterns in such relationships. They pursued the first objective outlined by Creswell et al. (2003)—to explain or elaborate on the initial quantitative results with subsequent qualitative data.

> • Specifically, they collected quantitative data to get an overall picture of the students' learning style distributions and the relationship of learning styles to learning strategies, while the qualitative interview data helped them explore the significant quantitative results to gain greater insights into the differences of using learning strategies by high and low achievers. (Ivankova & Creswell, 2009, p. 145)

▌• Task

Group work: Discuss the following questions in small groups.

1) Why do researchers choose to use mixed methods research approach?

2) What advantages does it offer?

11.2 Designing and Conducting a Mixed Methods Study

For student researchers, while designing and conducting a mixed methods study, it is useful to follow a set of logical steps. The following are eight basic research steps, which can also be used to evaluate mixed methods studies conducted by other researchers. This part is mainly adapted from "Mixed Methods" in *Qualitative Research in Applied Linguistics: A Practical Introduction* (Ivankova & Creswell, 2009, pp. 145–153).

The eight steps are described and illustrated below with Li and Qin's (2006) mixed methods study. They include

- determining if a mixed methods approach is the best;
- selecting a specific mixed methods design;
- writing a detailed mixed methods purpose statement;
- writing specific research questions;
- choosing the quantitative and qualitative data to collect;
- drawing a visual diagram of the procedures in your study;
- collecting and analyzing the quantitative and qualitative data; and
- writing the final report reflecting the mixed methods design used in the study.

Their order does not necessarily follow the logic of typical approaches to designing a study, but, in the end, the major aspects of design will be addressed. In this approach, the selection of a research design is completed early in the process, and this selection, in turn, informs many other aspects needed to design the study.

▶ Step 1. Determining if a mixed methods approach is the best

As mentioned earlier, for most research topics you can choose a qualitative, quantitative or mixed methods approach. Which type you choose depends on, among other things, whether you're taking an inductive vs deductive research approach; your research question(s); whether you're doing experimental, correlational, or descriptive research; and practical considerations such as time, money, availability of data, and access to respondents.

You need to decide if a mixed methods approach is the best choice for your study. Here are some questions to guide your decision:

- Would quantitative or qualitative data alone provide too limited an understanding of the research problem?
- Would the use of both quantitative and qualitative data enhance understanding?
- Are there advantages in having both a large sample representative of the population (quantitative data) and the views or experiences of selected individuals (qualitative data)?
- On the practical side, do you have the knowledge and skills necessary to conduct both quantitative and qualitative research?
- Is there enough time for collecting both types of data?

If you can answer "yes" to all of these questions, then a mixed methods approach would be better for your study than using a single method. From here, you need to clarify your rationale for choosing this approach. What is the specific purpose for using mixed methods research? Will it help you gain in-depth understanding of trends and patterns, develop a new measurement instrument, or produce well-validated conclusions?

> In Li and Qin's study, they expected that the quantitative data would help them get an overall picture of the learning style distributions of the participants and the relation of learning styles to learning strategies. Then, significant quantitative results could be explored through qualitative interviews to gain greater insights into the differences of learning strategy use between high and low achievers. Thus, the rationale for using mixed methods was that the qualitative findings were anticipated to help explain the results of the quantitative investigation.

▶ Step 2. Selecting a specific mixed methods design

Once you have decided that mixed methods research is the right approach, you must next determine which mixed methods design is the most appropriate for your study—explanatory, exploratory, triangulation, or embedded.

Think again about the purpose of the study and the rationale for using a mixed methods approach. Also, consider the timing of the quantitative and qualitative data collection and analysis, the weight given to quantitative and qualitative data sets in the study, and the stage in the research process where mixing or integration of the quantitative and qualitative aspects of the study would occur.

> Li and Qin used the explanatory design because the purpose of their study was to obtain a general picture of the relationship between learning styles and language strategies of foreign language learners, and then use the qualitative findings to obtain a more in-depth understanding.

The quantitative and qualitative data were collected and analyzed in two sequential stages, in which the qualitative phase was built on the quantitative through purposeful sampling. The weight was given to the quantitative data, and the two methods were connected after the quantitative data analysis was completed and the participants for the follow up qualitative interviews were selected.

▌• Task

Individual work: Based on the research topic and research questions you have chosen, consider and select the type of mixed methods design you would use in your project by referring to the mixed methods research design section.

▶ Step 3. Writing a detailed mixed methods purpose statement

Getting focused is an important part of the process of research in general. A mixed methods purpose statement can help you do that. It typically consists of three sentences and includes the overall purpose of the study and the purpose of each quantitative and qualitative component. It should also indicate the site and sample for each phase.

Model for purpose statement

Use the following sample script to assist in writing a purpose statement—fill in the information that applies to the study in the space between the parentheses (Ivankova, Creswell, & Plano Clark, 2007):

The purpose of this (*explanatory/exploratory/triangulation/embedded*) mixed methods study is to (*state the overall intent and the reason for collecting both types of data for this study*). The goal of the quantitative phase of the study is to (*state the purpose of the quantitative aspect of the study; indicate independent and dependent variables, instruments, participants, and site*). The goal of the qualitative phase of the study is to (*state the purpose of the qualitative aspect of the study; indicate the central phenomenon, type of data, participants, and site*).

For Li and Qin's study, the purpose statement can be written like this:

The purpose of this explanatory mixed methods study is to examine the relationship between learning styles and learning strategies of foreign language learners in China. The goal of the quantitative phase of the study is to obtain an overall picture of the learning style distributions of 187 Chinese tertiary-level English learners and the relationship of learning styles to learning strategies. The goal of the qualitative phase of the study is to more deeply explore the differences of learning strategy use between high and low achievers of the same learning style through individual interviews with six purposefully selected participants.

▶ Step 4. Writing specific research questions

Next you need to write up the specific questions that you are going to investigate. Specific research questions should be developed for both quantitative and qualitative aspects of the study.

- When writing the quantitative research questions or hypotheses, it is necessary to specify independent and dependent variables and focus on their relationship.

- When writing the qualitative research questions, it is necessary to indicate the central phenomenon that is to be explored.

- Developing a mixed methods research question that spans both quantitative and qualitative data collection and that reflects the rationale for choosing a specific mixed methods design.

> In Li and Qin's study, research questions for the quantitative and qualitative phases of the study were not specified; instead they listed three research questions which follow the quantitative-qualitative pattern of the explanatory design:
>
> - What are the learning style distributions of the Chinese tertiary-level English learners? (quantitative)
> - How do learning styles affect the use of learning strategies of tertiary-level English learners in China? (quantitative)
> - What differences relating to learning strategy deployment exist between high and low achievers of the same learning styles? (qualitative)
>
> These three questions are clear and focused, but they could add an overall mixed methods research question to emphasize the explanatory design of the study, such as: how do the qualitative findings explain the statistical results obtained in the quantitative phase about the relationship between learning styles and language strategies of foreign language learners?

▌• Task

♦Research topic and research questions for the mixed methods research

1. Individual work: Read the following example about a mixed methods study using podcast in English learning. Select a topic that is interesting to you and is also suitable for employing both qualitative and quantitative research. Do some preliminary readings of relevant research, formulating your research questions and describing your methodology. Finally, write each element, as illustrated in the example.

Topic: Using podcasts for learning English: perceptions of the Secondary ESL students in Hong kong of China*

Purpose statement: Previous research has seldom been carried out in Asia, and podcasting is still a very new technology in Hong Kong of China. This research investigates the Hong Kong ESL podcasting in our teaching.

Research questions: To study the students' perceptions of using podcasts, three questions were set as the main components of this research:

- What are Chinese Hong Kong students' attitudes towards podcasts?
- Do the students agree that podcasts are a useful tool in language learning?
- Are there any problems that are encountered by the students while using podcasts?

Research methodology

A case study approach was employed, which aims at providing a more subjective and interpretive stance in the education field (Gall et al. 1996; Johnson 1992; Stake 1994, 1995). Interviews and questionnaires are also undertaken for deeper investigation. Chappelle and Duff (2003) agreed that these instruments provide in-depth data which help in understanding the perceptions of students. Students' perceptions are reported individually in each case. Corresponding quotes from the interview transcripts and the journals are used to support the findings. Furthermore, the questionnaires are summarized and analyzed as statistical data.

2. Group work: Present your writing in small group, trying to give each other feedback and suggestions as to how to revise or improve each element.

▶ Step 5. Choosing the quantitative and qualitative data to collect

Your research questions should guide the decision about the types of quantitative and qualitative data to collect in the study; it is important to choose the types of data that will best answer the study research questions and that are not too difficult to collect.

Types of data collection

- Quantitative data collecting can include closed-response questionnaire items, test scores, checklists, and records.
- Typical qualitative data collection methods include open-response questionnaires, individual and focus group interviews, observations, and artifact analysis (documents and objects).

---

*The illustration is based on an undergraduate research paper by Li, H. C. (2010), "Using podcasts for learning English: perceptions of China's Hong Kong Secondary 6 ESL students" in *Début: the Undergraduate Journal of Languages, Linguistics and Area Studies*, 1(2), 78–90.

Quantitative and qualitative data can be collected using various methods. It is important to use a data collection method that will help answer your research question(s).

Weight of the data sets

At this stage in the process, it is important to decide on the weight that the quantitative and qualitative data sets will have in the overall study design. Where will your emphasis be?

Type and size of sample

Additional things to think about are the type and size of sample needed for each phase of the study.

- Quantitative research often requires a large random sampling to allow for the generalization of the study results to a wider population.

- Alternatively, qualitative research generally uses a small purposeful sampling to promote an in-depth understanding of the explored phenomenon.

- In a mixed methods study, it is typical to select both quantitative and qualitative samples from the same population. For example, all students in a class may be surveyed, and then a few of those students interviewed to investigate typical or extreme cases revealed in the survey findings.

Li and Qin's quantitative research questions, "What are the learning style distributions of the Chinese tertiary-level English learners?" and "How do learning styles affect the use of learning strategies of tertiary-level English learners in China?," led them to ask their 187 second-year undergraduate participants to complete the Myers-Briggs Type Indicator, Measure of Learning Styles, and a self-developed questionnaire on the use of learning strategies.

In addition, they used the scores on the final English tests as indicators of students' language learning outcomes. To answer the qualitative research question, "What differences relating to learning strategy deployment exist between high and low achievers of the same learning styles?" and to gain the students' perspectives, they interviewed six of the 187 participants, selecting three students from the top group and three others from the bottom group.

▐• Task

♦Data collection method

1. Individual work: Based on your own research questions, start collecting types of data for your research, using the samples given below as reference if necessary.

2. Group work: In a small group, discuss the samples below, and share your understanding of data collection based on your reading and your own research.

Sample 1: Data Collection*

Research questions

This study aims to overcome the inadequacies in the research design in most English-Chinese comparative textual studies. Its research questions are:

1. To what extent do Chinese university students employ thesis statement and topic sentences in their English and Chinese writing? If their writing contains thesis statement and/or topic sentence(s), where do they locate them?

2. To what extent do English university students employ a thesis statement and/or topic sentence(s) in their English writing? Where are any thesis statements or topic sentences located?

3. Are there any differences or similarities between Chinese and English university students in their uses of thesis statement and/or topic sentence(s)?

Method

Data collection

Three groups of university undergraduates participated in the study:

1. Thirty-one British university native English-speaking undergraduates who were specializing in English language and literature, politics, history or law.

2. Eighteen Chinese university Chinese-speaking undergraduates majoring in Chinese language and literature, economics or journalism.

3. Thirty-two Chinese university third-year English-majors.

In order to ensure that the texts produced by groups 1 and 2 were produced by competent L1 writers, they were assessed by two English and Chinese native-speaking linguists respectively. Eventually, 10 good English texts by native English-speaking students (hereafter known as EE) and 10 good Chinese texts by native Chinese-speaking students (CC) were chosen. They serve as the baseline reference data for English and Chinese writing respectively. Group 3 students wrote in English first (CEE) and then in Chinese (CEC) after a five-month interval. This was to reduce the possible translation effect between the two writing tasks. In order to reveal potential interaction between writing performance and the use of structural features, a high- and low-rated division of CEE and CEC texts was adopted. Two experienced

---

*The following excerpt is taken from the Method section of a research paper "A multidimensional comparison of discourse organization in English and Chinese university students' argumentative writing" by Xinghua Liu, published in *International Journal of Applied Linguistics*, Vol. 24, No. 1, 2014.

Chinese ELT staff evaluated CEE according to the official rating rubric for the National Test for English-majors Band 4 (TEM4) (NACFLT 2004) which is mainly concerned with expression and communication of main ideas, organization, coherence, logic, and supporting details, and eventually six high- and six low-rated CEE texts were identified (hereafter known as CEE-H and CEE-L respectively). Two Chinese linguists rated CEC according to the official rating rubric for Chinese writing in the National College Entrance Examination (NEEA 2008) which is mainly concerned with presentation of the theme/topic, richness of supporting details, organization, coherence and originality, and eventually seven high- and seven low-rated CEC texts were identified (hereafter known as CEC-H and CEC-L respectively).

All participants wrote an argumentative essay in response to the same topic on the role of Internet and online information. The writing instructions were given in the language of the task (See Appendix A). After the writing task, all participants were asked to fill in one writing experience questionnaire based upon Liebman (1992), Phung (2006) and Uysal (2008) (See Appendix B for a relevant excerpt); eight Chinese university English-majors were randomly chosen to attend an interview about what they have just written while EE and CC students answered the same questions in the format of the questionnaire rather than interview due to logistic constraints.

Appendix A: writing instructions

English writing prompt:

Some people say that the Internet provides people with a lot of information and much convenience. Others think access to so much information creates problems and brings potential troubles. What is your opinion? You are given 40 minutes to write a 250/500-word argumentative essay with specific reasons and examples to support your opinion.

Chinese writing prompt:

有人认为网络给人们提供大量的资讯，带来便利，也有人认为接触这么大量的信息会带来很多麻烦和潜在问题。您的看法呢？请用 40 分钟就这个现象写一篇 250/500 字左右的议论文，用具体的例子和推理来支持您的观点。

Appendix B: writing experience questionnaire (excerpt)

Note: For the sake of better understanding, the questionnaire was given in Chinese for Chinese-speaking university participants.

Part 1: writing experience at university

8. For argumentative writing, which of these things do you think that your teachers emphasize (tick as many as apply)

a. beauty of language [ ]
b. clarity of main idea [ ]
c. correct grammar and spelling [ ]
d. expressing your true feelings honestly [ ]
e. length of the paper [ ]
f. neatness and handwriting [ ]
g. creativity and imagination [ ]
h. truth of your ideas [ ]
i. topic sentence in each paragraph [ ]
j. thesis statement [ ]
k. using personal examples [ ]
l. referring to past histories and past/current events [ ]
m. quoting experts/important names and using other sources [ ]
n. directly arguing the opposition's points [ ]
o. using good logical examples and details to illustrate main ideas [ ]
p. others (please specify)_____[ ]

9. Which three things from the above list were emphasized the most?
   most important _____   second most important _____   third most important _____

Part 2: English writing knowledge and skills

1. What do you think makes a good English argumentative writing? Please explain.

Sample 2: Instruments*

Denzin (1978) discusses methodological triangulation, which is using more than one method to gather data to increase the credibility and validity of the results. In this study, three types of instruments are used—interviews, journal writing and questionnaires. The interview is divided into two parts: the pre-research period (Table 1) and post-research period (Table 2). The first interview is a structured interview with five questions. It mainly focuses on the interviewees' perceptions of using new technology in learning English.

---

*The excerpt is taken from Li's paper (2010) as cited on p.184.

Table 1   Pre-research interview questions

No.	Questions
1	Are you interested in using new technology?
2	Do you have an iPod?
3	Have you ever heard of podcasting?
4	Do you enjoy learning English?
5	Would you like to use a new technology to learn English?

Table 2   Post-research interview questions

No.	Questions
1	Do you like podcasts? Why?
2	Do you think podcasts are a useful tool in language learning? Why?
3	Are there any problems that you have encountered while you are listening to the podcast? What did you do?

Straightforward answers can be obtained from the structured interview (Wallace 1998) so I could determine whether the interviewee was willing to participate in the research. The second interview is semi-structured. Questions focus on the three objectives of this research.

Follow-up questions are also asked, so that the answers of the students can be interpreted more accurately. All questions are asked in English and the students can respond in Chinese. This allows them to share more complex ideas in their mother tongue. The quotes of the conversations are translated in the discussion of this article.

The second instrument was a journal (Table 3). It is used each week during the experimental period. Students were required to write a journal each week to show their participation in the podcasting activity. Brock et al. (1992) argue that journals can show the hidden affective variables that greatly influence the way students learn. During the experimental period, students are given feedback by the researcher on their journal entries (i.e. which programme is suitable for them to listen to), and hence their participation can be enhanced.

Table 3   Questions for journal entries

No.	Questions
1	Which podcast have you chosen this week? Why?
2	Do you enjoy listening to the podcast? Is there any problem? Why?
3	Has this podcast enhanced your interest in learning English? Why?

A questionnaire was used to collect the students' rating on the use of podcasting, which can also provide statistical data (Meyers and Well 1995). Within the questionnaire (Table 4), 13 questions are included. Some of the questions are either sharing the same meaning (e.g. 2 and 10) or contradicting each other (e.g. 6 and 13). This helps to control the accuracy of the data. This is particularly useful for distinguishing whether the participants are answering the questions thoughtfully or just randomly.

**Table 4   Questionnaire: Students' rating of their use of podcasts
put a tick in the appropriate box in each statement**

No.	Statements	Strongly disagree	Disagree	Fair	Agree	Strongly agree
1	I enjoy listening to podcasts					
2	I don't know how to handle this new technology					
3	Podcasts are difficult					
4	Podcasts are useful for language learning					
5	Podcasts bring me no fun at all					
6	I will not listen to podcasts again after this research					
7	I think podcasts help me a lot in language learning					
8	Podcasts are easy to handle					
9	I don't think podcasts are interesting					
10	Podcasts are too new to me					
11	The content of podcasts is not suitable for us					
12	I like listening to podcasts					
13	I will listen to podcasts in future					

▶ Step 6. Drawing a visual diagram of the procedures in your study

Since mixed methods studies are often complicated with multiple stages of data collection and analysis, it can be useful to create a visual diagram of all the procedures in your study.

- A visual diagram helps you envisage the big picture, so you can see the flow and timing of the quantitative and qualitative data collection, the weight given to the quantitative and qualitative data and where the mixing of the two methods will occur within a study.

- Including the visual diagram in a research report also helps the readers understand the study for specific rules for drawing mixed methods visual models.

A visual model of the explanatory design used in Li and Qin's study can be developed, as shown in the figure below.

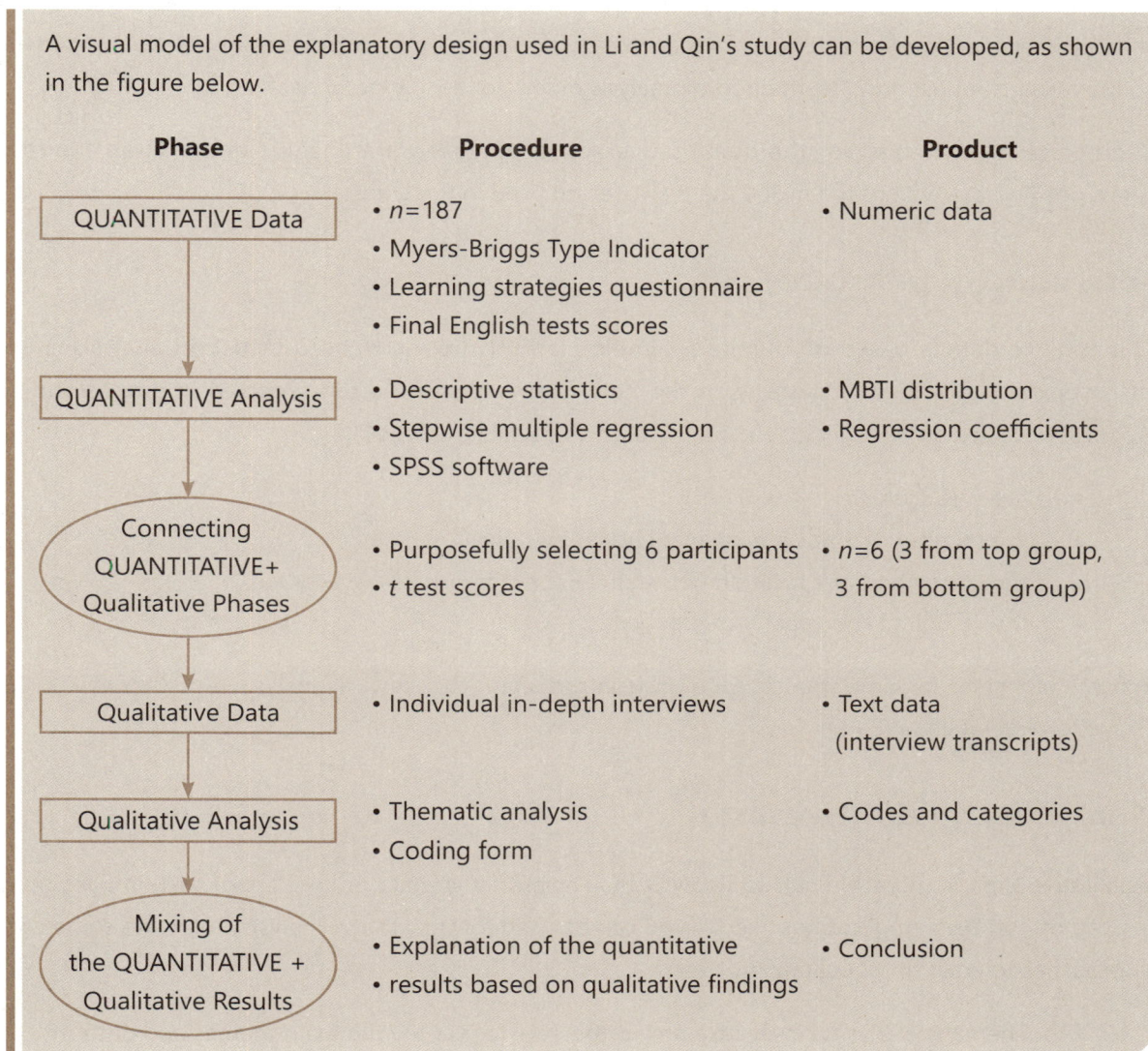

Phase	Procedure	Product
QUANTITATIVE Data	• $n=187$ • Myers-Briggs Type Indicator • Learning strategies questionnaire • Final English tests scores	• Numeric data
QUANTITATIVE Analysis	• Descriptive statistics • Stepwise multiple regression • SPSS software	• MBTI distribution • Regression coefficients
Connecting QUANTITATIVE+ Qualitative Phases	• Purposefully selecting 6 participants • t test scores	• $n=6$ (3 from top group, 3 from bottom group)
Qualitative Data	• Individual in-depth interviews	• Text data (interview transcripts)
Qualitative Analysis	• Thematic analysis • Coding form	• Codes and categories
Mixing of the QUANTITATIVE + Qualitative Results	• Explanation of the quantitative • results based on qualitative findings	• Conclusion

▐• Task

♦ Drawing a visual diagram

1. Individual work: Now, examine your own research design and process, trying to draw a visual diagram for your research project.

2. Group work: In small groups, work together to draw visual diagrams for the two sample studies presented in the previous sections. If there is any problem or difficulty encountered, discuss together the reasons and possible solutions.

▶ Step 7. Analyzing the quantitative and qualitative data

After the data is collected, you need to organize it into files to prepare for analysis. You should follow the basic procedures specified for each type of data, quantitative and qualitative. Quantitative or qualitative data by itself can't prove or demonstrate anything, but has to be analyzed to show its meaning in relation to the research questions. The method of analysis differs for each type of data.

The choice of strategies for the quantitative and qualitative data analysis depends on the research questions and the type of the mixed methods design used in the study.

Analyzing quantitative data

Quantitative data is based on numbers. Simple math or more advanced statistical analysis is used to discover commonalities or patterns in the data. The results are often reported in graphs and tables. Applications such as Excel, SPSS, etc. can be used to calculate things like

- average scores;
- the number of times a particular answer was given;
- the correlation or causation between two or more variables; and
- the reliability and validity of the results.

You can also refer to some sources for a basic introduction to statistical analysis, e.g., Creswell (2008) and Gravetter and Wallnau (2007).

Analyzing qualitative data

Qualitative data is more difficult to analyze than quantitative data. It consists of text, images or videos instead of numbers. Applications like NVivo8 can be used for qualitative analysis. There are some common approaches to analyzing qualitative data:

- Thematic analysis: closely examining the data to identify the main themes and patterns
- Content analysis: tracking the occurrence, position and meaning of words or phrases
- Discourse analysis: studying how communication works in social contexts

Please also see relevant sections in other parts of this book, or refer to "Organizing and Interpreting Data" section in some sources available to you.

Note that both quantitative and qualitative programs operate on different principles and require time to learn. Depending on the type of the mixed methods design, consider choosing one or more of the data analysis strategies discussed earlier within each design:

Data analysis in Li and Qin's study

- The quantitative analysis included descriptive statistics for the Myers-Briggs Type Indicator distributions of the participants and the stepwise multiple regression analysis for the examination of the relationship between learning styles and learning strategies. The stepwise regression analysis was aimed at revealing whether a learning style can be a significant predictor of the learning strategy choice.

- The qualitative data from individual interviews was analyzed using a specific coding form.

- Then the results of learning styles and learning strategies obtained from the qualitative data were compared against the participants' quantitative results for consistency.

Sample 3: Data Analysis*

Analysis of data 1: thesis statement

Native control groups' comparison between EE and CC

Figure 1 shows that both EE and CC texts all contained explicit thesis statements, which means that both EE and CC writers all stated their opinions on the topical issue in an explicit manner. In the questionnaire responses, 90% of EE and 100% of CC students reported that their teachers emphasized the importance of maintaining a clear main idea for argumentative writing. In addition, all CC students reported that a good piece of Chinese argumentative writing needs to have an explicit thesis statement. This all suggests that the requirement for an explicit statement of thesis in argumentative writing is well established among these English and Chinese students.

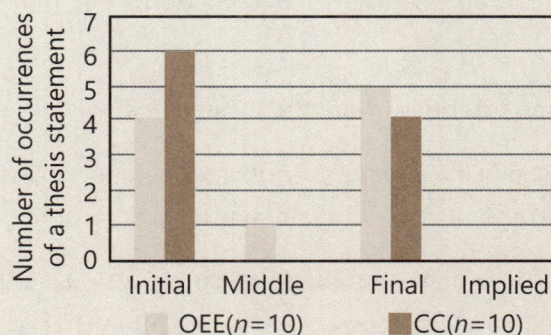

Figure 1   Placement of thesis statement in EE and CC texts

---

*The following excerpt is part of data analysis adapted from the research paper about English and Chinese students' argumentative writing mentioned in the earlier section. Study the sample and think about how you will write the data analysis for your project.

Figure 1 also shows an initial placement of the thesis statement in four EE and six CC texts (out of 10 texts in both cases) which means that, in this small sample, more CC students preferred a deductive style while the same number of EE students favored an inductive one. This finding is fundamentally different from the premise held by traditional contrastive rhetoric studies that English writing is deductive and direct while Chinese is inductive and indirect (Kaplan, 1966; Matalene, 1985). The result is also largely contrary to most English-Chinese contrastive rhetoric studies which have normally found that native English writers' English writing is more direct/deductive than native Chinese-speakers' Chinese writing. For example, Yang and Cahill (2008) found that, though both American and Chinese university students favoured a direct text organization, the American group's English writing was significantly more direct than the Chinese group's Chinese writing. In another study, Xing et al.(2008) found that native English-speaking university lecturers were more likely to put the thesis in an initial position in their English writing than Chinese university Chinese majors in their Chinese writing.

These seemingly conflicting results actually indicate the dynamic nature of writing practices and thus challenge any static and essentialist view of rhetorical practice in different languages and cultures. An examination of writing instruction materials in English and Chinese shows that the placement of a thesis statement is flexible and can be anywhere. According to Lin (2007), 中心论点 (Zhongxin Lundian, a central point) or thesis statement can be placed at any point in a text, such as the beginning, the conclusion, in the title or in the transition paragraphs. Lin (2007) also points out that the most often used method is to locate the thesis statement at the beginning to catch readers' attention. Though it has been widely acknowledged that English writing values an initial explicit statement of thesis (Silverman et al. 2004), this does not mean that an initial placement is the only choice for English writing. For example, in a university-level writing guidebook, Silverman et al. (2004: 67) suggest that the most important principle in positioning a thesis statement is to achieve "the most impact" and it is therefore perfectly acceptable to put the thesis statement at the end of a piece of writing and let the essay build up to this thesis.

Analysis of questionnaire and interview data: the influence of writing experience

Together with above mentioned questionnaire data, this study found that students' writing experience shapes both the way they perceive discourse organization and their writing practices.

The following excerpts are representative answers given by EE, CC and CEE students. In the following excerpts, Q stands for Question, S for students, and R for the researcher.

Q: Why did you organize the text structure in this way?
S: I was taught at school (both primary and secondary) that a piece of writing should have a strong introduction, a strong argument which covers both positive and negative points (in order to create a fair argument overall) and a definite conclusion.
(EE7, questionnaire answer)

R: Why did you organize the text structure in this way?

S: I feel this is just an ordinary general-specific-general format. The first paragraph is the general statement; the central two paragraphs present the specific information and then the last paragraph concludes with general statement.

R: Is there any significance for this kind of arrangement?

S: This is a routine format and looks like argumentative writing.

R: How did you learn to write in this way?

S: Teachers taught this format ... in the high school ... there is not a Chinese course in the college ... Kai Men Jian Shan (Open the door and see the mountain), Hua Long Dian Jing (bringing the painted dragon to life by adding the pupils of its eyes) ... giving readers the impression of being clear and straightforward.

(CC2, interview data)

As the above responses illustrate, qualitative data showed most participants reported that

- their English/Chinese teachers emphasized the importance of employing appropriate organization;
- for a good piece of argumentative writing, a clear and logical structure is essential; and
- they brainstormed the overall structure before they started writing.

▶ Task

♦ **Data analysis**

1. Individual work: Based on what you have learned from this section as well as from the above sample, try analyzing your data, both qualitative and quantitative. Then, by combining the individual parts you have done so far, try to write up your whole research project, including the major sections of Introduction, Literature Review, Methodology, and Results and Analysis, or you can make any change in this organizational, depending on the content and structure of your paper.

2. Classwork/Group work: Present your draft project in class or small groups, obtaining any feedback or comment from your peers or instructor, and then revise or edit your work.

▶ Step 8. Writing the final report reflecting the mixed methods design used in the study

The last step in any research study is writing up the report. The structure of your report should follow the type of the mixed methods design used. You should be careful to make clear distinctions between the quantitative and qualitative phases of your study, and indicate their weighting.

Depending on the sequential or concurrent timing of the data collection and analysis in the study, the procedures and the results should be reported differently.

Reporting the procedures and results

- In the explanatory, exploratory, and sometimes embedded designs, where the quantitative and qualitative data sets are collected and analyzed one following another, the procedures should be reported in different sections to emphasize the sequential order and the connections between the phases.

- In the triangulation, and sometimes the embedded designs, the procedures should be reported jointly to show the convergence of the two methods.

- The findings from the quantitative and qualitative components of the study should also be compared and interpreted in the Discussion section of the report.

Organizing various sections of a report

- More specifically, **the structure of an explanatory or exploratory design report** typically follows the sequential character of the design: the initial data (quantitative or qualitative) collection and analysis is described first, followed by the description of the further qualitative or the quantitative data collection and analysis. A separate section in the report discusses how the two phases were connected in the research process—for example, selecting follow-up cases in the explanatory design or developing a survey instrument in the exploratory design. The discussion of the study results explains how the qualitative findings helped elaborate or extend the quantitative results in the explanatory design, or how the qualitative findings lead to the quantitative results in the exploratory design.

- **In the report of a triangulation design study**, quantitative and qualitative data collection, analysis, and results are presented in separate sections. During the discussion of the overall study results, a researcher combines the interpretation of the quantitative and qualitative findings to see whether they support each other or diverge.

- **The structure of an embedded design study report** could follow either a sequential (the explanatory design) or concurrent (the triangulation design) design model depending on the timing of the data collection.

> The reporting structure in Li and Qin's study is consistent with the sequential nature of the explanatory design. First the quantitative procedures, including the description of the sample, data collection, and analysis, are presented; they are followed by a similar description of the qualitative procedures. The results are also presented in a sequential manner: first the results from the statistical tests are reported and then the findings from the individual interviews are provided. In the conclusion, the major findings from both phases of the study are discussed and integrated.

❗ Task

Individual work: Read and write.

1) Choose a mixed methods research study in ESL writing or foreign language education from *Journal of Second Language Writing*, *Journal of English for Academic Purposes*, *Journal of English for Specific Purposes*, or relevant CSSCI journals. Read the article, paying specific attention to how the authors implemented each of the eight steps for designing and conducting a mixed methods study discussed in this unit.

2) Consider a topic of interest to you. Using the eight steps for designing and conducting a mixed methods study discussed in this unit, write a short outline explaining each step that you will take in designing and conducting your study; draw a visual diagram of the mixed methods procedures of that study.

11.3 Improving the Quality of Mixed Methods Research

Like with any research, it is important that the results of a mixed methods study are reliable and valid. To ensure the quality of results generated from the quantitative and qualitative data sets in the study, it is recommended to carefully address each component separately and to apply procedures specific to each research tradition. These procedures are well described in quantitative and qualitative research literature and are recommended by mixed methods authors as initial steps in establishing the quality of a mixed methods study (Ivankova & Creswell, 2009).

▶ Reliability and validity

The reliability and validity of the quantitative data can be assessed using different reliability measures and different types of validity. The credibility and trustworthiness of the qualitative data can be established through the use of various verification procedures. In addition, since mixed methods research produces knowledge generated from the integration of the quantitative and qualitative data, it is also necessary to ensure that such knowledge is correct and legitimized. This is not an easy task because due to the different nature of quantitative and qualitative research approaches, different quality standards are applied.

In the mixed methods studies, validity is defined as the ability of the researcher to draw meaningful and accurate conclusions from all the data in the study, quantitative and qualitative. It is recommended to address validity from the standpoint of the mixed methods design chosen for the study and consider potential threats to validity that might arise during the data collection and analysis at each study stage.

▶ Potential threats to research quality

There are some potential threats that could affect the quality of research:

- Problems associated with different sampling strategies used in quantitative and qualitative research
- Choosing weak quantitative results for qualitative follow-up
- Using inadequate procedures for data transformation

To avoid or minimize these threats and achieve accurate and meaningful results from the integration of the two data sets in a mixed methods study, a researcher needs to design and conduct the study carefully (following the suggested eight steps), systematically apply the appropriate procedures in the quantitative and qualitative components of the study, and integrate the two methods as the mixed methods design dictates.

> In Li and Qin's study, to ensure the quality of the quantitative results, they used two validated questionnaires: the Myers Briggs Type Indicator and Measure of Learning Styles. For a self-developed questionnaire on the use of learning strategies they reported reliability for both pilot testing of the instrument and its use in the study. On both occasions reliability was high (.85 and .88), which indicated the obtained numeric scores were reliable. However, they did not report whether they assessed the credibility of the qualitative findings. Some useful procedures that they could have used include member checking (letting participants verify the accuracy of the interview transcripts) and inter-coder agreement (both researchers independently coding the data and then establishing themes based on the reached consensus). They did not discuss the validity of the integrated mixed methods results either or problems associated with the use of two different data sets; however, they addressed the limitations of the study, such as drawing conclusions based on a limited and nonrepresentative sample of the introductory level second-year students. (Ivankova & Creswell, 2009, p. 154)

Sample Research

Please scan the QR code below to acquire the sample article. Read the article and think about its research methods.

Sample Article

Unit 12

Ethnography

Ethnography is a type of qualitative research that involves immersing yourself in a particular community or organization to observe their behavior and interactions up close. Although it is not the most commonly used qualitative research approach in applied linguistics, it is an approach that has some unique offerings for the field. The main purpose is to learn enough about a group to create a cultural portrait of how the people belonging to that culture live, work, and/or play together. This is achieved through fieldwork—extended observation of and engagement with participants.

Ethnography is a flexible research method that allows you to gain a deep understanding of a group's shared culture, conventions, and social dynamics. However, it also involves some practical and ethical challenges.

12.1 Introduction

▶ What is ethnography?

Ethnography is the art and science used to describe a group or culture (Fetterman, 1998). The term "ethnography" refers to both the product—the presentation of the final analysis and interpretation of the completed study—and also the research process itself. According to Angrosino (2007), ethnographers search for predictable patterns in the lived human experiences by carefully observing and participating in the lives of those under study. Ethnography may also involve a full immersion of the researcher in the day-to-day lives or culture of those under study.

Ethnographic research originated in the field of anthropology. It finds its roots in anthropological work conducted in the early half of the twentieth century by researchers such as Bronisław Malinowski, Margaret Mead, and E. E. Evans-Pritchard. It often involved an anthropologist living with an isolated tribal community for an extended period of time in order to understand their culture. This type of research could sometimes last for years.

Although ethnography was begun by anthropologists, it did not take long for the use of the approach to be adopted by researchers in many other disciplines such as sociology, health, business, and education. Over time, the "classical" form of ethnography has metamorphosed, and today there are a wide variety of ethnographic forms, including critical ethnography, feminist ethnography, focused ethnography, confessional ethnography, autoethnography, and in the Internet age, virtual ethnography (Heigham &

Sakui, 2009).

In the field of applied linguistics, a commonly cited definition is "the study of people's behavior in naturally occurring, ongoing settings, with a focus on the cultural interpretation of behavior" (Watson-Gegeo, 1988, p. 576). Through ethnographic studies, researchers look at cultures for "what people do (behaviors), what they say (language), the potential tension between what they do and ought to do, and what they make and use, such as artifacts" (Spradley, 1980, qtd. in Creswell, 2007, p. 71), which include standardized test scores, photos, handouts, and surveys.

In brief, the use of ethnographic approaches has been encouraged by what has been called the "social turn" in language study which has led to the desire to develop in-depth understandings of language learning and teaching events in the specific (and frequently unequal) social contexts within which they are taking place. The combination of long-term observation and the collection of diverse forms of data provide understandings of participants' perspectives and meaning-making practices within the complex sociocultural worlds they inhabit that more traditional methodologies may not have succeeded in capturing.

▶ Key terms in ethnographic research

Culture

In order to fully understand ethnography, we need to take a closer look at a key term—culture—an understanding of which is crucial to appreciate this rich research tradition.

> Culture is an abstract concept used to account for the beliefs, values, and behaviors of cohesive groups of people. It is a narrower term than race (which accounts for biological variation); a racial group may contain many different cultures, and a cultural group may contain members of different races. Although cultural group may refer to a particular nationality, cultures may cross political boundaries and a nation may contain many cultural groups ... Within a cultural group, behaviors are patterned and values and meanings are shared. (Richards & Morse, 2007, p. 53)

Ethnographic research allows researchers to explore how people create, sustain, change, and pass on their shared values, beliefs, and behavior—in essence, their culture. It draws on an interpretive approach where "the researcher's intent ... is to make sense (or interpret) the meanings others have about the world" (Creswell, 2007, p. 21), meanings usually unexamined by these people themselves. Research topics are necessarily fairly broad because researchers usually choose ethnographic approaches when "the social issue or behaviors are not yet clearly understood" (Angrosino, 2007, p. 26), and they are looking for focus. The aim of ethnographers is to painstakingly develop an understanding of the particular cultural worlds which people build and live in and explain them to people outside those worlds.

Group

Since ethnography has a strong focus on culture, and culture only exists in groups, it is groups rather than single individuals that are studied in ethnography. However, the conception of "group" has evolved in recent years. When this research tradition began, ethnographers typically went into "exotic" or "uncivilized" cultures where the groups were considered "others"; the others typically spoke the same language as each other or lived in the same region, usually distantly located and little known by the researchers' culture.

Today, although some ethnographers continue to study such unknown cultures, more and more they are staying home and studying cultures closer to their own. In addition, it is now recognized that culture exists even in much smaller groups, such as organizations, industries, gangs, and schools—all of which are contexts ethnographers could investigate. In this shift from the unknown to the known, ethnography lost its defining feature as the study of "others," or at least others who differed dramatically from the ethnographer (Wolcott, 2008).

Location

Traditional ethnography typically focuses on location, not issues. Ethnographers choose to explore a group living in a particular place, with the aim of building a cultural portrait of the group found there. Such studies are exemplified by researchers entering the field with no preconceived focus and staying there for an extended period of time, allowing a comprehensive description of the culture to be developed (Richards & Morse, 2007).

Other ethnographic forms are quite different from traditional ethnographies. For example, in focused ethnography the focal point of the research is typically on an issue about which researchers may mold a guiding question before the study begins (Richards & Morse, 2007). With critical ethnography, researchers aim to go beyond rich cultural description to promoting change. Such nontraditional studies are often conducted in small cultures such as organizations or institutions. The group studied may be a sample of participants who share a particular feature, but not necessarily the same location, such as a group brought together in an online chat room (Angrosino, 2007). In such a situation, the researcher focuses on the common behaviors, experiences, or identities shared by the group in order to reveal the culture the people share.

▶ Topics or issues in applied linguistics

In the field of applied linguistics, there are types of topics or issues ethnographers might investigate. They might choose to study something like development of learning communities in a writing center, or relationships between native-English-speaking teachers and nonnative-English-speaking teachers in Chinese universities.

Notice that these topics are not well-defined research questions. Rather they are topics that a researcher cannot clearly understand and hopes to gain clarity of through research. The research in the latter case would likely take place in a narrowly defined site in Japan, and the participants would include native and nonnative-English-speaking teachers. The researchers might be interested in investigating the impact of administrative decisions on teachers' practices in the classroom, so the administrative staff might also become research participants.

Today, applied linguistics is almost by definition interdisciplinary, and a number of applied linguists are now working collaboratively with colleagues in fields such as health, the workplace, organizations of various types, the justice system and education broadly defined, carrying out ethnographic work on the communication practices at these sites.

▶ Characteristics of ethnography

Ethnography as a method has certain distinctive characteristics (Angrosino, 2007).

First, it is conducted on-site or in a naturalistic setting in which real people live.

Second, it is personalized since you as the researcher are both observer and participant in the lives of those people.

Third, ethnography also collects data in multiple ways for triangulation over an extended period of time. The process is inductive, holistic and requires a long-term commitment from you.

Finally, ethnography is dialogic since conclusions and interpretations formed through it can be given comments or feedback from those who are under study.

12.2 Uses of Ethnography in Applied Linguistics

First, ethnography provides the detailed and profound understanding of a given culture.

Compared with other research methods, ethnographic studies are fluid and flexible; the research question employed in these studies can be dynamic, subject to constant revision, and refined as the research continues to uncover new knowledge.

Since ethnographic research is generally conducted from within a target community, it allows for the recording of behavior as it occurs instead of depending on people's reports of their past or expected behavior. Thus, the behaviors researchers observe in the field should not be significantly different from the behaviors that occur in their absence, and this authenticity can help provide an accurate depiction of a given situation or culture.

An excellent example of deep cultural insight gained through ethnographic research is that of Heath (1983). Over a ten-year period, she examined two cultural communities in the southeast of the United States, a black working class community and a white working class community. By studying how the children learned to socialize through the use of language, she revealed how black children's verbal socialization significantly disadvantaged them when they entered school, as school norms were based on white culture. To achieve the depth of cultural illumination she gained, she had to devote an extensive amount of time to study these people's practices: she observed them in daily life, listened to their stories, participated in their cultural practices, and studied their related artifacts in detail. From a wide perspective that included sociocultural and political considerations, she continued to analyze her data throughout the course of her study and allowed her discoveries to direct, and redirect, her research. By doing this, she made important contributions well beyond her field. (Heigham & Sakui, 2009, p. 95)

Within the field of applied linguistics, many ethnographic works have shed light on the diversity of various cultures in our profession. For example, in Japanese secondary schools, where young teachers from English-speaking countries such as the US, UK, and Australia are invited to work as assistant teachers; in a Sri Lankan university, where a Sri Lankan teacher from a middle-class background meets with resistance to the Western textbooks she uses; and the controversial roles that English plays in the post-colonial era in Mexico are explored.

Second, the final reports of ethnography can reach a wide audience.

Other types of research are often presented in a conventional written format, but ethnographies are presented in many different ways, including narratives, novels, dramas, and documentaries, as well as traditional research articles. In the field of applied linguistics, the abstract nature of more quantitative research reports can deter some teachers and learners. In addition, since teachers frequently find the "stories" reported in ethnographic studies accessible, those reports may be read and understood by more people. Thus, ethnography has the possibility of having greater practical influence on what teachers are doing in their classrooms (Heigham & Sakui, 2009).

Elizabeth teaches English as a Foreign Language (EFL) at a medium-sized Japanese women's university that has a self-access center (SAC) for students. The SAC is designed to promote independent learning, and it aims to facilitate the development of communicative competence through learner-learner peer interaction and the development of learning communities. Uniquely, it is staffed entirely by third- and fourth-year students who act as peer advisors (PAs), and there is a strict "English only" policy. Although Elizabeth is not the SAC coordinator, she is very interested in the center and spends quite a lot of time there. She has noticed that in some years a strong supportive community of learners develops, but in other years it does not. She wonders why this is so, given that the freshman student orientation about the SAC is standardized. She has done research projects in the past, and decides that she would like to explore this situation by doing an ethnographic study of this small SAC culture. She talks about this with the SAC coordinator and the department chair, and they support her idea. Elizabeth then gets permission from her university's ethics board to begin a two-year research project, and the department chair, who feels the success of the SAC is important for the department and understands the time commitment that ethnography requires, arranges for her to teach one less class during the project period.

From the start of the next academic year, Elizabeth begins to spend about ten hours a week in the center. She often sits in the back of the room but sometimes wanders around mingling with students, and she makes extensive field notes of what she sees and hears. To find out how students view and use the SAC, with their permission, she also interviews the SAC coordinator, the PAs, some of the current students, and some of the alumni. She collects all of the posters and learning materials the PAs create. In addition, she reviews students' Test of English for International Communication (TOEIC) scores. Throughout the two years, Elizabeth continuously analyzes and interprets the data she collects, and this continues after she finishes her data collection. Over time Elizabeth is able to compile a "cultural portrait" of the SAC that reveals how the culture develops and changes and decides to present her findings to the department. She then begins to write up a report about the research that she hopes to have published.

Elizabeth considers different types of research approaches before deciding to use ethnography. She knows that ethnographic methods are particularly useful to investigate situations that are not clearly understood, like the one in the SAC. She also knows that she needs to "see" what happens in the center as well as "hear" the opinions and views of those who work in and use it in order to gain an understanding of the culture of the SAC. Thus, ethnography seems like the best choice. (Heigham & Sakui, 2009, p. 91; p. 96)

Task

◆**Choosing your research project**

Group work:

1) Work in small groups, discussing the features of ethnographic research and sharing with each other possible research topics.

2) Think of a topic or issue you would like to investigate using an ethnographic approach, either by yourself as an individual project or in teams as a group project. What site could provide you with useful data? How might you gain entry to the site? What types of data might be useful to collect for this study? How could you go about collecting them? Can you anticipate any problems you might have collecting your data? How might you overcome those problems? Write your answers and discuss them in groups.

12.3 Advantages and Disadvantages of Ethnography

There are a number of methodologies that can be chosen for a research project. It is important for us to know the advantages of choosing ethnography over other types of methodologies or approaches.

▶ Advantages

The main advantage of ethnography is that it gives the researcher direct access to the culture and practices of a group. It is a useful approach for learning first-hand about the behavior and interactions of people within a particular context. By becoming immersed in a social environment, you may have access to more authentic information and spontaneously observe dynamics that you could not have found out about simply by asking.

Ethnography is also an open and flexible method. Rather than aiming to verify a general theory or test a hypothesis, it aims to offer a rich narrative account of a specific culture, allowing you to explore many different aspects of the group and setting.

Here is a selective list of advantages of conducting ethnography, most selected from a list provided by Wolcott (2008):

- Ethnography can be conducted entirely by one individual.
- It is longitudinal in nature, allowing you as the researcher to observe and record changes over time.
- It can be carried out almost at any place.
- It focuses on working with others rather than treating them as objects.
- It provides you with a detailed and rich database for further investigation and writing.
- You can make the research not only interesting but adventurous.
- It requires no expensive or elaborate tools or equipment.
- It may present you with an opportunity to learn and use another language.
- It draws upon your personal skills and strengths to advantage.
- You often have exclusive domain or sole responsibility in the chosen setting or site.
- Your role is recognized.
- It offers you an opportunity to integrate professional and personal life.
- It allows you to get an insider's view of reality.
- It can provide deep insightful data.
- It can be used to study marginalized groups of people closed to other forms of research.
- It allows you to collect data in a realistic or naturalistic setting in which people act naturally, focusing on both verbal and nonverbal behaviors.

▶ Disadvantages

A major aspect that we need to think about when conducting ethnographic research is when or why we should or should not conduct ethnography. If you want to use ethnographic research in your thesis or research/term paper, it's worth asking yourself whether it's the right approach:

- Could the information you need be collected in another way (e.g. a survey, interviews)?
- How difficult will it be to gain access to the community you want to study?
- How exactly will you conduct your research, and over what timespan?
- What ethical issues might arise?

If you do decide to do ethnography, it's generally best to choose a relatively small and easily accessible group, to ensure that the research is feasible within a limited timeframe. Ethnography is a time-consuming method. In order to embed yourself in the setting and gather enough observations to build up a representative picture, you can expect to spend at least a few weeks, but more likely several months. This long-term immersion can be challenging, and requires careful planning (Heigham & Sakui, 2009).

Ethnographic research can run the risk of researcher bias. Writing an ethnography involves subjective interpretation, and it can be difficult to maintain the necessary distance to analyze a group that you are embedded in.

There are often also ethical considerations to take into account: for example, about how your role is disclosed to members of the group, or about observing and reporting sensitive information.

12.4 Process of Doing Ethnographic Research

There are general activities that need to be done before getting started (Roper & Shapira, 2000). First, you need to identify your research question. Second, you need to assess how much you know about the subject area. Third, you need to meet with the gatekeepers or those who will allow or give access to you to the setting. This can be difficult if you are unknown to a setting that you would like to access. Lastly, you need to assess your time and resources. Do you have the time to conduct the study? What about your other obligations and commitments? What types of resources do you have? What types of equipment will you need? Who will fund the study? These are important questions to ask and find answers before beginning your study.

Ethnographers must develop a deep understanding of the culture they study. Conventionally, this requires doing extended fieldwork within the culture, and with an open mind observing firsthand what happens there. To uncover hidden meanings of behavior, observation is usually supplemented with interviews to learn what those in the group make of their experiences. Related artifacts are also investigated. Rich, deep description is the hallmark of ethnography, and to build it, researchers make detailed field notes, creating meticulous descriptions of the context, participants, and events they witness. They also create maps of relationships between participants and chronologies of significant events (Heigham & Sakui, 2009). As a process, ethnography is "an emergent construction" (Fitzgerald, 1997, p. 53). That is, it is expected to change and evolve throughout the research process—it does not progress in a linear fashion. But this flexibility does not indicate a lack of rigor; ethnographers enter the field with an open mind, not an empty head.

There are no prescriptive chronological "steps" that ethnographers follow; however, the flow of typical ethnographic studies is somewhat predictable. It moves something like this: after you have determined that ethnography fits the research question or issue you would like to investigate, decide what type of data you want to collect (keeping in mind this will evolve throughout your study) and where you can collect it. Once you have decided these, you select your research site(s) and arrange entry. Gaining entry usually involves working with a gatekeeper, someone like a school principal who has the power to let you in—or keep you out of—a certain location. The next step is to begin the actual data collection. You analyze your data on an ongoing basis, and finally, you complete your analysis and interpretation, and write up a report or present your findings in some other manner (Heigham & Sakui, 2009).

Singleton and Straits (2005) identified the following seven stages in ethnographic field research:

- Formulating a problem
- Selecting a research setting
- Gaining access
- Presenting yourself
- Gathering and recording information
- Analyzing data
- Writing up an ethnographic report

▶ Step 1. Formulating the problem

First, you need to identify your research question. Define the main focus of the study by formulating the problem about which you wish to learn more. This can be done by asking the question that you want to ask and not that of someone else. Talking to others about your research project and consulting different sources for ideas can be helpful.

▌• Task

♦Formulating your research questions

Individual and group work: Read the following example* first. Then based on the example, think about the problem you want to solve concerning your topic, and write at least one specific research question. Finally, talk about it with your peer or instructor.

> Finders (1996) used ethnographic procedures to document the reading of teen magazines by middle-class European American seventh-grade girls. By examining the reading of teen zines (magazines), the researcher explored how the girls perceive and construct their social roles and relationships as they enter junior high school. She asked one guiding central question in her study: How do early adolescent females read literature that falls outside the realm of fiction? (p. 72)

Finders's (1996) central question began with *how*; it used an open-ended verb (read); it focused on a single concept—the literature or teen magazines; and it mentioned the participants, adolescent females, as the culture-sharing group. Notice how the author crafted a concise, single question that needed to be answered in the study. It was a broad question to permit participants to share diverse perspectives about reading the literature.

▶ Step 2. Selecting a research setting

The first question is knowing and deciding where to begin. The setting should permit clear observation. It is also helpful to select a setting that you can readily fit in but this does not mean that you are intimately familiar with it.

---

*The example here shows how to formulate a research question in ethnography research, selected from Creswell (2014, p. 242).

Open vs closed settings

The setting of your ethnography—the environment in which you will observe your chosen community in action—may be open or closed.

An open or public setting is one with no formal barriers to entry. For example, you might consider a community of people living in a certain neighborhood, or the fans of a particular baseball team.

     ✓   Gaining initial access to open groups is not too difficult …

     ✗   …but it may be harder to become immersed in a less clearly defined group.

A closed or private setting is harder to access. This may be for example a business, a school, or a special group.

     ✓   A closed group's boundaries are clearly defined and the ethnographer can become fully immersed in the setting …

     ✗   … but gaining access is tougher; the ethnographers may have to negotiate their way in or acquire some role in the organization.

▶ Step 3. Gaining access

How do you get into a group that you wish to study? You may need to seek formal permission which can be facilitated if you have a friend who can vouch for you. You can also get your foot in the door if you first participate in the group as a volunteer and not as a researcher.

Gaining access to a community

An important consideration for ethnographers is the question of access. The difficulty of gaining access to the setting of a particular ethnography varies greatly:

- To gain access to the fans of a particular sports team, you might start by simply attending the team's games and speaking with the fans.
- To access the employees of a particular business, you might contact the management and ask for permission to perform a study there.
- Alternatively, you might perform a covert ethnography of a community or organization you are already personally involved in or employed by.

Flexibility is important here too: where it's impossible to access the desired setting, the ethnographer must consider alternatives that could provide comparable information.

For example, if you had the idea of observing the staff within a particular high technology company but could not get permission, you might look into other companies of the same kind as alternatives. Ethnography is a sensitive research method, and it may take multiple attempts to find a feasible approach.

Working with informants

All ethnographies involve the use of informants. These are people involved in the group in question who function as the researcher's primary points of contact, facilitating access and assisting their understanding of the group.

This might be someone in a high position at an organization allowing you access to their employees, or a member of a community sponsoring your entry into that community and giving advice on how to fit in.

However, if you come to rely too much on a single informant, you may be influenced by his/her perspective on the community, which might be unrepresentative of the group as a whole.

In addition, an informant may not provide the kind of spontaneous information which is most useful to ethnographers, instead trying to show what they believe you want to see. For this reason, it's good to have a variety of contacts within the group.

▌• Task

♦ Selecting a research setting

Group work: Based on the preliminary work you have done, work in small groups, talking about the research setting you have selected to conduct your research, including the relevant issues mentioned above in this section. Then, make your own plan for the coming work.

▶ Step 4. Presenting yourself

You need to decide how you will present yourself to those in the field. Will you be conducting covert research? What roles will you need to adopt and relate to others? How active will you be participating in other people's lives? If you present yourself as a researcher, will others be able to accept you in their daily lives?

Overt vs covert ethnography

Most ethnography is overt. In an overt approach, the ethnographers openly state their intentions and acknowledges their role as a researcher to the members of the group being studied.

- √ Overt ethnography is typically preferred for ethical reasons, as participants can provide informed consent ...
- ✕ ... but people may behave differently with the awareness that they are being studied.

Sometimes ethnography can be covert. This means that the researcher does not tell participants about his/her research, and comes up with some other pretense for being there.

- √ Covert ethnography allows access to environments where the group would not welcome a researcher...
- ✕ ... but hiding the researcher's role can be considered deceptive and thus unethical.

▶ Step 5. Gathering and recording information

Sometimes it can be difficult to record and gather data at the same time. What are the types of information that should be recorded or taken as field notes? If you cannot fully record your observations while you are in the field, what should you do? Always carry a notepad for brief jottings. Sometimes there is no alternative but to wait and record observation after you leave the setting. You should record the observations as soon as possible to minimize recall problems. You may also rely on equipment such as audio-recorders, video cameras, etc.

There are three modes of data collection in ethnography: observation, interviewing and archival research. **Observation** is participant observation (recorded in field notes), which is the most often used method; **interviewing** (often transcribed and summarized), is the process of directing a conversation to collect information; and **archival research** (or artifact analysis) is the analysis of existing materials stored for research, service or other purposes officially and unofficially (Angrosino, 2007). Of these methods, participant observation is perhaps of greatest importance because it is crucial to develop an understanding of the culture.

Observation

Participant observation is unique in that it combines the researcher's participation in the lives of the people under study while also maintaining a professional distance. According to Angrosino (2007), observation is the act of perceiving the activities and interrelationships of people in the field setting.

Richards (2003) lists four main components that observers should make a conscious effort to note: **setting** (space and objects), **systems** (procedures), **people**, and **behavior**. At first, it will probably be difficult to know what to focus on in your observation. Most people begin with a "big net approach"—trying to focus on as many systems, people, and behaviors as possible in their observations until their focus naturally narrows to more specific issues or questions.

Active vs passive observation

Different levels of immersion in the community may be appropriate in different contexts. The ethnographer may be a more active or passive participant depending on the demands of their research and the nature of the setting.

An active role involves trying to fully integrate, carrying out tasks and participating in activities like any other member of the community, taking an **emic** position.

  √   Active participation may encourage the group to feel more comfortable with the ethnographer's presence...
      ...but runs the risk of disrupting the regular functioning of the community.

A passive role is one in which the ethnographer stands back from the activities of others, behaving as a more distant observer and not involving themselves in the community's activities, taking an **etic** position.

   √   Passive observation allows more space for careful observation and note-taking...

   ✕   ... but group members may behave unnaturally due to feeling they are being observed by an outsider.

Although the degree of immersion in the target culture might differ from study to study, an important criterion is that a researcher maintains an emic (insider or participant perspective) and etic (outsider or researchers' perspective) position simultaneously. By slowly adopting an emic position, over time you learn to understand certain cultural practices and routines, participate in them, and learn some of the jargon (and in some cases, the language) of the target culture. This allows you to develop knowledge about the culture from the inside (Heigham & Sakui, 2009).

While ethnographers usually have a preference, they also have to be flexible about their level of participation. For example, access to the community might depend upon engaging in certain activities, or there might be certain practices in which outsiders cannot participate.

Observing the group and taking field notes

The core of ethnography is observation of the group from the inside. Field notes are taken to record these observations while immersed in the setting; they form the basis of the final written ethnography. They are usually written by hand, but other solutions such as voice recordings can be useful alternatives.

Field notes record any and all important data: phenomena observed, conversations had, and preliminary analysis. Don't be afraid to also note down things you notice that fall outside the pre-formulated scope of your research; anything may prove relevant, and it's better to have extra notes you might discard later than to end up with missing data.

Thus, field notes should be detailed and provide rich contextual information derived from the setting itself rather than from preconceived ideas of the researchers. Careful attention to field notes prevents researchers from forming over-generalized impressions and interpretations, and allows them to describe the phenomenon or event observed more precisely.

> A field note taken while observing a language class states, "A student is sleeping and seems unmotivated." It is inadequate or thin. It does not describe the event and setting in detail, and it includes the researcher's subjective view as it describes the student as being "unmotivated." A better description would be as follows:
>
> A boy sitting in the second row from the back by the window has had his face down on the desk since the class began. It is the second period after lunch. Other students seem to be on task, but he has not participated in any learning activities for 20 minutes. He has not opened his textbook or notebook. They are covered by his head and arms. He has not moved much either. Cannot tell whether he is really sleeping or this is the way that he is resisting participation. (Heigham & Sakui, 2009, p. 98)

This description, a close emic look at a sleeping student, might be followed by a simple drawing of the classroom. Researchers might also add parenthetic remarks about what they are thinking about what they are observing. In this example, comments like these might be added: "Maybe he gets sleepy after lunch but is active in other classes." "I wonder why the teacher doesn't wake him up."

The above sketch is an example of thick description, as discussed earlier in case studies. When given this information, a reader can visualize the context and the boy's behavior. By using thick description, you can record the totality of what you observe so that your notes can help you remember both the events and their contexts when you return to analyze them later. Also, when thick description is put in a research report or article, it allows readers to picture the scene clearly, and since ethnography assumes an active role for its readers, this is essential. Furthermore, when recording what participants or informants say, try to capture not only the words but also the context in which they spoke as richly as possible, and later, share that richness with the reader.

It is important to note here that using meticulous description in your ethnographic report is key since these reports are not presented as definitive fact but as an informed interpretation, and readers are expected to read them and construct their own interpretations of them. The readers may then agree or disagree with what you argue. Thus, from the beginning of a study to the end, the role of maintaining thick description in field notes—descriptions that allow you to present clear pictures of what you experienced in the field—cannot be overemphasized (Heigham & Sakui, 2009).

Elements of field notes or description

You should take time to go over your notes, expand on them with further detail, and keep them organized (including information such as dates and locations). According to Singleton and Straits (2005), your field notes or detailed descriptive accounts of any observation made during a given period should include the following elements:

- **Running description:** This is the record of the day's observations. The objective is to record accurately what you observe. You should also avoid analyzing persons or events while in the field because there is no time and it will interfere with your observation of what is going on. What are things to watch for? The setting, the people, individual actions and activities, group behaviors, and perspectives.

- **Forgotten episodes:** These are accounts of previous episodes that you have forgotten but are remembering again while you are in the field.

- **Ideas and notes for further information use:** These refer to spur-of-the-moment ideas related to data analysis, data collection, speculations about relationships, etc. These are notes that you write to and for yourself, for example, plans for future observations, specific things or people to look for.

- **Personal impressions and feelings:** These refer to recordings regarding the subjective reactions you had while working in the field. They may provide clues to biases which might be clouding your observations.

- **Methodological notes:** These refer to any ideas related to the techniques you used to conduct research, for example, any difficulties you have in collecting data, any biases that might be introduced by the data collection techniques or any changes in how you can make and record observations.

Limitations of field research

Since most ethnographic research requires fieldwork, it also faces the same limitations that field research has.

First, ethnography can be very labor intensive and time consuming. Ethnographic researchers can spend years in the field. Because field research is rarely an entirely detached observation, field participation often becomes a question of "how much."

Second, balancing the requirements of both participating and observing can be very difficult. As you become more familiar with the setting and develops attachment and empathy for, and trust and rapport with those under study, you may be drawn into the lives of those people more as a participant than as an observer. When you become fully immersed in a culture or situation, you risk changing the events in which you observe and participate, perhaps even losing sight of your role as a researcher, thereby "going native" and over-identifying yourself with the group under study (Heigham & Sakui, 2009).

Third, field work lacks the level of structure and control found in laboratory settings that may help ensure objectivity. If you are not careful, your personal values and attitudes may lead to bias. Due to the sheer volume of rich data collected, you may also experience difficulty in both data analysis and interpretation. The ethnographic researcher also needs to know how to stay safe in unsafe settings, and cope with personal stress and conflicts in the field. These negotiations can be very difficult.

Finally, due to the nature of field research that personally involves the researcher in the social lives of other people, there are ethical dilemmas that you need to be considering. Issues of confidentiality and privacy, your unintentional revelation of identities, deception and misrepresentation of yourself, identification of your biases, your involvement with illegal behavior or activity, violation of your own basic personal moral standards in order to conform, your identification with those lacking power in society, your negotiations with the elite in power or authority, and your publishing field reports that may be truthful but unflattering are all ethical issues that may arise (Neuman, 2003).

Interview and artifacts

Interviews and artifacts are other fundamental parts of ethnographic research that will only be briefly mentioned here. Conducting good interviews is a skill that needs careful development, and, as we will only make a few comments here about them, please see the relevant section (Case Study) for a full discussion.

Each researcher formulates interview questions based on his or her own unique etic position. If another researcher went into the same field and were to interview the same people, the interview questions he or she chose to use would probably be different. Similarly, if the same interview questions were used by different researchers, interviewees would likely respond to the questions differently for reasons such as differences in age, gender, ethnicity, or class between themselves and the interviewers. As for who to interview, ethnographers have to find informants from within the target community to interview. Finding good informants, people who are articulate and gifted at description, is essential because the information researchers get from their informants can provide some of the mainstays of the research data. Using the "big net approach" mentioned above when entering a site can often help you discover good informants.

The artifacts ethnographers use in their research can take a variety of forms. They can be pre-existing documents such as past English writing grades, standardized writing test scores, handouts from lessons, end of term tests, or preexisting video footage or photos. As you are examining these, it is important to remain as skeptical of anything you read as you are of anything you hear or see. Every aspect of your research must be approached with the same questioning attitude (Heigham & Sakui, 2009).

Other considerations

Use of different data sources

The gathering and later comparison of different data sources by using a combination of methods is called "triangulation" and it is used to test the quality of information and ultimately to put the whole situation into perspective. Good ethnography is usually the result of triangulation (Angrosino, 2007), so doing it is crucial; it enables you to validate claims and discover inconsistencies that require additional investigation.

> In interviews teachers might emphasize the importance of teaching English communicatively, and field notes from classroom observations may also show the regular use of communicative activities, so a researcher might conclude that teaching students to communicate in English is the teachers' primary goal. However, when the artifact of the final test is examined, the researcher discovers that it focuses on students' grammatical knowledge rather than on their communicative skills. This kind of discrepancy revealed through triangulation could guide the researcher to examine why there is a difference between what teachers teach and what they test, and thus lead the researcher to important new discoveries. (Heigham & Sakui, 2009, p. 99)

Value judgements

As a researcher, you should be especially alert throughout the research process to remaining nonjudgmental and not imposing their own cultural norms on the people being studied (Fetterman, 1998). When you enter a new culture as a researcher it is difficult not to quickly make value judgments, but you need to resist that temptation. For example, an ethnographer might enter a language classroom and find an English teacher requiring students to copy pages from an English textbook into their notebook. One interpretation might be that this practice is outdated at best, and a waste of time at worst, and that the teacher is not teaching effectively. However, it might be the case that the teacher believes that the repetitive aspects of the writing activity, especially the kinesthetic aspect of hand-eye coordination that copying engenders, promotes learning. Whatever the deeper meanings in any context are, as an ethnographer you must take the time to find them out and avoid making quick, subjective judgments. Making hasty judgments can be dangerous because they can easily lead you to erroneous interpretations.

During her study, Elizabeth uses many different data collection methods. She conducts about 400 hours of observation in the center. She takes detailed field notes that include what she sees and hears, as well as her own reflections on these observations, which she records while consciously trying to keep an open mind. She interviews all of the PAs who work in the center, 16 students who use the center (four from each year), and six alumni. In addition, she reviews artifacts such as test scores, and flyers and posters made for the center by the PAs. The variety of data that she collects allows her to make thorough analysis and connections which help guide her ongoing research, analysis, and interpretation. (Heigham & Sakui, 2009, p. 101)

▶ Task

◆Data collection

1. Group work: After you have decided on the type of project you are planning to do, discuss in small groups what you will do to get data for your research project.

2. Individual work: Based on your reading and understanding of data collection introduced in this section, start collecting the data for your own research project, using observation, interview, or secondary library or documentary research.

▶ Step 6. Analyzing data

Ethnographers can collect great quantities of material to describe what people believe and how they behave in everyday situations; therefore, data analysis and interpretation can be challenging. First, you need to understand your materials.

The process of understanding is inductive in which you begin by learning from the data rather than starting with preconceived notions about your subject matter. The data analysis should also begin while the data are being collected so that the researcher can discover additional themes and decides whether to follow those leads for more intense investigation. The following are suggested strategies for ethnographic analysis (Roper & Shapira, 2000).

Coding for descriptive labels

Since the materials collected are in the form of written words, those words must first be grouped into meaningful categories or descriptive labels, and then organized to compare, contrast and identify patterns. Coding means that you give a label or categorization for a fairly small chunk of data, such as a line for an interview excerpt or a paragraph of field notes. First-level coding is done to reduce the data to a manageable size. Before one begins the coding process, it may be helpful to formulate basic domains that can categorize a broad range of phenomena, for example, setting, types of activities, events, relationships and social structure, general perspectives, strategies, process, meanings and repeated phrases.

Note: The process of coding is extremely time-consuming and can block the analyst from proceeding to "thick description." Some people do not do it, but it can enable researchers to discover themes or theories, rather than impose pre-existing ideas or categories on the data. If you do code, you can then use those codes to look for relationships among the categories. If you do not code, continue looking over the data, and group and regroup your ideas as you gradually work toward building assumptions and identifiable themes which are the basis for your final interpretation (Heigham & Sakui, 2009).

Sorting for patterns

The next step is to sort or group the descriptive labels into smaller sets. One begins to develop themes from those groupings and a sense of possible connections between the information.

Identifying outliers

Cases, situations, events or settings that do not "fit" with the rest of the findings may be identified. These cases should be kept in mind as the different steps in the research process are developed, for example, should we collect more information about those cases?

Generalizing constructs and theories

The patterns or connected findings are related to theories in order to make sense of the rich and complex data collected. Existing literature is also reviewed.

Memoing with reflective remarks

Memos are insights or ideas that one has about the data. They are written so that the researcher can know if anything needs further clarification or testing. It also helps the researcher to keep track of their assumptions, biases and opinions throughout the whole research process.

> Elizabeth knows that one of the keys to a successful ethnography is keeping her data well organized. At the end of each data collection session—no matter what type of data she collects—she always allows a few minutes to highlight points or make organizational memos. At the end of each week, she reviews all of her new data and inputs them into her computer into well-organized files. Sometimes she scans information, other times she types it in. This process not only keeps her organized but also acts as part of her ongoing analysis and interpretation since she has the opportunity to see the data again while they are still fresh and can add analytic memos. After her data collection is complete, she repeatedly reads over her data and makes additional notes. She is pleased with her progress, so she decides not to code her data. Over time, as she is working and reworking the data, she begins to see patterns of behaviors and values that she realizes are central to the SAC culture, and from there she is able to identify a number of central themes. (Heigham & Sakui, 2009, p. 103)

▌•Task

1. Individual work: Read carefully the steps and strategies introduced in this section, ask the instructor any question you have concerning the analysis, and write down in detail how you will conduct the analysis.

2. Group work: Work in small groups, talk about the difficulties or problems you may encounter in analyzing the data, and try to work out some possible solutions to the problem or give suggestions to your peer.

▶ Step 7. Writing up an ethnographic report

After observations are concluded, there's still the task of writing them up into an ethnography. This entails going through the field notes and formulating a convincing account of the behaviors and dynamics observed.

Organization of an ethnography

An ethnography is often organized around key topics that are presented in a way that progressively leads the reader through the researchers' interpretations or arguments. A final ethnographic report is often a cultural portrait of the group, incorporating the researchers' and the participants' viewpoints and terms of reference (Creswell, 2007), and it is often presented as a narrative. Thus, ethnographers' ultimate goal is to tell a "good story" about the experience of their research to an audience who may be unfamiliar with the culture. The tricky part of this is combining field notes, interview transcripts, and artifacts (from which you must maintain objective distance) together with subjective memos, which include your personal interpretations, reflections, and opinions to create a rich, thick description and compelling portrait that "rings true" for the reader. Here again, you must reflect on your emic and etic positions as you examine your data recorded from a *they* and *I* perspective and weave these different types of data into a consistent narrative form that fairly portrays the group you have studied.

The cultural portraits that Elizabeth constructs during her research reveal a variety of interesting issues that impact students, such as how the influence of periodic TV game-shows that use English, or Japanese actors appearing in popular English-language films, serve as transitory inspiration for interest in English and learning community building. In addition, as the research progresses, Elizabeth finds that the coordinator of the SAC seems to favor one type of student over another, based on her personal and cultural beliefs of how students should behave in autonomous ways. When students' behavior matches the coordinator's beliefs, she is encouraging and supportive. When they do not match, she is sometimes dismissive. Elizabeth feels this is a very critical point in her findings but at the same time does not know whether she can honestly report it because she and the coordinator have developed a positive rapport and Elizabeth fears that if she shares her interpretations, the coordinator might feel betrayed. This causes her some anxiety. In time, she finds that she is able to share her findings honestly with

> the coordinator, and their discussions together lead her to more discoveries. Later, Elizabeth gives a presentation on her discoveries to her department, and the faculty begins working on an action plan to improve the SAC orientation and PA support structure. To share her findings outside the department, she begins writing up a lengthy narrative about her research, which she hopes to have published. As she writes, she is careful to support her interpretations of the SAC culture by detailed description and expressive quotes from participants. (Heigham & Sakui, 2009, pp. 104–105)

The structure of an ethnography

An ethnography can take many different forms: it may be an article, a thesis, or an entire book, for example; the communicating of their findings also takes many forms. Today ethnographic products are presented in a multitude of ways including taxonomies, novels, novellas, short stories, poems, plays, dance performances, web-based texts and images, and films—all with varying proportions of description and interpretation (Heigham & Sakui, 2009).

Ethnographies often do not follow the standard structure of a scientific paper, though like most academic texts, they should have an introduction and conclusion. For example, the paper begins by describing the historical background of the research, then focuses on various themes in turn before concluding.

An ethnography may still use a more traditional structure, however, especially when used in combination with other research methods, that is, the standard structure for empirical research: introduction, methods, results, discussion, and conclusion.

The style of an ethnography

The goal of a written ethnography is to provide a rich, authoritative account of the social setting in which you were embedded—to convince the reader that your observations and interpretations are representative of reality.

Ethnography tends to take a less impersonal approach than other research methods. Due to the embedded nature of the work, an ethnography often necessarily involves discussion of your personal experiences and feelings during the research.

> During the second week, I became frustrated with my lack of progress in gaining the confidence of more than just my initial informants. The staff appeared to distrust me as an outsider...

Ethnography is not limited to making observations; it also attempts to explain the phenomena observed in a structured, narrative way. For this, you may draw on theory, but also on your direct experience and intuitions, which may well contradict the assumptions that you brought into the research.

> Despite the claims of Griffiths (2019), my own observations indicate that the ESL learners do not always develop any particular bond with one another in response to the stresses of their study. There are several possible reasons for this discrepancy: It may be that the layout of this particular classroom discourages such bond-forming interaction, or that my own presence was disruptive...

▶ Task

◆ Analyzing the ethnographic research papers

1. Group work: Choose one of the ethnographic research papers from the journals available in the school library or one of your own liking. While you are reading, try to pay attention to how the researcher describes the setting, systems, people, and behavior, as well as how he or she allows the voices of the participants to be heard. Then answer the following questions about the article.

1) What was the topic or issue investigated in the study?

2) What cultural group was studied?

3) How were the participants chosen, and who were they?

4) What types of data were collected?

5) How were they analyzed?

6) What was the role of the ethnographer in the study?

7) What claims were made? Do they "ring true" for you? Why or why not?

8) Consider the form in which the article was written. Does it work for you? What other ways might the report have been presented? Prepare to discuss your article and the answers to these questions within a group.

◆ Writing up the final project

2. Individual work: Read carefully the conditions and limitations for conducting ethnographic research, and think about how you will evaluate your own research. Then, complete your first draft of the project by combining all the work you have done previously.

3. Classwork: Present your work either individual or group in class, trying to get any comment or suggestion from your instructor and peers, make any relevant revision that you think is necessary, and finally, re-write it as the final draft.

12.5 Quality Control

There are three issues that need to be considered when you control for quality in ethnographic and field research: *reactivity*, *reliability* and *validity*.

▶ Reactivity

Reactivity is the degree to which your presence as the researcher influences the behaviors of others because they know they are in a study may cause those under study to act differently (Neuman, 2003). Being unobtrusive or disruptive, and familiarizing yourself with the lives of others may reduce the effect of reactivity.

▶ Reliability

Reliability in field research addresses the question of whether you are able to collect data that are internally and externally consistent, and credible (Neuman, 2003):

- Data are internally consistent when the researcher records behaviors that are consistent over time and in different social contexts.

- External consistency can be achieved by verifying or cross-checking data with other sources.

- Ethnographic researchers also depend on what others tell them; therefore, credibility of the source of information needs to be assessed. The information shared could be in the forms of misinformation, evasions, lies and omissions.

Reliability in field research will depend on your insight, awareness, questions and looking at behaviors and events from different angles and perspectives (Neuman, 2003).

▶ Validity

Validity in field research is the confidence placed in your ability to collect and analyze data accurately, representing the lives or culture under study (Neuman, 2003). Validity can be checked in the following ways:

- Ecological validity is the degree to which the data collected and described by the researcher reflects the world of those under study (Neuman, 2003). Natural history is a full description and disclosure of the researcher's actions, assumptions, and procedures for others to evaluate. If the study is accepted by or credible to others inside and outside the field site, it is valid in terms of natural history (Neuman, 2003).

- You should also check for member validation by taking the field results back to those under study to judge for adequacy and accuracy from their perspectives (Neuman, 2003). Additionally, you should have competent insider performance which is the ability of the researcher as a nonmember of the group or culture under study to interact effectively as a member (Neuman, 2003).

- Finally, the study should have pragmatic validity and transferability which is the degree to which the study results and conclusions have relevance beyond the study itself (Angrosino, 2007).

Elizabeth is vigilant in making meticulous field notes during her observations and reviewing them frequently. During her interviews she is careful to write thorough descriptions of how she believes her informants fit within their culture, and she frequently refers to these notes as she does her analysis. Throughout the research process, she takes her developing interpretations and conducts member checks with participants. In addition, to further strengthen her interpretations, she triangulates her different data. By doing these things, she feels that the results of her research will "ring true" with readers; moreover, through applying what she has learned, both she and the faculty believe the learning communities within the SAC can be improved. In her report, Elizabeth tries to clearly communicate to her readers in rich detail not only the cultural portrait of the SAC that she has developed, but also how she built her understanding of it. (Heigham & Sakui, 2009, pp. 106–107)

12.6 Application of Ethnography

Ethnography is an excellent way to explore the unique mysteries any culture contains; however, it is a challenging approach that takes skill and a lot of perseverance. When the aim of your research is to create a rich and detailed portrait of a given culture, ethnography is one of the best options there is. If you want to describe how a cultural group—be it a school system, a bilingual community, an ESL classroom, or a group of English teachers—works, and to explore the beliefs, values, and behavior of the people in that group, ethnography could be the right choice for you. But when you set out to choose a research approach, you should carefully consider its advantages and disadvantages, and decide if it's right for your research topic and for your qualitative research skills (Heigham & Sakui, 2009).

If you decide that ethnography is the most appropriate research approach for your research purpose and questions, the information in this unit can be a useful stepping-stone for you as you begin your research. If you decide on another approach, you might nevertheless still find it useful to train yourself to have an ethnographer's eyes, ears, and mindset so that as you conduct your research, you can see, hear, and question with patience and without judgment. No matter what research approach you finally adopt, having the open-minded attitude of an ethnographer will help you carry out well-balanced and revealing research.

Sample Research

Please scan the QR code below to acquire the sample article. Read the article and think about its research methods.

Sample Article

References

Afflerbach, P., & Johnson, P. (1984). On the use of verba reports in reading research. *Journal of Reading Behaviour*, 16(4): 307–22.

American Psychological Association. (2010). *Publication manual of the American psychological association*. American Psychological Association, Washington, D.C.

Angrosino, M. (2007). *Doing ethnographic and observational research*. Thousand Oaks, CA: Sage.

Bakhtin, M. (1986). *Speech genres and other late essays*. Austin, TX: University of Texas Press.

Barton, D. (2007). *Literacy: An introduction to the ecology of written language* (2nd ed.). Oxford: Blackwell.

Bereiter, C., & Scardamalia, M. (1987). *The psychology of written composition*. Hillsdale, NJ: Erlbaum.

Bruffee, K. (1986). Social construction: Language and the authority of knowledge. A bibliographical essay. *College English*, 48: 773–9.

Creswell, J. W. (2003). *Research design: Qualitative, quantitative, and mixed methods approaches* (2nd ed.) Thousand Oaks, CA: Sage.

Creswell, J. W. (2007). *Qualitative inquiry and research design: Choosing among five traditions* (2nd ed.). Thousand Oaks, CA: Sage Publications.

Creswell, J. W. (2008). *Educational research: Planning, conducting, and evaluating quantitative and qualitative approaches to research* (3rd ed.). Upper Saddle River, NJ: Merrill/Pearson Education.

Creswell, J. W. (2014). *Research design: Qualitative, quantitative, and mixed methods approaches* (4th ed.). Thousand Oaks, CA: Sage Publications.

Creswell, J. W., Plano Clark, V. L., Gutmann, M., & Hanson, W. (2003). Advanced mixed methods research designs. In A. Tashakkori & C. Teddlie (eds.), *Handbook on mixed methods in the behavioral and social sciences* (pp. 209–240). Thousand Oaks, CA: Sage Publications.

Connor, U. (1994). Text analysis. *TESOL Quarterly*, 28(4): 673–703.

de Saussure, F. (1986). *Course in general linguistics* (R. Harris, Trans.) (3rd ed.). Chicago: Open Court Publishing.

Dillman, D. A. (2000). The role of behavioral survey methodologists in national statistical. *International statistical review*, 68(2), 200–213.

Ede, L., & Lunsford, A. (1984). Audience addressed/audience invoked: The role of audience in composition theory and pedagogy. *College Composition and Communication*, 35: 155–71.

Elbow, P. (1998). *Writing with power: Techniques for mastering the writing process*. New York and Oxford: Oxford University Press.

Fairclough, N. (1992). *Discourse and social change*. Cambridge: Polity Press.

Fairclough, N. (2002). Language in new capitalism. *Discourse & society*, 13(2), 163–166.

Fairclough, N. (2013). *Critical discourse analysis: The critical study of language*. London: Routledge.

Fairclough, N., & Wodak, R. (1997). Critical discourse analysis. In T. Van Dijk (ed.), *Discourse as social interaction* (pp. 258–84). London: Sage.

Fetterman, D. (1998). *Ethnography: Step by Step* (2nd ed.). Thousand Oaks, CA: Sage Publications.

Fink, A. (1995). *How to Sample in Surveys*. Thousand Oaks, CA: Sage Publications.

Fitzgerald, M. (1997). Ethnography. In J. Higgs (ed.), *Qualitative research: Discourse on methodologies* (pp. 48–60). Sydney: Hampden Press.

Flower, L. (1989). Cognition, context and theory building. *College Composition and Communication*, 40: 282–311.

Flower, L., & Hayes, J. (1981). A cognitive process theory of writing. *College Composition and Communication*, 32: 365–87.

Foucault, M. (1980). *Language, counter–memory, practice: Selected essays and interviews*. Cornell University Press.

Fowler, F, Jr. (1993). *Survey Research Methods* (2nd ed.). Newbury Park, CA: Sage Publications.

Gass, S. (2015). Experimental Research. In B. Paltridge & A. Phakiti (eds.), *Research methods in applied linguistics* (pp. 88–99). London: Bloomsbury.

Gee, J. P. (1990). *Social linguistics and literacies: Ideology in Discourses*. (4th ed., 2011). London: Taylor and Francis.

Geertz, C. (1973). Thick description. In C. Geertz (ed.), *The interpretation of cultures* (pp. 3–33). New York: Basic Books.

Gravetter, F. L., & Wallnau, L. B. (2007). *Statistics for the behavioral sciences* (7th ed.). Belmont, CA: Wadsworth, Thomson Learning.

Grice, H.P. (1975). Logic and conversation. In P. Cole & J. Morgan (eds), *Syntax and semantics*, vol. 3, *Speech acts* (pp. 41–58). New York: Academic Press.

Habermas, J. (1973). What does a crisis mean today? Legitimation problems in late capitalism. *Social research*, 643–667.

Halliday, M.A.K., & Matthiessen, C. (2004). *An introduction to functional grammar* (3rd ed.). London: Edward Arnold.

Heigham, J., & Sakui, K. (2009). Ethnograph. In J. Heigham & R. Croker (eds.), *Qualitative research in applied linguistics: A practical introduction* (pp. 91–111). New York: Palgrave Macmillan.

Hood, M. (2009). Case study. In J. Heigham & R. Croker (eds.), *Qualitative research in applied linguistics: A practical introduction* (pp. 66–90). New York: Palgrave Macmillan.

Huckin, T. (1997). Critical Discourse Analysis. In T. Miller (ed.), *Functional Approaches to Written Text: Classroom Applications* (pp. 78–92). Washington, D.C: ERIC.

Hyland, K. (2009). *Teaching and Researching Writing* (2nd ed.). Harlow: Pearson.

Hyland, K. (2016). Methods and methodologies in second language writing research. *System,* 59: 116–125.

Ivankova, N. V., & Creswell, J. W. (2009). Mixed methods. In J. Heigham & R. Croker (eds.), *Qualitative research in applied linguistics: A practical introduction* (pp. 135–161). New York: Palgrave Macmillan.

Ivankova, N. V., Creswell, J. W., & Plano Clark, V. L. (2007). Foundations and approaches to mixed methods research. In K. Maree (Ed.), *First steps in research*. Pretoria, South Africa: Van Schaik Publishers.

Johns, A.M. (1997). *Text, role and context: Developing academic literacies*. Cambridge: Cambridge University Press.

Kinkead, J. (2015). *Researching writing: An introduction to research methods*. University Press of Colorado.

Kramsch, C. (1997).Rhetorical models of understanding. In T. Miller (ed.), *Functional approaches to written text: classroom applications* (pp. 50–63). Washington, DC: USIA.

Lave, J., & Wenger, E. (1991). *Situated learning: Legitimate peripheral participation*. Cambridge: Cambridge University Press.

Martin, J. (2004). Mourning—how we get aligned. *Discourse and Society,* 15(2–3), 321–344.

Matsuda, P. K., Canagarajah, A. S., Harklauc, L., Hyland, K., & Warschauere, M. (2003). Changing currents in second language writing research: A colloquium. *Journal of Second Language Writing*, 12: 151–179.

Moffett, J. (1982). Writing, inner speech and mediation. *College English*, 44: 231–44.

Murray, D. (1985). *A writer teaches writing* (2nd ed.). Boston, MA: Houghton Mifflin.

Neuman, W. L. (2003). *Social research methods: Qualitative and quantitative approaches* (5th ed.). Boston: Allyn and Bacon.

Nystrand, M. (1987) The role of context in written communication. In R. Horowitz & S.J. Samuels (eds), *Comprehending oral and written language* (pp. 197–214). San Diego, CA: Academic Press.

Nystrand, M. (1989). A social interactive model of writing. *Written Communication*, 6: 66–85.

Nystrand, M., Greene, S., & Wiemelt, J. (1993). Where did composition studies come from? An intellectual history. *Written Communication*, 19: 267–333.

Park, D. (1982). The meanings of 'audience'. *College English*, 44(3): 247–57.

Plonsky, L., & Oswald, F. (2014). How big is "big"?: Interpreting effect sizes in L2 research. *Language Learning*, 64(4): 878–912.

Prior, P. (1998). *Writing/disciplinarity: A sociohistoric account of literate activity in the academy*. Hillsdale, NJ: Lawrence Erlbaum.

Ramage, J. D., Bean, J. C., & Johnson, J. (2009). *The Allyn & Bacon guide to writing*. New York: Pearson.

Richards, K. (2003). *Qualitative inquiry in TESOL*. New York: Palgrave Macmillan.

Richards, L., & Morse, J. M. (2007). *README FIRST for a User's Guide to Qualitative Methods*. Thousand Oaks, CA: Sage Publications.

Roper, J. M., & Shapira, J. (2000). *Ethnography in nursing research*. Thousand Oaks, CA: Sage Publications.

Sangasubana, N. (2009). How to conduct ethnographic research. *The Qualitative Report,* 16(2), 567–573. Retrieved from http://nova.edu/ssss/QR/QR16–2/sangasubana.pdf

Silva, T. (1993) Toward an understanding of the distinct nature of L2 writing: the ESL research and its implications. *TESOL Quarterly*, 27: 665–77.

Singleton, R. A., & Straits, B. C. (2005). *Approaches to social research* (4th ed.). New York: Oxford University Press.

Sperber, D., & Wilson, D. (1986). *Relevance: Communication and cognition*. Oxford: Basil Blackwell.

Stake, R. (1995). *Case study research*. Thousand oaks, CA: Sage Publications.

Swales, J. (1990). *Genre analysis: English in academic and research settings*. Cambridge: Cambridge University Press.

Swales, J. (1998). *Other floors, other voices: A textography of a small university building*. Hillsdale, NJ: Lawrence Erlbaum.

Sytsma, S. (2009). The basics of experimental design [A quick and non-technical guide]. Retrieved November, 2, 2009. http://liutaiomottola.com/myth/expdesig.htm

Talmy, S. (2015). Critical research in applied linguistics. In B. Paltridge & A. Phakiti (eds.), *Research methods in applied linguistics* (pp. 153–168). London: Bloomsbury.

Tate, G. (2014). *A Guide to Composition Pedagogies* (2nd.). New York: Oxford University Press.

Teo, A. K. (2006). Social-interactive writing for English language learners. *The CATESOL Journal*, 18: 160–178.

Thompson, K. (2002). A critical discourse analysis of world music as the 'other' in education. *Research Studies in Music Education*, 19(1): 14–21.

Van Dijk, T. A. (1988). *News analysis*: *Case studies of international and national news in the press*. New Jersey: Lawrence.

Watson-Gegeo, K. A. (1988). Ethnography in ESL: Defining the essentials. *TESOL quarterly,* 22(4), 575–592.

Wagner, E. (2015). Survey Research. In B. Paltridge & A. Phakiti (eds.), *Research methods in applied linguistics* (pp. 75–87). London: Bloomsbury.

Wodak, R. (1996). *Disorders of discourse*. Harlow: Longman.

Wolcott, H. F. (2008). *Ethnography: A way of seeing* (2nd ed.). Lanham, MD: AltaMira Press.

Yin, R. K. (2003). Designing case studies. *Qualitative research methods*, 5(14), 359–386.

Yin, R. K. (2009). *Case study research: Design and methods* (Vol. 5). Thousand Oaks, CA: Sage Publications.

Young, L., & Harrison, C. (2004). Introduction. In L. Young & C. Harrison (eds), *Systemic functional linguistics and critical discourse analysis* (pp. 1–11). London: Continuum.

Zamel, V. (1983). The composing processes of advanced ESL students: Six case-studies. *TESOL Quarterly*, 17: 165–87.